Enduring Issues in

Law and Society

First Edition

Edited by Michelle Foster
Kent State University

cognella
academic publishing

First published in the United States of America in 2014 by Cognella, Inc.

Printed in the United States of America

ISBN: 978-1-62131-328-1 (pbk)/ 978-1-62131-329-8 (br)

cognella
academic publishing

www.cognella.com 800-200-3908

Dedication

To my family (my dad, husband, and children) and my dear friends (you know who you are) who have always supported me no matter what crazy new endeavor I've undertaken. Thanks for being there for me!

Table of Contents

Section III: Policy and Social Justice

Section IV: Social Ills and Social Justice

Acknowledgments

I wish to express my gratitude to the wonderful staff at Cognella Publishing, without whom this book would not have been possible. First and foremost, I would like to thank both Melissa Barcomb and Sarah Wheeler, who reached out to me with the idea for this project, Jessica Busch for the book cover design, and to all of the other individuals at Cognella who helped me. To Dr. David Kessler, Dr. Stephen Brown, and Dr. Ryan Claassen—faithful guides and instructors at Kent State University who are always there to provide support and advice. To Dr. Mary Wilson, a dear friend and excellent professor at Kent State University, who never fails to impress me in all she does. To Dr. Christopher Bellas, a good friend and professor at Youngstown State University, who could not wait to help me with writing a chapter for this book. Additional thanks to Chris for providing recommendations for the book's title and cover design. Thanks to Andrew Spriegel, a wonderful person and attorney, who always knows what is important in life; no matter what emergency we face at the law firm, you always tell me it can wait if I have something to do for my students or family. To my lifetime friends, Julie Evans and Lisa Gerdes, for your kind promptings to complete this project; I thank you and I love you both. And, finally, sincerest thanks to Kent State University and my students—this really is the best job in the world!

Preface

Compiling a selection of readings for inclusion in a classroom textbook is not an easy task. It is an even more challenging endeavor to put together a text that contains important and interesting information particular to today's culture that people (other than me) would find beneficial. Given the vast amount of literature available, it is often hard to select just one perfect piece. Reflecting upon issues that carry the most importance in society was the simplest part of this project. The core concerns of today are the same as those of yesterday, a decade ago, a century ago, and so on. These issues are all related to equality, fairness, and justice. How do we, a society of many, with diverse interests, goals, hopes, backgrounds, etc., live together without causing harm to others? It is simple as long as one remembers this: equality, fairness, and justice. With these three words in mind, I put together these readings.

Section I

Understanding Crime, Law and Justice

Introduction to Section I

Understanding Crime, Law, and Justice

By Michelle Foster

As long as there are people, there will be crime. It is basic human nature to be self-interested and do for oneself or one's family over others. But understanding exactly "why" crime occurs enables individuals to be more cognizant about prevention and protection from criminal activities. Concern about crime is real and necessary, but how much crime is there? Should people fear being attacked every time they walk to their vehicles at night? Should people fear for their safety and belongings every time they leave their homes? Or leave their doors unlocked? Maybe not, but being aware of potential dangers can reduce risk and increase people's perceptions of safety. The media feeds into this fear by sensationalizing criminal activities because of their newsworthiness. Crime stories make interesting news and television shows. Those who work in law enforcement know that criminal investigations are not handled the way they are depicted on television. But the hype and excitement these shows portray are in stark contrast with the horror felt by those victimized by the acts. Of course, victims are not always overlooked, but the focus is always on catching the "bad guy" rather than making someone feel whole or safe again after being subjected to violence. In addition, preventing and understanding why the crimes occurred in the first place probably would not make for an exciting television drama or an evening news broadcast.

Chapter 1 has been borrowed from Marcus Felson and Rachel Boba's book, *Crime and Everyday Life*. This chapter is just a glimpse of the crime problem, which they explain in a simple, practical manner. Felson and Boba demonstrate that much of the crime that exists today occurs as a result of *opportunity*. Thus, if you diminish the opportunity for crime to occur, either against your person or property, then you clearly reduce the chance of becoming a crime victim. Of course, the crime still may occur but—again, if the opportunity presents itself—to someone else. You have, however, just prevented harm to yourself. It is interesting to realize that individuals have to think about prevention. However in a society of many, prevention is a necessary part of the solution—the reduction of crime.

To highlight some of the reasons why our country has become an "incarceration nation," Travis Pratt's offerings from his book, *Addicted to Incarceration*, is provided in Chapter 2. Pratt explores how misconceptions about crime have been used in political discourse to justify filling our correctional institutions to and beyond maximum capacity. For decades, criminal justice policy translated basically into "if you build it, they will come." This quote has been repeated by many in corrections, as if jokingly concluding there will always be criminals and places to house them. What society does not realize is that we are creating this revolving door either because of unintended consequences of stringent sentencing policies or owing to our own ignorance and failings in realizing another old adage, "what goes around comes around." Thus, sentencing low-level offenders (i.e., non-violent offenders) to long prison terms does not achieve the goals of modern sentencing. Incapacitation is the Band-Aid solution to crime.

Addressing the crime problem then is not just an issue involving policy endeavor or criminal justice, but *social justice*. Chapter 3 from Matthew Robinson focuses on the concept of social justice through the lens of theorists John Rawls and David Miller. Social justice can only be achieved once individuals are treated as equals—and then punishments for violations of the law can be dispensed after considering the seriousness of the offense. If punishment is provided without placing individuals on an even keel, then true justice cannot be realized. Of course, many may argue this is socialism and that socialism does not work either. Rawls and Miller, however, have a point that unless the least advantaged members have the same opportunity as others, then they will always be treated differently in all stages of the criminal justice system (i.e., law enforcement, courts, and corrections).

Chapter One

Chemistry for Crime

By Marcus Felson and Rachel Boba

The whole is more than the sum of its parts. In a school science class, you may have mixed baking soda, vinegar, and dish detergent, producing a small eruption. Mixes make surprises for crime, too, for people mix in different ways.

- Two "innocuous" individuals mix badly, getting into a fight.
- Two drug sellers compete, with one driving the other out of business, even away from crime.
- Two teenagers who behave well in the presence of parents get drunk and wild when together.
- A middle-aged man, conventional at work, gets caught somewhere else with his pants down.

Many people are volatile and reactive. Almost everyone has ups and downs, ins and outs, feelings of anger and calm, moods of conformity and defiance, and legal and illegal behavior. Emotional ups and downs are even more common for people who commit a lot of crime (Cogan, 1996). This is why you, as a student of crime, should pay attention to the specific circumstances affecting people at particular times, and how they act together.

The Setting

More than 40 years ago, Professor Roger Barker (1963) developed tools for studying these variations in how people behave together. He and his students studied thousands of details of daily life after dividing a small Kansas town into hundreds of "behavior settings," namely, slices of space and time. Barker noted exactly what people were doing, when and where, in what group sizes and what ages, in each of the settings studied.

These settings ranged from a school history class to guys hanging out on a street corner or at a gas station. Barker's students took special note of how each setting sets up individual choices. For example, the same individual would read in the library and play ball on the ball field—different activities in different settings. That town provided teenagers few settings for escaping adults for very long, but still helps us study youth processes in larger places and today's world (see Chapter 6). For each of us spends part of the day in some settings and part in other settings, affecting what we do ourselves and what happens to us.

Just as economists study markets, crime analysts can use settings. A setting is a location for *recurrent* behavior at known times (Felson, 2006, p. 102). A crime setting is where people converge or diverge—influencing their crime opportunities. Some settings are largely abandoned, except for the offender and target of the crime. On a street with few pedestrians, a robber can pick off a straggler. Other, busier streets make crime more difficult. Some settings invite people to get drunk or abuse drugs. Other settings are sobering. Clearly, settings help us understand a very physical process such as crime.

Moreover, one setting can set the stage for another nearby. This is well illustrated by the *ambush sequence:*

1. A public setting (e.g., a bar) is packed with strangers.
2. One of these strangers leaves, walking down a deserted street nearby.
3. A second stranger leaves the bar, following the first until there is nobody else around to interfere.
4. At the right moment, the second stranger attacks the first.

Dennis Roncek (1981) studied dangerous places, including bars that set the stage for nearby crime. He even found that living near high schools exposes people to risk of burglary and other crimes. P. L. Brantingham and P. J. Brantingham (1984, 1993, 1999) found that the tough bars in town were the likely origin of nearby crimes, including property crimes and violence alike (see also Scott & Dedel, 2006). Our point is that settings are the central organizing feature for everyday life. Most human activities occur in settings, and the features of some settings make them more risky for crime, whereas other settings are not very risky at all. To understand this, you should learn the stages of the crime sequence and the basic elements whose presence or absence make crime likely.

The Stages of a Criminal Act

A crime incident can be meaningless without information about what led up to it. For example, one man punches another in the face and breaks his nose. But why did this happen? What led up to the event? What happened afterward? Your task as a student of crime is to think about the behavior sequences of everyday life. You should figure out when those sequences set the stage for crime. As you think about everyday sequences, you will better understand how the setting and the people in it get involved in crime.

You can divide the sequence for a criminal act into three stages (Felson, 2006, p. 42):

Stage 1. The *prelude.* The events that lead directly up to and into the criminal act, such as getting drunk, driving through a neighborhood, or waiting until no one is looking
Stage 2. The *incident:* The immediate criminal act, such as punching someone, breaking a window, or stealing a purse out of a car
Stage 3. The *aftermath:* Whatever happens after or as a result of the incident, such as the offender fleeing the scene, fencing stolen goods, or using a stolen credit card.

Notice that other criminal acts are often committed in the aftermath. Thus, a burglary sets the stage for a second crime, fencing stolen goods, and maybe a third crime and a fourth. Now that we've covered the sequence of a criminal act and its stages, let's dissect the criminal act into its elements.

The Almost-Always Elements of a Criminal Act

Most criminal acts occur in a favorable setting. Criminal acts have three *almost-always elements:*

- A likely offender
- A suitable target
- The absence of a capable guardian against the offense

Starting with the likely offender, anybody might commit a crime. Yet the best candidate is a young male with a big mouth who does poorly in school, loses jobs, gets into traffic accidents, and ends up in the emergency room (Gottfredson & Hirschi, 1990). Daily life helps some people reach their full criminal potential, whereas others have a stunted criminal growth. Although most active offenders start young, some criminals may be late bloomers. The march of life provides new criminal opportunities, hence changing the pool of likely offenders as time goes on, while making some previous offenders more efficient or less so.

A suitable target is any person or thing that draws the offender toward a crime, whether a car that invites him to steal it, some money that he could easily take, somebody who provokes him into a fight, or somebody who looks like an easy purse-snatch.

"Guardians" should not be mistaken for police officers or security guards, who are very unlikely to be on the spot when a crime occurs. The most significant guardians in society are ordinary citizens going about their daily routines. Usually, you are the best guardian for your own property. Your friends and relatives also can serve as guardians for you and your property, as you can for theirs. Even strangers can serve as guardians if they are nearby, and the offender thinks they might turn him in or otherwise interfere with his plans. Some guardians are employees, such as a store clerk or other employee who helps protect against business crime.

With a guardian present, the offender avoids attempting to carry out an offense in the first place. *The guardian differs from the offender and target, because the* absence *of a guardian is what counts.* A guardian is not usually someone who brandishes a gun or threatens an offender with quick punishment, but rather someone whose mere presence serves as a gentle reminder that someone is looking.

The Crime Triangle

You recall the not-me fallacy from the first chapter—the idea that "I'm too good for crime." Yet most people commit some crime sometimes. When will otherwise "good" people do bad things? The answer to that question has to do with temptations, opportunities, and controls. Professor John Eck of the University of Cincinnati devised the basic crime triangle (Figure 1.1), another tool for thinking about crime settings[1] (Center for Problem-Oriented Policing, 2009). You can always come back to that triangle if you get lost when studying crime. This triangle can be applied to anything from loud music to murder.

The small inner triangle in the center of the figure gives the three features of each crime problem: the offender, the crime target, and the place or setting where the crime occurs. These three elements need to converge in space and time.

But for that to happen, the offender must evade supervision of three types. The outer triangle tells us about this supervision. A handler supervises potential offenders; for

Figure 1.1 The Basic Crime Triangle

Figure 1.2 The Dynamic Crime Triangle

example, mom, dad, the football coach, and the teachers are handlers whose presence or controls (e.g., curfew) discourages misbehavior. A place is supervised by a place manager, whose presence and alertness discourages crime from happening there. A target of crime within that place is any relevant person or piece of property. It can include money to steal, a person to attack, or somebody selling illegal drugs.

After evading the handler, the likely offender must find a place containing a crime target whose place manager is absent or indisposed. Then he must find a target with no guardian watching it. In sum, the offender moves away from handlers toward a place without a manager and a target without a guardian. This mix of divergences and convergences is summed up in the Dynamic Crime Triangle (Figure 1.2).

Pay close attention to place managers. Examples are hotel or store clerks and apartment building managers. They control the physical environment, set and enforce rules, oversee behavior, and thus influence crime. A school principal or mall manager might influence thousands of people and affect whether or not crime occurs. A bar owner with lax policies on underage drinking makes possible more drunk driving, fights, and sexual assaults in and around his bar. Managers are especially important for minimizing illegal drug sales and controlling public drinking.

Suppose two teenagers break into your car in the university lot, stealing your phone while you're in class. The teens escaped their parental supervision, found a car whose guardian (you) is absent. The parking manager is either absent or indisposed, and perhaps had not thought out well the design of lighting, video surveillance, or location of parking spaces.

The Often-Important Elements of a Criminal Act

These almost-always elements of a crime are supplemented by its *often-important elements:*

- Any props that help produce or prevent a crime, including weapons or tools
- Any camouflage that helps the offender avoid unwanted notice
- Any audience the offender wants either to impress or intimidate

Thus, an ideal crime provides the offender a target in the absence of a guardian against crime. A setting is even more ideal if it contains things that offenders like to use, audiences they wish to impress, and camouflage to hide their illegal action from anybody who might interfere. Additional features of daily life affect criminal acts, as you shall see in the progress of this book. Figure 1.3 depicts a setting containing almost-always and often-important elements of crime. The almost-always elements are shown in the upper half of the setting. The often-important elements are shown in the bottom half of the setting, where the camouflage hides the target, the props are accessible to the offender, and any audience can see the target and be seen by the offender. The general crime setting depicted in Figure 1.3 will, of course, vary among the great variety of criminal acts.

Notice in Figure 1.3 that the offender and target have entered the setting, and the guardian has exited. The offender may have props (such as tools to cut away what he's going to steal) and perhaps an audience (such as his other offenders, easily impressed by his mischievous display). And so it goes with everyday crime.

The direct-contact predatory crime predominates, even in a computerized age. True, the Internet and phone systems make many remote predatory crimes possible, but direct physical contact remains the most common criminal technique. That is why crimes are still so dependent on settings. This is true for each of three major categories of illegal action: predatory crimes, fights, and consensual criminal acts.

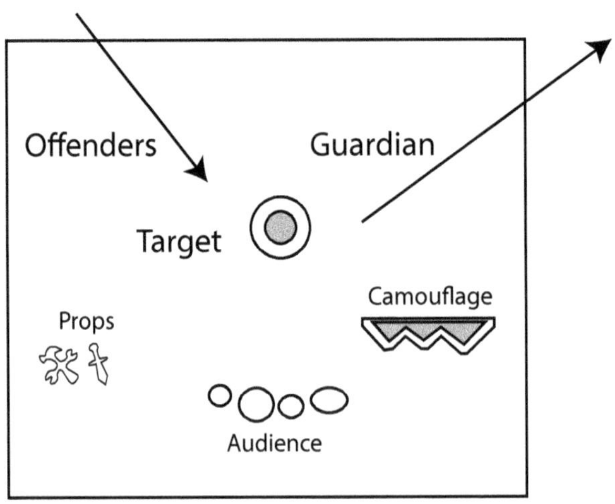

Figure 1.3 The Setting for the Crime

Predatory Crimes

Although we often think of crime as predatory, with clear victims, in fact, ordinary crime also includes fights and consensual criminal acts.

Predatory crime occurs when the offender is clearly different from the victim, and the victim objects to the offender's actions. Notably, most Part I crimes are this type—rape, robbery, burglary, theft, auto theft. Other examples include child abuse, bullying, and identity theft. An ideal predatory offense requires at least one clearly guilty offender preying on at least one clearly innocent person or a property target the offender has no right to.

Predatory offenders are mostly impersonal. They do not care how the victim feels. Robbers just want the money, and if you give it to them politely, they usually just go away. There are exceptions. Some predatory attacks are personal, made by someone mad at someone else. For example, a local boy may get even with the neighbor who scolded him by vandalizing his car. But these noteworthy offenses do not negate the general rule that the offender is most oriented toward himself, not his victim. Indeed, we prefer the word "target" to "victim" because the offender is usually oriented toward either property or a person treated largely in physical terms.

The *predatory sequence* typically works like this:

1. A likely offender enters a setting.
2. A suitable target enters, too.
3. A guardian leaves.
4. An offender attacks the target.

Some settings are called *crime attractors* (Brantingham & Brantingham, 1998, 1999) because they are especially likely to draw offenders. In such cases, the first and second steps are reversed. In other settings, likely offenders and suitable targets are around for other purposes, but criminal acts emerge. These are called *crime generators.* Given enough time, settings may themselves transform, as shown in the following crime attraction sequence:

1. A setting has normal legal activities.
2. It assembles crime elements and becomes a crime generator.
3. Active offenders figure this out.
4. The setting becomes a crime attractor, with crime getting still worse.

You can readily see why the setting is central for crime analysis. That's where the action is. In most settings most of the time, crime does *nut* occur. The question to ask is whether the almost-always and often-important elements are present. You can see that a setting is not fixed in time. It transforms itself, altering crime opportunities and outcomes. That process occurs not only for predatory crimes but also for other offenses.

Fights

Fights are violent interactions involving two or more persons in the same conflict role. Most fights emerge from quarrels in which neither party is fully innocent. Often they are equally guilty, or almost so. They frequently have a pre-existing relationship, but sometimes strangers or near-strangers get into a fight.

True, one guy might have thrown the first punch, but if the other guy insulted or taunted him, it is hard to call that a predatory crime. Fighting words and a fighting response usually incriminate both sides. Typically, the police take the winner of the fight to jail and the loser to the hospital.

The *escalation sequence* typically works like this:

1. One party perceives an insult from the other.
2. He responds to the insult and escalates the confrontation.
3. That answer evokes a similar escalation.
4. Someone throws the first punch, and so it goes.

In a fight, the audience is especially important, for it enhances the embarrassment of being insulted and compels a response. If someone in the audience acts as peacemaker and face-saver, escalation can be averted. Comments like "Don't pay any attention to Joe" or "You guys knock it off" generally suffice to quiet the waters. On the other hand, some members of an audience may act as troublemakers or provokers. Statements such as "Are you going to let him say that to you?" tend to encourage escalation. These individuals are considered handlers because they are influencing the behavior of the offender(s).

Many social psychologists have investigated this escalation process in laboratories. The professor hires a "stooge," another student pretending to be a subject. An observer sits behind a one-way mirror watching. The undergraduate "subject" enters the room, thinking the experiment has not started. The stooge insults him, perhaps saying, "That's an ugly shirt you're wearing." The observer notes whether the subject responds to the insult and escalates the encounter, or shrugs it off. Some experiments introduce different audiences, or peacemakers, or provokers. The general picture of escalation given above is substantiated over many experiments (Kennedy & Forde, 1999; Tedeschi & Felson, 1994).

Consensual Crime: Illegal Markets

Consensual crimes involve at least two parties as illegal counterparts. For example, an illegal drug sale involves a buyer and a seller. A knowing buyer and seller of stolen goods also engage in consensual crimes.

Which markets are illegal may vary among nations and even American states, but they have a common pattern. The buyer and seller are cooperating. Neither wants to get caught. The offenders in an illegal sale, acting in different roles, are symbiotic in a biologist's sense: They depend on each other like flowers and bees.

Illegal markets for goods. These are for selling drugs or contraband, counterfeit money or products, as well as goods known to be stolen. Many stolen goods are also sold without the knowledge that they are stolen. Illegal markets also include legal items sold illegally. Thus, the beer you might buy as an underage college freshman, even though from a legitimate store, fits the "illegal market" definition.

Illegal markets for services. Illegal markets may link buyers and sellers of prostitution, illegal sex shows, or even contract killings. A less sinister example is the ongoing chain of illegal services that makes New York's Chinatown work. The restaurants and their suppliers are mostly unlicensed and untaxed, and the delicious plate of noodles you can buy there at a cut rate reflects this.

Illegal markets for persons. These include slaves, women sold into prostitution, and persons smuggled into work arrangements across borders (see Chin, 1999, 2001; David, 2000; Zhang & Chin, 2002; Zhang, Chin, & Miller, 2007). Yet millions of people are smuggled into the United States with their own consent, and hired willingly by American employers.

Settings for illegal markets. These illegal transactions have physical requirements and depend on suitable settings. Figure 1.4 shows some of the settings for drug sales. Ideal for recruiting new customers are the outdoor, round-the-clock settings, such as the edges of parks or liquor stores. These are readily available to strangers who can spot what is happening quite easily. Next best are small apartment buildings or abandoned houses, but as these become well-known sources of drugs, offenders may move toward the previously described "ideal" places. Personal ties are less suitable for recruiting new users because the seller is (in the short run) limited to those he or she already knows. However, personal networks do fan out and can, in time, spread illegal sales to a broader audience.

Research on drug sales now pays very close attention to settings (Eck, 1995; Green, 1996; Jacobson, 1999; Natarajan, 2006; Natarajan & Hough, 2000; Rengert, 1996;

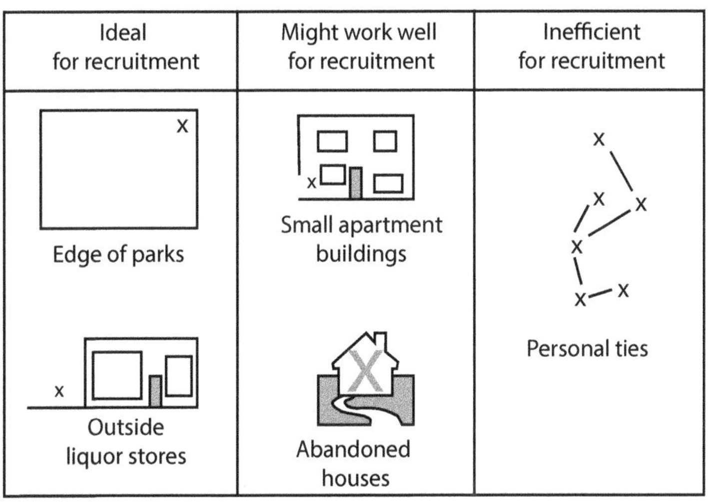

Figure 1.4 Types of Drug Sale Setting and Recruiting New Customers

Rengert, Chakravorty, Bole, & Henderson, 2000; Reuter, 1998). A remarkable private entrepreneur, Severin Sorensen, has achieved major reductions in outdoor drug sales and related crime by redesigning settings where drugs are sold. Police crackdowns on the ideal settings for selling drugs serve to reduce the problem greatly (Knutsson, 2000; see also Rengert, 1996; Weisburd & Green, 1995). After such settings are denied, the population of drug abusers tends to get older and older. It is short-sighted for police or other officials to say, "Those drug sellers just went indoors; I'm giving up." The outdoor settings provide the best *recruitment of new drug abusers,* hence replenishing a sick and aging clientele. Denying the best settings, as Rengert et al. (2000) explain, serves a serious purpose.

Calming the Waters and Looking after Places

Several roles have already been described for people who calm the crime problem. Guardians can prevent properly crime and illegal sales. Handlers or peacemakers in particular can discourage fights. Managers also serve to prevent crime settings from deteriorating because they oversee and monitor the settings:

- Homeowners and long-time renters
- Building superintendents, doormen, and receptionists
- Bartenders, managers, and owners
- Small-business persons and store managers
- Street vendors
- Security people with focused responsibilities
- Park and playground supervisors
- Train station managers
- Bus drivers

Each place manager has an incentive to prevent crime. The owners and long-time residents want the place to be safe. The businesspeople want to make money. The others want to keep their jobs and be safe, too. Society has other guardians, but place managers are probably the most important of all. On the other hand, they cannot watch everything everywhere.

Crime analysts have also paid a good deal of attention to natural surveillance. That includes ordinary citizens going about their daily lives, but providing by their presence some degree of security. We can learn a great deal from Oscar Newman's (1972) classic distinction:

1. Private space,
2. Semiprivate space,
3. Semipublic space, and
4. Public space.

Private space might include the inside of your home. The area just outside your home—such as an apartment lobby—is probably semiprivate. That means you have a good deal of control over who goes there. Semipublic space is farther out, such as a yard in front of an apartment building, where the public might not always go but can get to rather easily. Public space, such as a street or sidewalk, is especially difficult for you to control, and hence provides the least security. But you can never be entirely sure of keeping any space secure from crime. That's why you must pay close attention to crime targets themselves.

Risky Settings

Daily life is divided into different types of settings, some of which generate a lot of crime (see Clarke & Eck, 2005, Step 15; Clarke & Eck, 2007; Felson, 1987). The riskiest types of settings are

a. *Public routes,* especially foot paths, parking facilities, and unsupervised transit area
b. *Recreation settings,* especially bars and some parks
c. *Public transport,* especially stations and their vicinities
d. *Retail stores,* especially for shoplifting
e. *Residential settings,* especially for burglary and theft
f. *Educational settings,* especially on their edges
g. *Offices,* especially when easily entered for theft
h. *Human services,* especially hospitals with 24-hour activities
i. *Industrial locations,* especially warehouses with attractive goods.

Hot Products

Some products are stolen much more than others. Start with cars. The Highway Loss Data Institute (http://www.carsafety.org) shows that specific makes and models differ greatly in their probability of being stolen. Table 1.1 sums up the theft loss data for 2003 to 2005 two-door car models, as reported in September 2006. It shows that the Honda Civic hatchback generates *9.8 times so much theft risk* as the Mini Cooper. The Honda Accord creates about twice as much insurance theft problem as the Chevrolet Cavalier (see Brown & Billing, 1996; Clarke, 1999). Even trucks vary greatly in their ability to attract thieves (Brown, 1995). Clearly, some products attract the attention of thieves much more than others. Jewelry, cash, and small electronic goods are more likely to be stolen in burglaries than most items in the house.

According to the National Retail Security Survey, in recent years, those products most stolen from stores have been magazines, shirts, jeans, items with the Hilfiger or Polo label. CDs, videocassettes, beauty aids, cigarettes, batteries, condoms, sneakers. Nike shoes, hand tools, jewelry, and action toys (Hayes, 1997b, 1999, 2000, 2003). As

Model	Theft Index
Honda Civic Hatchback	236
Chevrolet Monte Carlo	156
Acura RSX	146
Mitsubishi Eclipse	141
Honda Accord	112
Pontiac Grand Am	111
Dodge Stratus	111
Hyundai Tiburon	102
Toyota Celica	91
Volkswagen Golf	90
Honda Civic Coupe	86
Chrysler Sebring Convertible	66
Chevrolet Cavalier	66
Scion tC	63
Toyota Camry Solara	56
Ford Focus	49
Pontiac Sunfire	49
Audi A4 Cabriolet Convertible	48
Volkswagen New Beetle Convertible	42
Saturn ION Quad Coupe	32
Volkswagen New Beetle	28
Hyundai Accent	27
Mini Cooper	24

Table 1.1 Theft losses for Two-Door Cars, 2003–2005 Models, United States
*Calculated from average loss payments per insured vehicle-year, then indexed to the average for all two-door cars. Thus, 104 is 4% worse than average.

times change, types of products stolen change as well; we are seeing iPods, DVDs, and video games being stolen often today.

Past studies have compared retail value per pound of most stolen goods (see Cohen & Felson, 1979; Felson & Cohen, 1980). Washing machines are worth several hundred dollars, but only about $5 per pound. They are not usually stolen. In contrast, electronic consumer goods are high in value per pound and attractive targets of crime. Clarke's (1999) pamphlet *Hot Products* tells us a good deal about which items are most likely to be stolen. That and other sources help us understand an important issue in the chemistry of crime. What features of crime targets make them so inviting?

Items That Invite Theft

The property offender wants to steal something valuable, enjoyable, and available. He wants to be sure he can remove it from the property. As he removes it, he wants to be able to conceal it. After he removes it, he wants to have a way to dispose of it, perhaps selling it to somebody else.

Clarke (1999) rearranged those words to form this acronym for goods "craved" by thieves. Hot products tend to be

Concealable
Removable
Available
Valuable
Enjoyable
Disposable

Cash solves all six problems, so it will be a hot product as long as we are still printing it. Jewelry is often desirable, too, for it is easily concealed on one's person. A very common car is easier to conceal than an unusual model (such as a Rolls Royce) that is easy to spot. Small items and those on wheels are the easiest to remove. Light televisions are more vulnerable than the heaviest models. If thieves had to carry the car on their backs, there would be no car theft.

Items produced in great numbers and placed near a door are most likely to be stolen because they are available (Clarke, 2002). Valued items to young thieves might be popular CDs, but not Beethoven. Old-style maternal minivans are almost never stolen because young car thieves do not want them. Offenders are more likely to steal products that are fun to own or consume. They tend to enjoy alcohol, tobacco, expensive clothes, fancy shoes. DVDs, or condoms. Thieves also prefer items easy to dispose of.

Hot Products Are Affected by Their Settings

Hot products are affected by the setting that contains them. A household burglar targets both the home and the goods inside it. Many burglars assume that something good is inside, paying attention to the building in making their decisions. The offender considers tall bushes that could conceal entry and exit and may take into account the proximity to the Street and driveway, enabling removal of what is taken. The offender also considers the environment and whether people are in the building, which is why residential burglaries happen predominantly during the day when the residents aren't home. Subsequent chapters of this book will go into more detail on how settings affect offender decisions, which also then provide tools for preventing crime.

Stores that hide their cash-counting operations in an upstairs office gain some protection by not tempting people needlessly. Being out of sight also helps protect some illegal transactions from prying eyes. Access is the ability of an offender to get to the target and then away from the scene of a crime. With enough effort and sufficient tools, every offender can get to every target, but the whole idea of crime is to get things the easy way, acquiring few skills and applying little effort over a short time. Easy access is essential for ordinary crime. Many offenders are probably even more concerned with their exits than their entrance, wanting a safe getaway. Flashing money, leaving valuables out, making obvious the lack of locks, putting valuables by the front window where people pass by, living on a busy street, inviting too many people to see your new stereo, putting a shiny new car on the street, letting the hedges overrun the back windows—all of these can generate extra crime risk.

Targets Vary by Offender Motive

Legal definitions of criminal acts often hide human differences. For example, auto thieves differ in their motives and hence in the targets they pick (Clarke & Harris, 1992):

- A joyrider takes a trip for fun, picking a flashy and fun car.
- A "traveler" chooses almost any car that's convenient and drives home.
- A felon steals a car to perform another crime, picking a fast model.
- A parts chopper selects a common model 3 to 5 years old for which parts are in demand.
- A "shipper" takes a luxury car to sell abroad.

As motives shift, so do targets.

When Heavy Items Are Stolen

We noted earlier that washing machines and other heavy appliances are worth a lot of money but too heavy for the average thief to remove quickly. But the exceptions illustrate how relative these concepts really are. Washers, dryers, dishwashers, and similar appliances are sometimes burgled from rural homes, vacation homes in the off-season, or construction sites. In these three cases, pickup trucks are probably common, making the burglary easier to conduct and less likely to stand out.

As a general rule, the weight of items burgled increases as one goes farther from the city center. Inside the city, burglars are more likely to work on fool, doing their best to carry off money or jewels. In suburbs, more burglars use cars and can remove televisions or other electronic goods. In rural areas, with pickup trucks at hand and guardians away, offenders may find it easier to load up with whatever they want. At construction sites, burglars may look and act like construction workers and have the equipment and trucks to uninstall and drive away with the appliances (Boba & Santos, 2008; Clarke & Goldstein, 2002).

Heavier items are also stolen when wheels provide a getaway. Cars, motorcycles, mopeds, and bicycles face high risk. A family returned from vacation to find that someone had broken into their garage, taking the two cheaper bikes but leaving the expensive one that had no air in the tires. On some college campuses, bicycles are often stolen. In nations such as the Netherlands and China, where bicycles are a primary form of transportation, their theft is endemic.

Theft Trends

To learn which targets offenders crave, find out what is popular among youths. What brands of shoes are in style? What video games are in demand? What clothing labels are in current fashion? What items are getting lighter? Has the packaging changed? Are items being stored where they are more subject to theft?

Changes in goods and money are very important for crime rate trends. Cohen and Felson (1979) have shown that one of the major causes of the mushrooming crime rates in the United States after 1963 was the proliferation of lightweight durable goods that were easy to steal. Knutsson and Kuhlhorn (1997) in Sweden and Tremblay (1986) in Quebec. Canada, demonstrated that easier use of checks and credit cards without careful identification produced a proliferation of fraud. Americans using far less cash helped to produce the declining U.S. crime rates since 1990 (Felson, 1998). You can see that the CRAVED model tells us a great deal about theft variations and trends. These practical features also apply to targets of violent crime and how offenders select these targets.

Craving Violent Targets

Like property offenders, those who commit violence also have problems to solve. The CRAVED model applies well, especially if we shift to verbs. A violent offender generally needs to *conceal* the violent act, as well as steps before and after it. He must *remove* himself safely from the scene; *avail* himself of a convenient human target for violent attack; find a target of *value* in his own mind; *enjoy* the criminal act, or at least avoid pain to himself; and *dispose of* incriminating evidence, even the victim.

To solve these problems, offenders pick dark and isolated alleys or parks, spots with easy entry and exit for themselves and a good chance to ambush someone, victims who are weak and alone, and victims who give pleasure and cannot easily inflict pain; they even consider simple ways to dispose of weapons. Kidnappers, for instance, probably wait until the victim is most available. They may pick a victim from a wealthy family. They may enjoy getting even with that family or someone in it. And they may find a remote location that permits disposal of their victim without being seen. A blitz rape (LeBeau, 1987) is also a highly physical crime. An example is when an offender grabs a victim from a dark street and then rapes her in nearby bushes. The target and setting are concealed. The target is usually small and weak enough to be removed from one spot to another. The offender may live, work, shop, or prefer recreation in certain areas where he finds a victim available. Rapists normally are attracted to victims of younger ages, reflecting their pursuit of pleasure (R. Felson, 2002; Tedeschi & Felson, 1994; for some reason, this point is controversial). Some rapists even kill victims and dispose of the bodies, or at least try to dispose of any evidence of their own criminal behavior.

Store robbers attack cash registers that are concealed by advertisements plastering the windows. They seek removable cash near the door and available stores near the freeway or large boulevards. These robbers would generally prefer stores that have no drop safe and whose employees are in some sense, compliant. Stores with lots of small bills assist the offender's disposal of the loot. Moreover, those offenders who use a mask or disguise need a place to dump it unseen.

The literature increasingly recognizes the physical side of assaults as more than incidental. Richard Felson (1996) explained in *Big People Hit Little People* how physical size and strength influence assaults. The classic book by Olweus (1978), *Aggression in the Schools: Bullies and Whipping Boys,* explained how larger and stronger children abused those smaller and weaker. Studying Norway and learning from other nations not known for their violence, Olweus showed that violence between children is probably universal among nations and very common in schools (see also Baldry & Farrington, 2007; Espelage & Swearer, 2004; Greif & Furlong, 2006; Smith et al., 1999). Bullying also applies to other ages and settings, as explained in Randall's (1997) book *Adult Bullies* and Barron's (2000) work on "workplace bullies"

Those who crave sexual release with children or young teenagers can also be pragmatic. James M. Mannon (1997) considers how easy it is for stepparents to gain access to stepchildren, priests to choirboys, and child care workers to young children. Offenses usually occur in settings with guardians absent and unable to intervene. Family members are also more vulnerable to intimate victimization when isolated. Baumgartner (1993) found that wives with the support of family members have less risk of being beaten by husbands (see also Davis, Maxwell, & Taylor, 2006; Felson, Ackerman, & Yeon, 2003; Felson & Outlaw, 2007; Zolotor & Runyan, 2006). Opportunities for sexual coercion also seem to be linked to physical access (Tedeschi & Felson, 1994; Wortley & Smallbone, 2006).

The essential point is that both property and violent offenses are physical acts involving tangible targets whose specific features make them more suitable for offenders to attack.

The General Chemistry of Crime

Each crime type has its particular chemistry. Crimes also have a common chemistry. For each setting, consider its presences and absences, its entries and exits, and how these make a particular crime likely to occur. Even solo drug abuse depends on the absence of anyone to interfere. Some settings favor one offense but not another; for example, a crowd drives away most offenders but invites pickpocketing. Some settings enhance many types of crime. Scholars have shown that blocks containing bars or high schools have more crime (Roncek & Lobosco, 1983; Roncek & Maier, 1991). Other work uses the medical term "hot spots" to show that a small number of addresses (such as a large retail store or a tough bar) generate many more than their share of calls for police service (Sherman et al., 1989). Even within a high-crime area, most specific addresses appear to be quite safe, whereas a few addresses generate most of the problem.

To understand where many types of crime risk occur, Brantingham and Brantingham (1998, 1999) offer three terms:

1. *Nodes:* settings such as homes, schools, workplaces, shopping or strip malls, and entertainment areas. They provide particular crime opportunities and risks. A node that favors one type of crime might not favor another, but specific crime risks differ greatly among nodes.
2. *Paths:* leading from one node to another, also offering crime opportunities and risks. Not only do paths conduct more people per square foot—hence providing offenders, targets, and guardians—but also lead people to nodes that might involve them, one way or another, in crime.
3. *Edges:* places where two local areas touch. Crime is often most risky here. At the edges of an area, outsiders can intrude quickly and then leave without being stopped or even noticed. For example, college students might find their cars broken into when they park at the edge of campus. Those who can only find parking at the edge of a high-crime area suffer greater properly or even personal risk.

Finally, some human categories face the greatest general risk of crime victimization, including young males, especially if they are single, living alone, drinking a lot, and staying out late. Those who are past victims or are themselves frequent offenders also face extra victimization hazards (Hindelang, Gottfredson, & Garafolo, 1978; see also Fattah, 1991; Kennedy & Forde, 1990; Lasley & Rosenbaum, 1988). If you put together hot products, young males, people living alone, heavy drinking, late hours—at risky nodes or along edges of areas—you have created the ideal chemistry for crime. But this is just a generalization; in this book, you will learn details that vary from that theme.

Conclusion

As you read this book, you should look at life from the offenders point of view. The offender sees targets and considers whether guardians are absent. The offender picks suitable settings from his own point of view. The offender is the one who takes offense, gets in a quarrel, and then gets into a fight, so his viewpoint is the one you need to consider to understand how that happens.

Yet offenders are but one element in a crime, and probably not even the most important. Predatory crimes need targets with guardians absent. Fights thrive on audiences and troublemakers without peacemakers. Illegal sales depend on settings where buyers and sellers can converge with camouflage present and place managers absent. Offenses depend on quick entry and exit. Targets most craved by offenders are concealable, removable, available, valuable, enjoyable, and disposable. We shall argue in the course of this book that *opportunity is a root cause of crime* (Felson & Clarke, 1998). Everyday life tempts and impairs potential offenders, influencing their decisions about crime, as the next chapter considers in detail.

Main Points

1. A setting is a location for recurrent use, for a particular area, at known times; a crime setting is where people converge or diverge to influence crime opportunities.
2. The sequence of a criminal act can be broken down into three stages: the "prelude," the "incident," and the "aftermath."
3. A criminal act has three elements almost always present: a likely offender, a suitable personal or property target, and the absence of a capable guardian against a crime.
4. The crime triangle illustrates the relationships among offender, target, place, and time and mechanisms that can influence crime opportunities, handlers, guardians, and managers.
5. Predatory crime occurs when the offender is clearly different from the victim, and the victim objects to the offender's actions.
6. A fight begins with an insult and then escalates, often affected by an audience and alcohol. Peacemakers can quiet things down and prevent that escalation.
7. Illegal markets are those in which participation is voluntary and consensual. Types include illegal markets for goods, services, and persons.
8. Place managers have a large span of control, making their role in crime opportunities important.
9. Settings, some of which are at higher risk for crime, include public routes, recreation settings, public transport, retail stores, residential settings, educational settings, offices, human services, and industrial locations.
10. Offenders "crave" hot products and targets of violence for specific reasons.
11. Crime risks occur at nodes, paths, and edges.
12. Opportunity is the root cause of crime.

Projects and Challenges

Interview projects. (a) Interview any retail store owner, manager, clerk, or someone who worked in a retail store about what gets shoplifted. If you yourself worked in a store, supplement the interview with your own experience. (b) Interview a bartender, bar owner, or server about conflicts—how they develop and are prevented in a bar setting, and how to keep them from escalating.

Media project. Find a rich newspaper account of any plain crime and describe the prelude, the crime incident, and the aftermath. Draw from this chapter to make sense of the account.

Map project. Draw (a) the floor plan of a retail store and consider the vulnerable places for shoplifting based on layout and types of goods, or (b) the inside of two bars and consider which one is more likely to have people bumping into each other and other conflicts.

Photo project. Find four different places on campus most suitable for a crime to occur. Photograph each one and then describe it.

Web project. Use the Internet to gather information that helps you elaborate any point in this chapter. You might find the Web page one author [MF] has designed (crimeprevention.rutgers.edu) useful to you.

Note

1. Also called the "problem analysis triangle."

Chapter Two

Misinformation About the Crime Problem

By Travis C. Pratt

In recent decades, it has become fashionable for political figureheads to decry the nation's "crime problem." News-friendly quips from political pundits come in many flavors, but most often they are merely slight variations of the common theme that crime in the United States is "out of control." Such claims are aided by high-profile violent incidents such as the rise in the number of school shootings—over 20 incidents since 1996, with over 70 deaths and over 100 injured—and the terror brought on by the Washington, D.C.-area snipers in 2002 and the Virginia Tech University shootings in 2007. These events are certainly tragic in their own right, yet they also tap into our deepest fear of crime: stranger-to-stranger violent victimization.

The end result of such tragedies is that policy makers have continued to feel justified in their message to the American citizenry that it is reasonable for all of us to be afraid of the random victimization experienced by those on television since, as evidenced by such horrific events, the crime problem in this country is off the charts. And it is not just crime, but the *kind* of crime—those offenses that citizens buy deadbolts for their doors to shield themselves against—that is important. After all, the message implies, this is not some socially constructed "moral panic" over nothing, but rather a rational response for us to want to protect ourselves from what John Dilulio and colleagues (including former Drug Czar and Department of Education Secretary William Bennett) have dubbed "superpredators"—those intrinsically flawed evildoers who are apparently growing in number (Bennett et al. 1996).

Curiously, this position seems to be at odds with the recent "crime drop" in the United States during the 1990s, which has been described by criminologists as "extraordinary" (Conklin 2003, vii) and "remarkable" (Blumstein and Wallman 2000, 1). Despite this potential call for optimism, some criminologists, such as James Alan Fox (who also frequently appears before Congress on matters of crime policy), still warn us of impending doom: "We are facing a potential bloodbath of teenage violence in years ahead that will be so bad, we'll look back at the 1990s and say those were the good old days" (quoted in Austin and Irwin 2001, 239).[1] Based on comments like this and others like it, DiIulio appeared to make the ongoing exponential growth of the prison system in this country a personal crusade during the 1990s (see, e.g., DiIulio and Piehl 1991). Such growth would be necessary, according to DiIulio (1995, 15), to give us a fighting chance of winning the battle against the "fatherless, Godless, and jobless" superpredators.

This chapter examines the validity of these claims by tracing how three misconceptions about the nature of crime in the United States have served as political fodder for advocates of the expanded use of incarceration. The first misconception is that increases in the "fear of crime" among Americans simply reflect increases in the objective probability of being victimized. This myth is necessary for policy makers to justify the continued growth of incarceration as a means of addressing the fears of their voters. The second misconception is that low-level offenders (e.g., drug and property offenders) will inevitably graduate to violent offending in the absence of a stiff criminal sanction. This erroneous assumption has been the key for stiffening the sanctions associated with virtually all criminal offenses—not just violent crimes. The third misconception is that chronic, life-course persistent offending can be accurately predicted using variables that are given the most "weight" in criminal justice processing: the severity of the offense and the offender's prior record. These factors play directly into enhanced sentencing schemes by being the primary axes for determining an offender's punishment in the sentencing grids that have been adopted by states. By themselves, the acceptance of any one of these mistruths would be enough to cause advocates of mass incarceration to salivate in anticipation and to cause critics of the current state of imprisonment to lose their appetites. When taken together, however, like the combination of heroin and cocaine, these individual slices of misinformation have merged to create a "speed-ball" political justification for sustaining the incarceration addiction.

Victimization and the Fear of Crime

Prior to the 1960s, crime was not cited by the American public as being a major issue of concern (Chambliss 1999). Even when President Reagan formally launched his "War on Drugs" in 1982—which effectively tied the issues of crime and drugs together for years to come—less than 2 percent of American citizens cited drugs as the nation's most pressing problem. This figure had changed dramatically by the time Reagan's understudy, George Herbert Walker Bush, took office in 1988 (and appointed a "Drug Czar"), at which time 64 percent of Americans believed that the drug problem was the most salient issue facing the nation (Beckett 1997). This trend also followed public concern over crime in general, where even as late as June of 1993—under the leadership of President Bill Clinton this time, and right before Congress began its debate over his "crime bill" proposal—only 7 percent of Americans cited crime as the nation's most important problem. Just 6 months later, and largely as a result of the intense publicity these legislative sessions received, that number had increased to 30 percent (Braun and Pasternak, 1994). By August of 1994, that figure had reached 52 percent, which public opinion pollsters attributed to Clinton's discussion of the crime bill in the State of the Union Address, and to the extensive media coverage of how Congress was considering the bill (Moore 1994; see also Alderman 1994).

It is clear, therefore, that Americans' concern over the crime problem has increased substantially in recent years and, despite stable and even falling crime rates, fear of crime continues to be high (Gallup 1999). As can be seen in Figure 2.1, the trends in American citizens' perceptions of both the crime rates in their local communities and nationally are that crime is not only increasing, but it is doing so dramatically. Even so, these patterns are not new; as Figure 2.2 shows that over the last couple of decades around half of all American citizens have thought that crime is on the rise, regardless

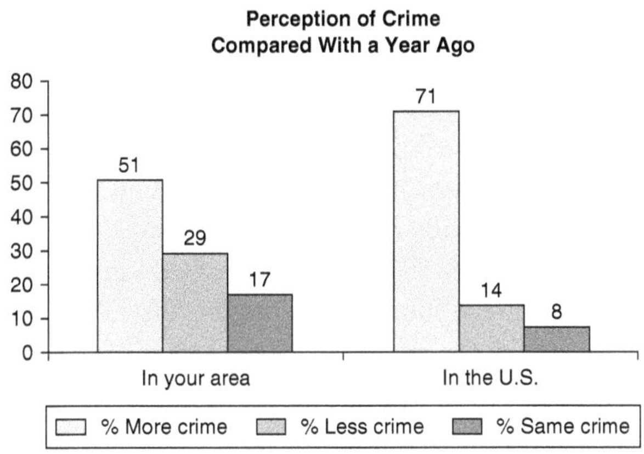

Figure 2.1 Citizens' Perceptions of Local and National Crime Rate Changes
Source: Gallup Poll, 2007.

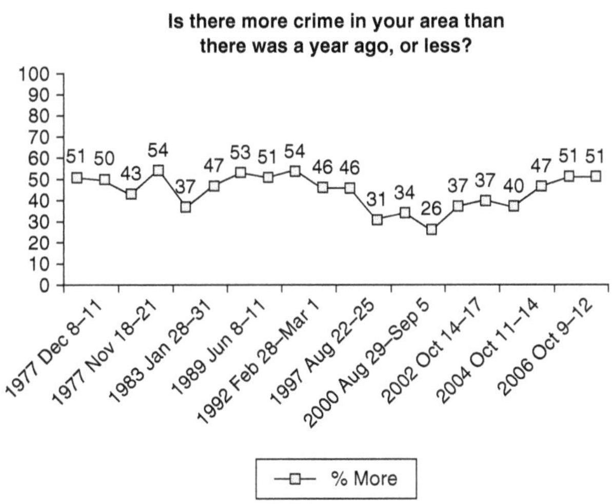

Figure 2.2 Citizens' Perceptions of Local Community Crime Increases From 1977–2006
Source: Gallup Poll, 2007.

of actual changes in rates of criminal behavior. Even in 2002, when the media blitz concerning the crime drop of the 1990s was at its strongest, a quarter of the population still believed that crime rates were increasing. In short, criminal victimization, it turns out, bears a surprisingly inconsistent relationship to fear of victimization (Lewis and Salem 1986; Taylor and Hale 1986; see also Hale 1996). If crime itself does not drive fear of crime, what does?

To answer that question, an understanding of the disconnect between citizens' perceptions of risk and the objective probability of victimization can be reached when it is examined through the lens of school shootings. For example, Brooks, Schiraldi, and Ziedenberg's (2000) analysis of national opinion polls that were taken after the shootings in Jonesboro, Arkansas, and Littleton, Colorado, found a 49 percent increase in parents' anxiety about their children's safety in the classroom. This increase occurred despite studies by the U.S. Department of Justice and the National School Safety Center that showed a 40 percent decrease in school-associated violent deaths in 1998–1999, the school year including the Columbine shooting.

While these violent incidents are undoubtedly serious social problems, their prevalence has been severely blown out of proportion. Although the probability that a child would be the victim of lethal violence in school is 1 in 2 million, an overwhelming majority of parents still feel as though it is likely that a tragic event such as this will occur in their child's school in the future (Bonderman 2001). Misplaced public fear over this issue has even resulted in an increase in the number of kids being homeschooled, presumably in an effort by parents to insulate their children from the inevitable violence that they believe must surely come with going to school with other (unpredictable) youths (Hargrove 2001).

This "knowledge gap" between the reality of crime and the public's perception of that reality is mirrored in the American news media's reliance on crime-related issues to generate advertising revenue. For example, Klite, Bardwell, and Salzman's (1997) survey of 100 television stations found that 72 of them began their evening news programming with a crime story, and that a third of all stories dealt with crime-related issues. Furthermore, Angotti's (1997) study of local news programming in eight major media markets—including the 12 million citizens in New York City's market—found that instances of crime news were twice as common as instances of political news. The reliability of crime stories to attract viewers even led KREM 2 News in Spokane, Washington, to place the phrase "Crime Is Bad" in bold letters across the screen in their 2008 television promotional ads, as if their viewers were unaware of this bit of information and therefore needed to be informed of it.

Put simply, the media have discovered that, in the United States, "crime sells," and Americans are constantly bombarded by images of crime and victimization whenever they turn on their television set or open a newspaper. Nevertheless, some scholars still contend that "media effects" on fear of crime are absent, and have effectively dismissed the existence of a "knowledge gap" outright. For example, J. Young (1987, 337) argued that "popular conceptions of crime … are, in the main, constructed out of the material experiences of people, rather than fantasies impressed upon them by mass media."

Rubin, Perse, and Taylor (1988, 126) made the similar argument that "television's influence on social reality is overshadowed by direct personal and interpersonal experience" with the reality of crime. Sparks (1992, 2) echoed these sentiments in his contention that "fear is so plainly a product of the real conditions of existence ... as to leave no space for the role of the mass media in accounting for it."

Statements like these perpetuate the misconception that citizens' fear of crime is a natural consequence of their objective probability of victimization and that the media does nothing to elevate levels of fear beyond one's own personal experiences. The fundamental problem with these arguments, however, is that they are based merely on speculation as opposed to solid, social scientific evidence. Recent empirical work on criminal victimization and the fear of crime sheds light on the myth that American citizens' fear of crime—which has been used to justify the prison boom in recent decades—is solely a function of their own immediate experiences.

Media Influences on Fear of Crime

The relationship between media influences and fear of crime has been well studied (see reviews by Eschholz 1997; Heath and Gilbert 1996). Only three studies of this relationship, however, have been conducted using data more recent than 1981—the time at which rapid prison expansion began. Furthermore, studies rarely differentiate between local and national news media effects (for an exception, see Barzagan 1994). Finally, no studies have included controls for the crime rate (as a measure of the "reality" of crime), and studies that do control for the effect of personal victimization on fear of crime (see Chiricos, Eschholz, and Gertz 1997) have been limited to single communities.

In an effort to address these methodological shortcomings, Chiricos, Padgett, and Gertz (2000) have conducted the most rigorous study of the effect of television news content on citizens' fear of crime to date. In a statewide survey of Florida residents, they isolated the independent effect of news media programming (both local and national) on fear of crime by controlling for citizens' prior victimization experiences and even their perception of the level of safety in their neighborhood. Their results indicated that, even after controlling for such experiences, exposure to both local and national news media sources significantly increased citizens' fear of crime. These effects are even more telling when the magnitude—or "strength of effects"—is taken into account. In particular, the magnitude of the media effects (local and national combined) on fear of crime was nearly twice as large as the effect of personal victimization experiences on fear of crime. These results therefore suggest that American citizens' fear of crime, while to a certain extent rooted in personal experience, is to a greater degree determined by their level of exposure to the spectacle of human horrors depicted by news media organizations.

Linking Fear to Leniency

Beckett's (1997) analysis of national public opinion surveys from 1964 to 1992 also found that changes in public concern over crime (which included indicators of concern over drugs) were unrelated to changes in crime rates. Like Chiricos and colleagues (2000), Beckett found that public concern was instead predicted by media coverage of issues associated with crime and drugs. Furthermore, and perhaps more important, public concern about crime over time was most closely tied to what she referred to as "political initiative," which is defined as "the number of speeches, statements, policy initiatives, or summaries pertaining to crime ... made by federal officials and reported in the mass media" (1997, 116).

After placing the crime issue at the top of the political agenda, policy makers—abetted by a willing media—were then able to cultivate the public's fear of crime. Even so, throwing gasoline on the fear fire was not enough, by itself, to justify a dramatic increase in prison population growth. To do that, policy makers needed to frame the apparent crime problem as a consequence of excessive leniency on the part of the criminal justice system—the techniques for which have been honed to perfection by political elites over the last 30 years. It is clear, however, that their ability to do so has been predicated on misinformation about the degree to which citizens' fears about being victimized are driven by their own experiences versus the lurid images of crime and victimization they are flooded with on a regular basis. In short, our state of mass incarceration cannot be justified on the basis that it is necessary to allay the portion of citizens' fear of crime that can be attributed to instances of personal victimization since such experiences have little to do with fear of crime.

Nonserious Crime as Gateway Offending?

In 1981, Nancy Reagan's advisors sought to change her image from a china- buying White House decorator to something with more political substance. Determined not to be stuck in some budgetary role or in some policy job (after all, these were tasks tackled by her predecessors), Mrs. Reagan informed her projects director that she wanted to address the issue of "drug abuse" (see Baum 1996, 141). Despite the warnings from the media-savvy Communications Director Michael Deaver—who instead suggested focusing on something "fun" along the lines of volunteerism or historic preservation—Nancy went forth with the drug abuse issue. What followed was the memorable "just say no" antidrug campaign, which spawned a number of subsequent generations of antidrug television spots, from "parents who use drugs have children who use drugs" (recall the defiant youth shouting at his father, "You, alright? I learned it by watching you!") to the father figure in the kitchen cracking eggs into a bacon grease-filled cast iron pan who says, "this is your brain; this is your brain on drugs." To push the "just say no" message a step further, Mrs. Reagan even made a cameo appearance alongside Gary Coleman on the television comedy *Diff'rent Strokes* in a storyline about drug use among school-aged children.

The underlying theme of the antidrug movement throughout the 1980s was not simply that drug use, in and of itself, is harmful. Rather, the message being sent to kids and, more importantly, to their parents, was that drug use is a type of "gateway offense" that opens the door to the full spectrum of criminal behavior for youths. Rising levels of violent offending during the 1980s, which were often linked to inner-city drug markets by the media and by political entrepreneurs, led the public and policy makers to adopt a misconception about the "escalation" of the severity of offending by individuals.[2] Specifically, the political culture surrounding crime—especially since the early 1980s—makes the implicit assumption that if someone is committing low-level offenses now (such as drug abuse or theft), it is only a matter of time until the person graduates into committing violent offenses such as robbery, rape, and murder. It is my contention here that this concern is misplaced, and that it is inconsistent with the reality of criminal-offending trajectories.

Categorical Contagion

The image of a young punk stealing someone's bike does not generally cause people to go and buy state-of-the-art alarm systems for their houses, to clip cans of pepper spray to their key rings, or to avoid walking home alone in the dark. These types of reactions are instead attributed to the fear of violent victimization, especially the threat of lethal violence, which is the major source of fear and anxiety for Americans. Of course, the fear of lethal violence is not unique to Americans. Kristof (1996) notes that the fear of gunshot wounds is even quite prevalent among Japanese citizens, despite the fact that there were only 32 gun-related homicides in 1995 (roughly half of the total for Newark, New Jersey, in any given year). But the United States does experience a higher rate of homicide victimization than any other Western industrialized nation (Pratt and Godsey 2003), so American citizens' fears of being murdered, in particular, are not necessarily unfounded relative to citizens of other nations. What is uniquely American, however, is that our fear of lethal violence has spread like a virus into a universal fear of all forms of crime—even those that pose no credible threat to our physical safety.

Zimring and Hawkins (1997, 13) referred to this phenomenon as "categorical contagion," which they defined as "the agency whereby citizens come to fear many forms of criminal behavior because they imagine them all committed by extremely violent protagonists." Even some criminologists, such as James Q. Wilson and George Kelling (1982), have perpetuated this pattern of overgeneralization in their argument that low-level instances of incivility and disorder in a community will inexorably lead to direct, violent, predatory victimization in the absence of some formal intervention.[3] In short, today's thief or burglar is tomorrow's rapist and killer. Yet, if this is true, why do we not find the same level and quality of fear of crime among citizens living in nations where the rate of property offending is comparable to ours, such as the United Kingdom? If there really is some sort of "law of escalation" in the severity of offending, fear of crime should be directly commensurate with the supply of potential criminal offenders in any given social context.

Upon closer examination, this proposition simply does not hold up. There is no credible empirical evidence of a progression of increasing severity in the offenses committed over the length of a criminal career (Shannon 1991; Wolfgang, Figlio, and Sellin

1972). On the one hand, offenders—even chronic offenders—are quite versatile in their offending patterns (i.e., they generally are not too picky about which offense to commit when the opportunities to do so are easy; see Piquero, Farrington, and Blumstein 2003). Nevertheless, recent work based on a large sample of high-risk, persistent offenders found no evidence of either offending "specialization" in violence or of systematic escalation of lower-level offending (e.g., drug and property offending) to violent personal crimes (McGloin et al. 2007; C. J. Sullivan et al. 2006). In short, the evidence suggests that although offenders may exhibit a lot of bad behavior, we have no reason to believe that engaging in more mundane misbehavior will, by definition, lead to the kinds of serious violent offending that tend to *really* scare people.

To illustrate this point, Zimring and Hawkins (1997) noted that for every 10 theft offenses reported in Sydney, Australia, there are just over 13 reported in Los Angeles, and for every 10 burglaries reported in Sydney, there are 9 in Los Angeles. Thus, it appears as though the overall supply of criminal offenders is roughly the same across the two cities. However, for every 100 homicides in Los Angeles, there are only 4.8 in Sydney. It is clear, therefore, that (1) despite comparable numbers of potential offenders, the nature of crime differs considerably across these two communities, and (2) a general fear of "crime" has little to do with crime at all, but rather with lethal violence, which, again, is a condition somewhat unique unto itself in the United States.

Implications for Corrections Policy

The problem is that this categorical contagion has had major implications for prison growth in this country. Here lies the fundamental paradox: as states create stiffer sanctions—presumably in an effort to rid the streets of those who would commit acts of life-threatening violence—the bulk of enforcement efforts will typically be directed toward *nonserious offenders*. Even before the creation of baseball metaphor-enhanced sentencing policies such as "Three Strikes and You're Out," offenses such as armed robbery, aggravated sexual assault, and murder almost always resulted in a prison sentence. Even with limited prison space, we can always find a bed for folks like Jeffrey Dahmer, Ted Bundy, and Gary Ridgeway (the infamous "Green River Killer"). As prison space expands, who are we going to fill prison cells with if we are already locking up serious violent offenders?

The answer, of course, is nonserious offenders. Austin and Irwin's (2001) analysis of prison admissions confirms this recent trend. Their work indicates that the most frequent crime resulting in a prison sentence is drug possession (22 percent), which is followed by burglary (20 percent), theft and fraud (20 percent), and drug delivery (15 percent), and that these four nonviolent crimes constitute 77 percent of all prison admissions. It is therefore quite obvious that in our efforts to round up violent offenders, a sizeable portion of nonviolent—and nonserious—offenders have been caught in the net. This has resulted in a dramatic shift in the composition of the inmate population in this country. What we have now is a rather large gap between violence and imprisonment—one that is aided, at least in part, by the third misconception about crime in

America: that we can accurately predict whether someone is likely to be a chronic, life-course persistent offender by taking into account the severity of his or her current offense and the extent of the person's prior record of offending.

Incapacitation and Errors in Prediction

The notion of incapacitation as a legitimate goal of punishment—incarcerating an offender so that he or she cannot break the law, at least for the duration of the individual's stay in prison—is a recent phenomenon in American correctional policy. The problem in the past has been that we believed that through imprisonment, some sort of "incapacitation effect" was inevitable (and therefore theoretically uninteresting), which contributed to incapacitation's status as a secondary purpose of punishment at best (Zimring and Hawkins 1995). In essence, incapacitation suffered from the "no duh" syndrome, where lawmakers knew they would get a marginal incapacitation effect through the incarceration of offenders. The risk of focusing on this potential benefit, however, seemed to come at the cost of admitting to the failure of both rehabilitation- and deterrence-based correctional philosophies (Feeley and Simon 1992; see also Pratt and Cullen 2005).

This all changed with Wolfgang et al.'s (1972) "birth cohort" study of Philadelphia youth, which found that 6 percent of the kids in their cohort were responsible for over half of the arrests or police contacts—a finding that has been replicated rather consistently in subsequent research (see, e.g., Chaiken and Chaiken 1984; Shannon 1991; J. D. Wright and Rossi 1986). To lawmakers in the 1970s and 1980s (see J. Q. Wilson 1975), the policy implications of this body of research were as clear as could be: since most criminal offenses are committed by a small proportion of the offender population, crime rates could be substantially reduced if we could lock up those "high-rate" offenders before they embark on their lifelong pattern of criminal activity.

Selective Incapacitation

Like any sexy policy proposal, this concept was given a catchy name to help it resonate with policy makers and the American public: "selective incapacitation." To assess the potential social value of a selective incapacitation strategy, the National Institute of Justice funded a multisite, longitudinal study of "criminal careers"—the result of which was a study published by the Rand Corporation in 1982 (Greenwood and Abrahamse 1982). Using a sample of inmates convicted of robbery and burglary from three states (Texas, Michigan, and California), Greenwood and Abrahamse constructed a seven-factor predictive scale that was composed largely of items tapping into an offender's prior criminal history (e.g., prior convictions and incarcerations, age at first conviction, substance abuse).[4] Using items such as these was critical for the successful implementation of the selective incapacitation model, since information about these factors is easily accessible to prosecutors and judges—the primary "players" in the sentencing process. Put simply, the selective incapacitation model is only seductive for policy makers if it is fairly easy to predict (with easily obtainable information) whether a particular offender will be a career criminal.

To determine if this is so, Greenwood and Abrahamse (1982) correlated their predictive scale with the self-reported estimates of offending from the inmates in their sample. Based on their analyses, they concluded that their predictive scale is accurate enough at identifying high-rate offenders that it should be used during the sentencing decision. More specifically, the high-rate offenders identified by the predictive scale should receive longer sentences so that the maximum benefit to public safety (crime reduction) could be achieved. By that same token, low-level offenders, as identified by the same predictive scale, should be given shorter sentences in order to maximize the efficient use of finite correctional resources.

It is simple to see why this model for corrections policy became so popular. The idea of reducing crime by locking people up for an extended period of time—as opposed to wasting our energy trying to change offenders' behavior through rehabilitative practices—was consistent with the social and political climate of the 1970s and 1980s. Thus, such a policy proposal "made sense" in the social context of the time. The conservative shift in correctional ideology during this time was even powerful enough to cause policy makers—as well as their constituents—to ignore the ethical and due process concerns associated with a selective incapacitation strategy. In particular, the selective incapacitation framework *punishes offenders for crimes that have yet to be committed*—a practice that legal scholars generally denounce as being inconsistent with the basic precepts of justice and the foundation of American criminal law (Packer 1968; von Hirsch 1984, 1985; see also Dworkin 1985). As problematic as this may be, such ethical concerns ended up playing second fiddle to the proposed public safety benefits of selective incapacitation, especially since "rigorous social scientific research" had clearly demonstrated that the identification of high-rate offenders is both practical and possible, and that it does not require the detailed knowledge of each offender's battery of social and psychological factors.

Errors in Prediction: False Positives

Like any human endeavor—from forecasting the weather to guessing someone's age—predicting who will be a high-rate offender will come with a certain degree of error. In the context of selective incapacitation, one kind of error is the "false negative," where some decision rule (perhaps Greenwood and Abrahamse's predictive scale) labels someone as low or medium risk when he or she is actually a high-rate offender. Should this offender receive a shorter sentence on the basis of the person's designated risk level under a selective incapacitation sentencing scheme, there may be an enhanced risk to public safety if that offender is released into the community too early.

Although this issue is certainly important, the corollary problem of "false positives" has been of greater concern for researchers and policy makers interested in constructing a rational and efficient sentencing system, as well as for advocates of due process and fair sentencing practices, where there is a heightened concern that incarceration resources should be judiciously reserved for the worst of the worst criminal offenders. In this case, the errors come in the form of "overprediction," where low- (or medium-) risk offenders are erroneously predicted to be chronic, high-rate offenders. Again, given that selective incapacitation involves extending the period of incarceration for an individual according to offenses not yet committed, the problem of false positives means that we may be locking people up for crimes that they probably would not commit anyway. This definitely raises ethical and due process concerns, but the practical downfall of the existence of false positives is that correctional resources are squandered on people who have been incorrectly identified, thus raising the costs of incarceration for public budgets that are already stretched to the limit.

This problem would be moot, however, if the rate of accurate identification to risk-level categories was high—as claimed by Greenwood and Abrahamse (1982). Unfortunately, nothing could be further from the truth. In fact, one might be surprised that, although we can predict with a certain measure of confidence that a small proportion of offenders in any given community will be career criminals (or high-rate offenders), our success rates for predicting just *who* those folks will be at the individual level is truly dismal. Even Blumstein, Cohen, and Farrington (1988), some of the most respected experts in criminal career research, each of whom had access to information on a host of personal, social, and environmental characteristics of offenders, readily confessed to the inability to identify chronic criminal "persisters" until they were already well into their criminal careers (see also Petersilia 1980).

The problem gets even worse when we start looking at the error rates associated with the purported predictive scale offered by Greenwood and Abrahamse (1982) themselves. Specifically, their analysis indicates an overall success rate of only 51 percent in correctly classifying criminal offenders. Their false positive rate—where offenders are incorrectly classified as high-risk—is 48 percent, and reanalyses of the same Rand data conducted by J. Cohen (1983) and by Visher (1986) placed that figure even higher, at 55 percent. Perhaps the most damaging blow to the selective incapacitation argument came with Auerhahn's (1999) replication of Greenwood and Abrahamse's work on a sample of California inmates. Not only did she continue to find relatively low (yet slightly better) overall predictive accuracy at 60 percent, her results also indicated serious problems with the reliability of the original Greenwood and Abrahamse predictive scale. For example, various items contained in the predictive scale—all of which purportedly tap into the same dimension of "seriousness"—were, at best, only weakly related to one another. In other words, knowing how someone scored on one dimension of the scale (e.g., substance abuse) provides little insight into how he or she will score on another dimension of the scale (e.g., age at first arrest).

In the end, the lure of selective incapacitation as a strategy for corrections policy rests on the assumption that we can identify high-rate offenders in a prospective manner, and that we can do so early enough in each offender's criminal career that we can get the largest potential reduction in crime for our correctional dollar by throwing such miscreants in prison for lengthy periods of time. The problem is that no credible social scientific evidence exists that indicates this can be done. Our inability to correctly identify who among our offender population will come to resemble Wolfgang et al.'s (1972) "chronic 6 percenters" does not exactly conjure up images of Nostradamus; it instead tends to evoke the more arbitrary image of a coin flip. Regardless of the metaphor, so long as political pundits continue to boast about the potential incapacitative effects of enhanced sentencing policies, they can only do so by ignoring the fact that such claims are based on faulty assumptions regarding the ability of a few criminal history variables to predict complex human behavior over the life course.

Summary

The purpose of this chapter was not to trivialize the issue of crime—especially violent crime and the fear that it engenders—in the United States. To be sure, our rates of violent interpersonal offending are well above those of our Western industrialized peer nations, particularly our levels of homicide victimization. Decision makers in the policy and media arenas have taken this unfortunate reality, however, and have stretched, nipped, and tucked it so much that the face of truth about crime in America is barely recognizable.

This might not be such a problem if the systematic distortion of information was used solely for entertainment purposes. Obviously, this is not the case. Beckett and Sasson's (2003) recent work highlights how receptive Americans are to such misinformation with the popularity of reality TV programming such as *Cops* and *To Catch a Predator*. Nevertheless, political entrepreneurs (and their media sidekicks) have methodically used misinformation about why Americans are so fearful of crime, about patterns of escalation in the seriousness of offenders' criminal careers, and about our ability to predict long-term chronic criminal behavior over the life course with a few simple variables, in an effort to gain political capital.

What we are left with is a caricature of the picture of our current crime problem, complete with exaggerated features that American citizens now consider the "real thing." The purpose of this chapter, therefore, was to highlight how various pieces of misinformation about the crime problem in this country have been used by policy makers to support initiatives—such as the war on drugs and all forms of enhanced sentencing policies—that have fueled our dependence on the incarceration "solution" to the crime problem.

Notes

1. It is worth noting that other criminologists, although not quite as zealous as Fox, also caution against the blatant "triumphalism" (see Currie 1999, 3) of those claiming credit for the crime drop of the 1990s. What may seem like an extreme downward swing in crime rates may just be part of a larger trend of reestablishing an equilibrium following unusually high levels of crime in the 1980s (see also Donohue 1998; Friedman 1998; LaFree 1998).

2. It is important to note that increases in violent crime during this time period were, in fact, highly correlated with patterns of drug use, drug distribution, and gang violence (B. A. Johnson, Golub, and Dunlap 2000). The problem, however, comes when policy makers cling to the false assumption—and claim publicly— that the social processes that lead to the problems of drug use and gang violence are somehow independent of those that influence rates of violent crime. In short, one set of problems (drugs and gang violence) cannot "cause" another problem (violent crime) if the two emerge from a common source (e.g., concentrated disadvantage in urban communities; see W. J. Wilson 1987).
3. Despite its popularity among police agencies and policy makers, the notion that low levels of disorder actually cause an increase in more severe forms of crime has yet to receive much in the way of serious empirical support (see the discussion in Harcourt 2001). Instead, the social scientific evidence on the subject attributes serious crime to social conditions that lead to both disorder and crime (i.e., disorder cannot cause crime since the two are both consequences of the same social processes; see Sampson 2006; Sampson and Raudenbush 1999). Moreover, recent evidence also suggests that citizens do not even make a mental distinction between their perceptions of disorder and of crime (Gau and Pratt, forthcoming), which lends further evidence to the categorical contagion thesis.
4. Only one item in Greenwood and Abrahamse's (1982) predictive scale was not related to prior offending history: whether the offender had been employed less than 50 percent in the preceding 2 years.

Chapter Three

Assessing Criminal Justice Practice Using Social Justice Theory

By Matthew Robinson

Introduction

Criminal justice agencies have been facing serious criticisms from scholars in criminal justice, criminology, and related disciplines. One main claim is that criminal justice agencies are ineffective at meeting their goals, especially achieving justice (Robinson, 2009). Others say the "criminal justice system" may actually be aimed at controlling certain segments of the population—the dangerous classes—in order to serve ideological interests of the powerful (Reiman, 2003; Shelden, 2000).

Whatever the case, few would argue with the point that there are major inconsistencies between criminal justice practice and efforts to bring about social justice (Arrigo, 1998). "Social justice" is generally equated with the notion of equality or equal opportunity in society. Although equality is undeniably part of social justice, the meaning of social justice is actually much broader (Scherlen & Robinson, 2008). Further, "equal opportunity" and similar phrases such as "personal responsibility" have been used to diminish the prospective for realizing social justice by justifying enormous inequalities in modern society (Berry, 2005). The most recent theories of, and scholarly statements about, social justice illustrate the complex nature of the concept.

Two of the most prominent statements about social justice, each of which posits its own theory of social justice, are John Rawls' (2003) *Justice as Fairness* and David Miller's (2003) *Principles of Social Justice*. Both conceptions of social justice are similar, so there is significant overlap between the main ideas of the theorists; this is likely due to the fact that they are founded on like principles and based on previously posited theories from significant historical political philosophers (Brighouse, 2005).

In this article, I thoroughly summarize the social justice theories of John Rawls and David Miller. Then, I utilize the two theories to assess the current state of criminal justice practice as it relates to social justice. One goal of this article is to show how America's "criminal justice system" is both consistent and inconsistent with these theories of social justice—i.e., how criminal justice not only helps bring about but also interferes with the realization of social justice. Another goal is to make suggestions to make criminal justice practice more consistent with social justice as laid out in the theories of Rawls and Miller.

My effort is not the first to examine criminal justice practice for the presence of biases based on extra-legal factors such as race, social class, and so forth; many of the problems with criminal justice identified in this article have been documented elsewhere (e.g., see Omi, 1994; Sidanius & Pratto, 2001). The main contribution of this article is that I specifically show how these problems in criminal justice threaten the realization of social justice, at least as social justice has been characterized by John Rawls and David Miller.

John Rawls

Goal and Assumptions

John Rawls posits a theory of social justice commonly referred to as "justice as fairness." Rawls (2003, pp. 5–6) set out to sketch a theory of social justice that would answer the questions: "once we view a democratic society as a fair system of social cooperation between citizens regarded as free and equal, what principles are most appropriate to it?" and "... which principles are most appropriate for a democratic society that not only professes but wants to take seriously *** that citizens are free and equal, and tries to realize that idea in its main institutions?"

Rawls develops his theory for a democratic system of government, and he assumes that society is composed of a fair system of social cooperation between free and equal citizens. He also assumes that society is well-organized and regulated by a public perception of justice. Further, he assumes that society is guided by rules and procedures that are publicly recognized and agreed to, that the rules specify fair terms of cooperation and are rooted in the notion of reciprocity or mutuality so that each person has a chance to promote his or her own advantage or good. Thus, his theory is aimed at determining the "political conception of justice for specifying the fair terms of cooperation between citizens regarded as fair and equal and as both reasonable and rational***" (Rawls, 2003, pp. 7–8).

Rawls' conception of social justice is developed around the idea of a social contract, whereby people freely enter into an agreement to follow certain rules for the betterment of everyone, without considering the implications of these rules for their own selfish gain. Rawls posits that rational, free people will agree to play by the rules under fair conditions and that this agreement is necessary to assure social justice because public support is critical to the acceptance of the rules of the game. These rules or principles "specify the basic rights and duties to be assigned by the main political and social institutions, and they regulate the division of benefits arising from social cooperation and allot the burdens necessary to sustain it" (Rawls, 2003, p. 7), Thus, social justice is about the advantages and disadvantages of society and how they should be distributed.

This also is asserted by David Miller (2003), whose theory of social justice is reviewed later in the article.

Rawls does not suggest that everyone will agree with what justice specifically requires in given situations, but rather that his conception of justice as fairness can fit into "conflicting doctrines" because of what he calls "overlapping consensus." That is, people agree enough about the basic principles of justice he offers that even when they disagree about larger moral, religious of philosophical issues they can still agree about issues of social justice (Rawls, 2003, pp. 32–37).

Finally, Rawls does not posit an unrealistically utopian vision of what is justice but instead offers a theory of social justice that is realistically utopian" (Rawls, 2003, p. 4). Rawls attempts to answer "[w]hat would a just democratic society be like under reasonably favorable by still possible historical conditions, conditions allowed by the laws and tendencies of the social world?"

What is Social Justice?

According to Rawls, social justice is about assuring the protection of equal access to liberties, rights, and opportunities, as well as taking care of the least advantaged members of society. Thus, whether something is consistent with social justice depends on whether it promotes or hinders equality of access to civil liberties, human rights, opportunities for healthy and fulfilling lives, as well as whether it allocates a fair share of benefits to the least advantaged members of society.

Rawls' theory of "justice as fairness" can be summarized with three primary principles. They are:

1. Each person has the same indefensible claim to a fully adequate scheme of equal basic liberties, which scheme is compatible with the same scheme of liberties for all[1];
2. Social and economic inequalities are to satisfy two conditions: First, they are to be attached to offices and positions open to all under conditions of fair equality of opportunity[2]; and
3. Second, they are to be to the greatest benefit of the least-advantaged members of society[3] (Rawls, 2003, pp. 42–43).

By the least advantaged, Rawls is referring to those who lack what he calls "primary goods" (Rawls, 2003, p. 53). Primary goods, according to Rawls, include "things needed and required by persons seen in the light of the political conception of persons, as citizens who are fully cooperating members of society, and not merely as human beings apart from any normative conception. These goods are things citizens need as free and

1 This can be called the "equal liberties principle."
2 This can be called the "equal opportunity principle."
3 Rawls calls this the difference principle."

equal persons living a complete life; they are not things it is simply rational to want or desire, or to prefer or even to crave" (Rawls, 2003, p. 58). Such goods include:

- The basic rights and liberties: freedom of thought and liberty of conscience, and the rest;
- Freedom of movement and free choice of occupation against a background of diverse opportunities, which opportunities allow the pursuit of a variety of ends and give effect to decisions to revise and alter them;
- Powers and prerogatives of office and position of authority and responsibility; Income and wealth, understood as all-purpose means (having an exchange value) generally needed to achieve a wide range of ends whatever they may be; and
- The social bases of self-respect, understood as those aspects of basic institutions normally essential if citizens are to have a lively sense of their worth as persons and to be able to advance their ends with self-confidence (Rawls, 2003, p. 58–59).

It should be noted that Rawls (2003, p. 13) acknowledges the importance of "human rights" as well. He writes: "A just world order is perhaps best seen as a society of peoples, each people maintaining a well-ordered and decent political (domestic) regime, not necessarily democratic but fully respecting basic human rights." Human rights are expansive and include many rights relevant to criminal justice including but not limited to the rights to life; liberty; security; equality before the law; fair and public hearings by independent and impartial tribunals; presumption of innocence until proven guilty; freedom of peaceful assembly and association; the right to participate in government; freedom from slavery, servitude, torture or cruel, inhuman or degrading treatment or punishment; discrimination; arbitrary arrest, detention, or exile; arbitrary interference with privacy; among many others.[4]

According to Rawls, liberty is the most important element of social justice because the three principles are ordered in terms of importance; this means the first principle (the "equal liberties principle") should be achieved before efforts to achieve the second principle (the "equal opportunity principle") and third principle (the "difference principle") are attempted. The second and third principles should "always to be applied within a setting of background institutions that satisfy the requirements of the first principle (including the requirement of securing the fair value of the political liberties)" (Rawls, 2003, p. 46). Background institutions refer to basic structures of society (e.g., family, school, religion, economy, polity), which, when just, can be referred to as "background justice" (Rawls, 2003, p. 10). Logically, agencies of criminal justice are included in these societal institutions.

---

4 For other examples, see the Universal Declaration of Human Rights, Covenant on Civil and Political Rights. Covenant on Economic, Social, and Cultural Rights, and other similar documents."A Summary of Agreements on Human Rights." Retrieved from http://www.hrweb.org/legal/undocs.html.

The Scope of the Principles

Not only can Rawls' first principle be differentiated from the second in terms of priority or importance, each also has its own scope. That is, each is meant to have its own unique applications. According to Rawls, the first principle applies to the "constitutional essentials" whereas the second applies to "the background institutions of social and economic justice in the form most appropriate to citizens seen as free and equal" (Rawls, 2003, pp. 47–48).

Rawls explains that the principles of justice as fairness are adopted and applied in a four-stage sequence. The first is the adoption of the principles of justice to regulate a society. Rawls (2003, p. 15) asserts that these must be adopted behind a "veil of ignorance," which exists when there is a limit on information because "parties are not allowed to know the social positions or the particular comprehensive doctrines of the people they represent. They also do not know persons' race and ethnic group, sex, or various native endowments such as strength and intelligence, all within the normal range."[5]

The second phase is the constitutional convention, which sets forth the institutions and basic processes of governance. The third stage is the legislative stage, where just laws are enacted. Finally, the fourth stage is the application of the rules by administrators, the interpretation of the constitution and laws by the judiciary, and the following of the rules by members of society in the conditions required by justice as fairness.

David Miller

Goal and Assumptions

David Miller posits a pluralistic and circumstantial theory of social justice that is built around those principles of justice that people actually hold. Miller (2003) develops his theory for a democratic system of government, and he assumes that society is a living organism composed of individuals, groups, and so forth who believe in social justice because it specifies the institutional arrangements that allow for full contributions by and well-being of members of the society. Further, his theory assumes a bounded society with members: that there are specific institutions to which the principles of social justice apply; and that the state is the agency capable of changing structures when necessary. The theory can be considered pluralistic or circumstantial because different parts of his conception of social justice are more or less relevant depending on the circumstances. That is, social justice depends on the context of given situations.

Millers' goal was to discover those principles people actually use when judging whether parts of society are just or unjust. Miller created his theory from public opinion polls and studies of public opinion with regard to different elements of justice. He does this in part because, while social justice must be "critical" in nature so that changes

5 Criminal justice scholars often refer to 'blind justice" when discussing how factors such as race, ethnicity, gender, social class, and other extra legal factors should not impact outcomes of justice (Robinson. 2009).

toward more fairness in society can be achieved, it must not be utopian. That is, it must be supported by citizens and can realistically be achieved; this is something with which John Rawls agreed.

It is important to note that Miller finds that people's views of justice are actually pluralistic in that they are determined by the context of a situation. This suggests that whether something is judged as just or unjust depends not only on the principles of justice that people hold but also in part on the nature of the situation.

What is Social Justice?

According to Miller, social justice deals with the distribution of good (advantages) and bad (disadvantages) in society, and more specifically with how these things should be distributed within society. Further, social justice is concerned with the ways that resources are allocated to people by social institutions. Some of the advantages relevant for social justice include money, property, jobs, education, medical care, child care, care for the elderly, honors and prizes, personal security, housing, transportation, and opportunities for leisure. Some of the disadvantages include military service, dangerous work, and other hardships. Logically, punishment for wrongdoing would also be considered a disadvantage. Keep in mind that Miller's theory applies to both public goods as well as private commodities.

Whether something is just or unjust thus depends on whether advantages and disadvantages are distributed appropriately in society. Miller (2003, p. 1) explains that when "we attack some policy or some state of affairs as socially unjust, we are claiming that a person, or more usually a category of persons, enjoys fewer advantages than that person or group of persons ought to enjoy (or bears more of the burdens than they ought to bear), given how other members of the society in question are fairing."

Miller clearly points out that, when considering policies to allocate advantages and disadvantages, we must not judge them based on how they benefit us personally: Justice is about assigning benefits whose values are established by their worth to the relevant population taken as a whole, and it must be blind to personal preferences (Miller, 2003, p. 8, emphasis added). Further, Miller (2003, p. 22) says that "justice fundamentally requires us to treat people as equals; or we should understand justice as what people would agree to in advance of knowing their own stake in the decision to be reached."[6] Social justice efforts can not merely be rationalizations of self-interest; this is another concept agreed to by John Rawls.

According to Miller, social justice is a social virtue that pertains to what you are due or owed, as well as what you owe others. It requires that everyone agrees to treat others as equals in a manner that is not egocentric or selfish. This does not mean that everyone has to agree on all procedures to bring about justice, for people generally agree on what justice demands (this is called the stability of justice).

6 This is similar to Rawls' claim about the "veil of ignorance" and reminds us of the need in criminal justice practice for "blind justice."

Miller's theory focuses on the concepts of need, desert, and equality. Need is a claim that one is lacking in basic necessities and is being harmed or is in danger of being harmed and/or that one's capacity to function is being impeded (Miller, 2003, pp. 207, 210). Desert is a claim that one has earned reward based on performance, that superior performance should attract superior recognition (Miller, 2003, pp. 134, 141). Equality refers to the social ideal that society regards and treats its citizens as equals, and that benefits such as certain rights should be distributed equally (Miller, 2003, p. 232).

Modes of Human Relationships

Miller's (2003, p. 25) theory asserts that whether need, or desert, or equality takes precedence depends on which "mode of human relationship" is being considered. This is because "we can best understand which demands of justice someone can make of us by looking first at the particular nature of relationship." A mode of human relationship refers to the different kinds of relationships that people have with one another.

Miller specifies three basic modes of human relationships, including the solidaristic community, instrumental associations, and citizenship. A solidaristic community "exists when people share a common identity as members of a relatively stable group with a common ethos" (e.g., family relations). In this mode of human relationship, the principle of distribution according to need is most relevant: "Each member is expected to contribute to relieving the needs of others in proportion to ability, the extent of liability depending upon how close the ties of community are in each case *** Needs will be understood in terms of the general ethos of the community. Each community embodies, implicitly or explicitly, a sense of the standards that an adequate human life must meet, and it is in terms of this benchmark that the much-contested distinction between needs, which are matters of justice, and mere wants is drawn" (Miller, 2003, p. 27). Miller is clear in differentiating needs (meeting what is minimally necessary to avoid harm) versus wants or preferences. Needs are also held to be community-specific rather than individual-specific and thus can vary across places.

Instrumental associations exist when "people relate to one another in a utilitarian manner; each has aims and purposes that can best be realized by collaboration with others" (e.g., economic relations). In this mode of human relationship, the principle of distribution according to desert is most relevant: "Each person comes to the association as a free agent with a set of skills and talents that he deploys to advance its goals. Justice is done when he receives back by way of reward an equivalent to the contribution he makes. A person's deserts, in other words, are fixed by the aims and purposes of the association to which she belongs; these provide the measuring rod in terms of which relative contributions can be judged" (Miller, 2003, p. 28). Desert is measured based on actual performance rather than efforts or attributes. It assumes that superior performance (not superior talents) should attract superior reward. Desert lies at the heart of a meritocratic system.

Finally, citizenship refers to "members of a political society" in "modern liberal democracies" who "are related not just through their communities and their instrumental associations but also as fellow citizens. Anyone who is a full member of such a society is understood to be the bearer of a set of rights and obligations that together define the status of citizen." In this mode of human relationship, the principle of distribution according to equality is most relevant because everyone in the society is deemed equal in terms of certain rights (Miller, 2003, p. 30). Here, every citizen deserves equal rights.

Because of the citizenship mode, human rights play a significant role in Miller's theory of social justice. Miller (2003, p. 13) explains that "a central element in any theory of justice will be an account of the basic rights of citizens, which will include rights to various concrete liberties, such as freedom of movement and freedom of speech *** an extensive sphere of basic liberty is built into the requirements of social justice itself." As introduced earlier, human rights are expansive and include rights in many areas.

Summary of and Overlap in Rawls' and Miller's Theories of Social Justice

In order to summarize the theories, each social justice theorist posits three major principles. John Rawls' principles assert: (1) Every person should have the same liberties; (2) Inequalities are acceptable if every person has the same opportunity for success; and (3) Inequalities are acceptable if they are arranged to the greatest benefit of the least-advantaged members of society. David Miller's principles assert that; (1) Every person's basic needs should be met and not hindered; (2) Every person should enjoy benefits and carry burdens to the degree he or she deserves them: and (3) Each person should be treated equally.

There is obviously significant overlap in the theories of Rawls and Millers. For example, Rawls' equal liberties principle is most similar to Miller's principle of equality (every citizen deserves the same basic civil liberties and no societal practices should interfere with these rights). Rawls' difference principle is most similar to Miller's principle of need (arrangements in society should take care of the basic needs of all people in society and no societal practices should interfere with these needs). And Rawls' equal opportunity principle is most similar to Miller's principle of desert (every citizen should have the same opportunity to compete for reward based on performance and societal practices should be set up to assure this outcome). As noted earlier, the overlap in the theories is likely due to the fact that both theories are founded on like principles and based on previously posited theories from significant historical political philosophers.

Finally, recall that each principle has its own scope. For example, according to Rawls, the equal liberties principle applies to the establishment of "constitutional essentials." Thus, the equal liberties principle can be used to assess if citizens enjoy equal liberties according to the law. Rawls' other principles apply to the main institutions of society, which would include the law, policing, courts, and collections. As such, the equal opportunity and difference principles apply to the interpretation and application of the law by important societal institutions, including the police, courts, and corrections.

Similarly, according to Miller, each principle is more or less relevant depending on the mode of human relationship being considered. In matters of citizenship, the principle of equality is most important. Following this logic, as citizens in the United States, all of us should be treated equally in the eyes of the law (and in its application by agencies of criminal justice).

As for the principle of need, this is most relevant for solidaristic communities such as families. However, it is not irrelevant for criminal justice for at least three reasons. First, to the degree that all citizens of a society see themselves as members of an extended family e.g., an "American family" where all members are "in this together," need becomes even more important. Second, to the degree that criminality is driven by efforts to satisfy basic needs (e.g., stealing food to eat), need becomes relevant since punishing people for trying to satisfy basic needs will logically interfere with the ability of people to satisfy their basic needs (Little & Steinberg, 2006). Third, criminal justice processing can interfere with the basic needs of citizens as well, especially minorities and the poor (Lurigio & Loose, 2008).

As for the principle of desert, this is most relevant for instrumental associations such as work. However, it is also not irrelevant for criminal justice for at least three reasons. First, many criminological theories assert that criminality is driven by a desire to seek monetary gain; these crimes are even referred to as "instrumental crimes" (Baumer & Gustafson, 2007). Second, if people cannot obtain wealth and their other goals through legal means, some will turn to criminality through "innovation" (Merton, 1938). To whatever degree people innovate because of diminished opportunities for legitimate success, criminal justice processing may be less deserved because of "mitigating" factors such as poverty and unemployment (Ashworth, 1994). Third, it is well accepted among legal scholars that punishment is aimed at satisfying desert; that is, giving offenders what they deserve (Ristroph, 2006).

How to Use the Theories

For the above reasons, it is entirely appropriate to use the theories of John Rawls and David Miller to assess the performance of government institutions, including the law, policing, courts, and corrections. We can use Rawls' theory of "justice as fairness" to determine whether any institution, process, or outcome in society is consistent with social justice. When an institution, process, or outcome does not comport with any of Rawls' principles, we can conclude that it is not consistent with social justice. That is, something is not consistent with Rawls' conception of social justice if it interferes with any person's indefensible claims to equal basic liberties (the "equal liberties principle"); or if inequalities in society are not attached to offices and positions open to all under conditions of fair equality of opportunity (the "equal opportunity principle"); or if inequalities in society are not arranged to the greatest benefit of the least-advantaged members of society (the "difference principle").

Similarly, we can use Miller's pluralistic theory of social justice to determine whether any institution, process, or outcome in society is consistent with social justice. When an institution, process, or outcome does not comport with any of Millers' principles, we can conclude that it is not consistent with social justice. That is, something is not consistent with Miller's conception of social justice if it interferes with one's necessities or hurts one's capacity to function, if it interferes with claims based on desert, or if it impedes equal opportunity or treatment.

These theories can be used to assess any government policy to determine whether it is consistent or inconsistent with this theory of social justice. Thus, any criminal justice policy from law-making to policing, judicial processes, correctional punishments, and so forth *** can be judged as consistent or inconsistent with social justice based on whether it is consistent or inconsistent with Rawls' and Miller's principles of social justice. This article is the first to assess criminal justice practice using these theories of social justice.

How Does Criminal Justice Help Realize and Interfere with Social Justice?

Table 3.1 identifies key policies, laws, and programs within criminal justice, which are consistent with the theories of social justice put forth by John Rawls and David Miller. These are efforts that help bringing about social justice in the real world. Each entry is discussed below.

Table 3.2 identifies key policies, laws, and programs within criminal justice, which are inconsistent with the theories of social justice put forth by John Rawls and David Miller. These are efforts that hinder bringing about social justice in the real world. Each entry is also discussed below.

A review of these tables leads to the overriding conclusion that the criminal law (e.g., the Bill of Rights in the U.S. Constitution) was set up to protect civil liberties and to provide for equality, at least ideally. Further, American criminal justice agencies are ideally dedicated to outcomes consistent with social justice (e.g., due process and equal protection). Yet, the reality of criminal justice practice puts criminal justice at conflict with social justice in many ways. I shall discuss some of the ways that criminal justice practice is consistent and inconsistent with social justice as put forth in the theories of John Rawls and David Miller. I start with the law and then move onto police, courts, and corrections.

Table 3.1. How criminal justice is consistent with social justice

Law	Police	Courts	Corrections
Bill of rights	L.E. Code of Conduct	Due process	Care, custody of inmates
Due process	Rights protector	Adversarial system	Inmate classification
Equal protection	Service provider	Indigent defense Sentencing guidelines	Education, vocational training
Defines crimes	L.E. Code of Conduct		
Public order	Law enforcement		
Citizen protection	Crime prevention Peace preserver		

Table 3.2. How criminal justice is not consistent with social justice

Law	Police	Courts	Corrections
Differential access Voting	Enforce biased laws	Enforce biased laws	Enforce biased laws
Lobbying	Abuse discretion	Unequal access to defense	Unequal application of sanctions/punishments
Do not define crimes based on harm	Differential arrest, force	Plea bargaining	
Criminalize need Biased laws	Racial profiling	Determinate, mandatory sentencing	Limited access to satisfy needs

The Law

Starting with the Bill of Rights of the U.S. Constitution, the law establishes due process rights and equal protections for all citizens under the law (Orth, 2007). Thus, it can be seen as consistent with Rawls' "equal liberties principle" and Miller's principle of "equality." Recall that Rawls suggested that his first principle (the "equal liberties" principle) applies to the "constitutional essentials." The ideal of American criminal justice as found in the U.S. Constitution appears on its face to be consistent with Rawls' first principle. Also recall that Miller's conception of equality is to be applied in matters of citizenship, suggesting that all members of a political society in modern liberal democracies be granted the same rights by law. The ideal of American criminal justice as found in the U.S. Constitution thus appears to be consistent with Miller's equality principle.

However, it should be pointed out that historians, sociologists, and other scholars have interpreted the U.S. Constitution differently. That have argued that the Constitution was not written behind a veil of ignorance (and was thus not "blind to personal preference," as Miller would say). This raises the possibility that the founders may have acted with their own personal interests in mind when they wrote the U.S. Constitution.

For example, Charles Beard suggests that the construction of the Constitution was biased against the poor. For example, of the five economic groups that existed in 1787, when the document was drafted in Philadelphia, "the four poorest groups had no representatives at the convention: women, slaves, indentured servants, and propertyless white men" (Harrigan, 2000, p. 45). Every delegate involved in drafting the Constitution was a white male who owned enough property to be allowed to vote. According to Beard, of the 55 delegates, 38 owned government bonds, 24 earned their living through banking or some other financial investment, 15 owned slaves, and 14 had investments in western lands. Further, of the 55 delegates, "at least 40 percent have been or are slave owners, and a significant proportion of the others profit to some degree as merchants, shippers, lawyers, and bankers from the trade in slaves, commerce in slave-produced agricultural products, or supplying provisions to slaveholders and slave-traders" (Feagin, 2001, p. 9).

Harrigan (2000, p. 47) suggests that three different types of provisions were written into the Constitution to protect the limited financial interests of wealthy, white male delegates:

- Those that protected their private property rights;
- Those that insulated the national government from popular rule; and
- Those that minimized the influence of the lower-status population in the ratification process.

The protections of private property rights included provisions that benefited businesses engaged in trade and economy, bankers and creditors, slave holders, and holders of securities under the Articles of Confederation.

Feagin (2001, p. 10) explains that:

> At the heart of the Constitution was protection of the property and wealth of the affluent bourgeoisie in the new nation, including property of those enslaved. For the founders, freedom meant the protection of unequal accumulation of property, particularly property that could produce a profit in the emerging capitalistic system. Certain political, economic, and racial interests were conjoined. This was not just a political gathering with the purpose of creating a new major bourgeois-democratic government: it was also a meeting to protect the racial and economic interests of men with substantial property and wealth in the colonies.

Popular rule was not set up in the Constitution because people did not directly vote for the president, the Court, or the Senate. Only House members were originally elected by the people, and people could vote only if their congressional districts had at least 30,000 people. This benefited the wealthy. Barriers to voting (such as property ownership requirements) were constructed to discourage a large percentage of people from voting. Because of this, Harrigan concludes:

> The lower-status population did indeed have nothing to say about the drafting of the Constitution and (whether by choice or coercion) had little to say about ratifying it. Important provisions in the Constitution protected economic interests that were more valuable to the upper-status population than to the lower-status population (p. 53).

Similarly, Joe Feagin (2001), traces the roots of American racism to the U.S. Constitution and early Colonial America. He suggests that many of our country's founders, including Thomas Jefferson, Benjamin Franklin, and James Madison, were greatly influenced by assumptions in Europe about the inherent inferiority of African Americans to Caucasians. Thus, African Americans would specifically to be counted only as three-fifths of a man according to the Article I, Section 2 of the U.S. Constitution.

Feagin (2001, p. 14) asserts that the U.S. Constitutional Convention was something other than what we have learned about in school. He suggests the structure of the nation, as laid out in the Constitution, "was created to maintain separation and oppression at the time and for the foreseeable future. The framers reinforced and legitimated a system of racist oppression that they thought would ensure that whites, especially white men of means, would rule for centuries to come."

According to Feagin (2001, p. 15), the country's founders owned slaves and benefited from the unequal treatment of African Americans with Caucasians. "Men of politics like Thomas Jefferson, George Washington, Alexander Hamilton, Patrick Henry, Benjamin Franklin, John Hancock, and Sam Houston enslaved black Americans. Ten U.S. presidents (Washington, Jefferson, James Madison, James Monroe, Andrew Jackson, John Tyler, James Polk, Zachary Taylor, and Ulysses S. Grant) at some point in their lives enslaved African Americans." Many lawmakers (members of both houses of Congress) were also slave owners, as were those who would interpret the law (members of the U.S. Supreme Court). Not surprisingly, few major decisions made by the federal legislative and judicial branches went against the interests of the nation's slaveholding oligarchy, and foreign and domestic policies generally did not conflict with the interests of those centrally involved with the slavery system" (p. 56).

To the degree that the claims of these scholars are accurate, then the U.S. Constitution was not written behind a "veil of ignorance" but rather was actually a rationalization of self-interest on the part of wealthy, large land holders and slave owners. This would make those parts of the U.S. Constitution that serve limited interests inconsistent with social justice.

The criminal law defines crimes to maintain public order and to protect citizens from harms (Davenport, 2008). Since government protection from willful harmful acts like crimes can be seen as a basic human right or need, this is consistent with Miller's principle of "need." To the degree that all citizens are viewed as a family, as noted earlier, this is especially important. Defining crimes to protect citizens and society is also consistent with Rawls' notion that "primary goods" should be available to all because primary goods include the right of people to live freely and safely.

However, from the very beginning of the criminal justice practice, there is differential access to law-making in the form of voting and lobbying activities (Lynch, Michalowski, & Groves, 2000). The poor and people of color are underrepresented among voters and legislators themselves and are also least likely to donate money to political campaigns (Robinson, 2009). This raises the significant possibility of bias in the criminal law, the outcome being that certain groups have their voices and interests represented more than others and that certain acts will be more and less likely to be criminalized not based on degree of harm caused but instead on other political and ideological grounds (Remain, 2003). Differential access to the criminal law and criminalization of various harms based on differential access to the criminal law are outcomes that are inconsistent with Rawls' equal opportunities principle as well as Miller's equality principle. In order to be consistent with social justice, every citizen should have an equal chance to influence the criminal law and have his or her interests reflected in the criminalization process.

Further, it is obvious that the rules and procedures of criminal justice are not created behind a "veil of ignorance," raising a significant possibility that criminal justice practice is not blind to personal preferences and may thus be created as rationalizations of self-interest (McGarrell & Flanagan, 1987). In fact, all criminal justice policies are lobbied for and against by powerful interests. Groups behind current criminal justice policy are not necessarily motivated by concerns for social justice. One likely outcome of this reality is that many forms of harmful behaviors will not be legislated as crimes and targeted by criminal justice agencies, simply because of who commits them. In fact, although the criminal law is aimed at protecting people from harmful acts, those acts that pose the greatest threats to citizens (i.e., white-collar and corporate crimes) are the ones that are least likely to legislated as crimes and especially as serious crimes (Simon, 2007). Thus, the most dangerous criminals often do not get what they "deserve" (Robinson & Murphy, 2008). This is not consistent with Miller's concept of desert.

In order to reiterate, since Miller's concept of desert is most relevant for instrumental associations such as work, the application of desert to the criminalization process may not be viewed as all as entirely appropriate. However, it is well established that being labeled a "criminal" and suffering sanctions from governmental institutions such as the police, courts, and corrections will likely produce outcomes such as "felony disenfranchisement" that interfere with the ability of citizens to engage in instrumental associations such as work (Sennott & Galliher, 2006). Thus, forms of punishment such as incarceration can be seen as inconsistent with social justice to the degree that they interfere with one's ability to engage in activities such as work that allow people to be rewarded for their contribution to society (Wheelock, 2005).

Simultaneously, relatively minor criminals often get far more than they "deserve" based on the harms caused by their behaviors (Meier & Geis, 1997). As one example, Robinson and Murphy (2008) demonstrate, using government data, that corporate and white-collar crime cost Americans at least one trillion dollars in direct losses every year, compared to only $20 billion in losses cause by street crime. Yet, less than five percent of police officers are focused on the former, and about 99% of all people incarcerated in the United States are incarcerated for committing the latter. This is inconsistent with Miller's concept of desert. The argument is that the "worst of the worst" offenders should be subjected to the "worst of the worst" criminal sanctions. In the United States, this is simply not the case.

Further, crimes of the poor (e.g., theft) are at times aimed at satisfying basic human "needs" (Agnew, 2005). Thus, the application of the law to stop such acts can be seen as interfering with social justice, at least when the means to achieve one's goals are blocked for reasons such as discrimination, which itself is not consistent with social justice (Simons & Gray, 1989). That is, if opportunities to succeed through legal means are not truly equally available to all (as they should be according to Rawls), and some people respond through "innovation" by creating new, illegitimate (i.e., criminal) means to achieve their goals (Merton, 1938), then we can see the labeling of some behaviors as crimes as the criminalization of efforts to meet needs.

In a nutshell, to the degree that the criminal law is aimed at the crimes committed disproportionately by the poor and people of color while it simultaneously ignores the harmful and culpable acts of the powerful (e.g., wealthy whites), it is unequal, undeserved, not focused on helping people achieve their basic needs, and clearly not aimed at providing the greatest advantage to the least advantaged. Thus, it violates Rawls' and Miller's conceptions of "need," "equality," "desert," and the "difference principle."

Further, since police, courts and collections enforce the criminal law (through arrest, conviction, sentencing, and punishment), any bias in the criminal law will logically be perpetuated through enforcement of that law (Reiman, 2003; Robinson, 2009; Shelden, 2000). This is likely the greatest threat to social justice in criminal justice practice. As shown in Table 2, this threat to social justice (enforcing biased law) is found in policing, courts, and corrections.

Policing

In policing, the Law Enforcement Code of Conduct specifies that one of the fundamental duties of police is to protect people's rights, provide important services to the community, as well as enforce the law, prevent crime, and uphold the peace (International Association of Chiefs of Police, 2008). Since all of these which can be seen as "needs" of the community and basic rights of the people, the written functions or roles of police are consistent with Miller's principle of need and Rawls' conception of primary goods. Further, rights protection can be seen as a form of policing activity that is consistent with Rawls' "equal liberties" principle. One good example is at the point where arrest is imminent, police officers read suspects their rights to remain silent in order to protect their Fifth Amendment right against self-incrimination (Stuart, 2008).

Yet, since officers have discretion, it can be abused (Alpert, Dunham, & Stroshine, 2005). When it is, it leads to differential police outcomes. For example, poor people and people of color are disproportionately likely to be stopped, searched, arrested, and have force use against them (Walker, Spohn, & DeLone, 2007). They are also more likely to be victims of racial profiling (Withrow, 2005). These are outcomes that are inconsistent with Rawls' "equal liberties" as well as Miller's equality principle." All citizens deserve to be treated the same by the police and other agents of government, unless their own actions lead them to "deserve" more attention. Racial profiling implies that certain groups in society are being targeted more based on extra-legal factors such as race rather than legal factors such as criminality (Miller, 2007).

Further, since criminal justice involvement can interfere with legitimate opportunities such as school and work, it can be seen as a threat to Rawls' "equal opportunities principle." And since differential involvement with police tends to harm the least advantaged (Shelden, 2000), it is inconsistent with Rawls' "difference principle." In order to be consistent with Rawls' difference principle, activities of government institutions such as law enforcement agencies should be arranged to assist the least advantaged not to hinder or hurt them.

Recall that historians have pointed out that, historically, law enforcement agencies were used to maintain current power arrangements. Examples include slave patrols, disruption of labor organizing and demonstrations, strike busting, interfering with civil rights, and so forth (Loewen, 2007; Zinn, 2003). Clearly, this is not consistent with Rawls' or Miller's principles of social justice.

Courts

In courts, because of due process rights, every citizen has the right to trial, as well as other constitutional protections that are supposed to be upheld in an adversarial process whereby prosecutors and defense attorneys represent different actors in a battle to determine the truth (Neubauer, 2007). Due process is clearly part of Rawls' "equal liberties" principle as well as Miller's "equality" principle. Further, efforts are made e.g., through sentencing guidelines to produce fan sentences based on legal variables such as offense seriousness and prior record, which is also consistent with Miller's conception of "equality" (Walker, 2005). Finally, there are clearly measures in place to protect the weak (e.g., indigent defense) and this is consistent with Rawls' "difference principle" (National Association of Criminal Defense Lawyers, 2008).

However, there is unequal access to quality defense representation in criminal cases. For example, those that can afford private attorneys are less likely to sit in jail awaiting trial and are less likely to be incarcerated upon conviction (Bureau of Justice Statistics, 2008), suggesting that the ability to pay for private defense protection does lead to differential outcomes. This is not consistent with Rawls' "equal liberties" or Miller's "equality principle." It is also a threat to Rawls' "difference principle" because access to quality defense representation is not arranged for the benefit of the least advantaged.

Quality of defense can be considered incompatible with Miller's principle of "desert" for some clients do not have their case adequately defended based merely on their inability to pay. Wrongful convictions, caused mostly by overzealousness on the part of police and prosecutors, as well as faulty eye-witness testimony, are obviously inconsistent with the concept of "desert" (Bell, Clow, & Ricciardelli, 2008). This is true for two reasons: first, no one deserves to be punished for acts they did not commit; second, when wrongful, conviction occurs, the factually guilty do not receive the punishment they rightly deserve; they are also free to commit further crimes, causing even more harm to society.

The imbalance of power in the courts that exists in America is also not consistent with the values on which the court system was supposedly founded due process and "innocent until proven guilty." Currently, the prosecution has much more power than the defense as evidenced by more employees and a much larger budget nationwide. This threatens the ability of defendants to seek and obtain meaningful trials, which necessitates plea bargaining (Walker., 2005). Research shows that plea bargaining occurs for two main reasons: first, the police make too many arrests; second, the courts receive only about 20% of all resources devoted to criminal justice, meaning they do not have enough resources to justify having a trial for every one accused of even serious crimes.

The very practice of plea bargaining is not consistent with due process (Fisher, 2003), and thus is not compatible with Rawls' "equal liberties" principles. In essence, the right to a criminal trial is more myth than fact. Plea bargaining is also inconsistent with Miller's "equality principle" since plea bargaining is much more likely to occur with poor clients who are not well represented by quality defense attorneys (Pad field, 2009).

Plea bargaining also tends not to assign punishments that achieve proper "desert" of guilty criminals. Further, plea bargaining leads to too much punishment for those who are innocent but plead guilty anyway (Siegel, 2005). Walker (2005) shows that both "conservatives" and "liberals" do not like plea bargaining because it satisfies neither the requirements of punitive justice or procedural justice.

When trials (rarely) happen, they are plagued by serious threats to principles of social justice. For example, the "voir dire" process routinely results in African Americans being excused from jury service through the use of peremptory challenges (Walker et al. 2007). This is a significant threat to equal treatment, due process, and even "desert" (if defendants are convicted in part due to the racial composition of a jury). Research by the Capital Jury Project shows just how important the racial makeup of juries is for outcomes such as conviction and sentencing, even in death penalty cases where someone's life is literally at stake (Brewer, 2004).

The practice of mandatory sentencing is consistent with Miller's principle of "desert" when it is utilized for the worst offenders (who thus deserve the worst punishment). However, mandatory sentencing is inconsistent with the notion of desert when it is used against relatively harmless criminals who do not deserve such punishment based on the small amount of harm they cause to society. For example, "three strikes" laws have generally been used against non-violent offenders, leading to life imprisonment sentences. Meanwhile, white-collar and corporate offenders rarely are punished at all, even when serious injury or death results (Robinson, 2009). Three strikes laws have also been applied in a racially discriminatory manner, thereby threatening Miller's "equality" principle (Macallair & Males, 1999; Brown & Jolivette, 2005; Rand Corporation, 2005).

Corrections

In corrections, inmates are classified based on various criteria including their personal needs, inmates are provided care by facilities, and to some degree they are offered educational and vocational opportunities (Clear, Cole, & Rising, 2008). This is all consistent with Rawls' "difference principle" and Miller's conception of "need," Further, the protection of inmates' First, Fourth, Fifth, Sixth, and Eighth Amendment rights is also consistent with social justice (American Civil Liberties Union, 2008).

Yet, the limited educational and vocational opportunities available to inmates can be considered a threat to the "needs" of inmates (Ross & Richards, 2002). Additionally, any and all unequal application of sanctions in America is a threat to Rawls' and Miller's principles of "equal liberties," "equal opportunity," "equality," "desert," and the "difference principle." Recall that the practices of criminal justice institutions should respect the civil liberties of all citizens, should be applied in an equal fashion, should be based on desert, and should be arranged to the benefits of the least advantaged.

The poor and people of color are disproportionately likely to be exposed to probation, jail, prison, and executions (Barak, Leighton, & Flavin, 2006). To the degree that this is not due to disparate criminality of these groups, it is not consistent with social justice. For example, African American men tend to commit roughly half the murders and robberies in the United States in any given year. In 2006, they accounted for 51% of those arrested for murder and 56% of those arrested for robbery (Sourcebook of

Criminal Justice Statistics, 2008). While some use these data to suggest that African Americans are thus more dangerous than whites (New Century Foundation, 2005), murder is but one form of culpable killing and robbery is but one form of taking property. If one were to focus on all forms of culpable killing and property taking behaviors, the vast majority of offenders would be white, for the vast majority of white-collar and corporate offenders are white (Robinson, 2009). Thus, the disproportionate focus on African American offenders owes itself to the fact that criminal justice agencies are aimed at pursuing only certain types of criminals (the sheet crime variety), and this is inconsistent with the concept of desert that is key to social justice (Lynch, McGurrin, & Fenwick, 2004; Ross & Rome, 2007; Rothe & Friedrichs, 2006).

The harsh conditions of prison commonly referred to as the "pains of imprisonment" (Sykes & Western, 2007) are also a threat to social justice. While incarceration is supposed to achieve the goal of incapacitation for the protection of society, imprisonment entails much more than mere removal of one's freedom. Inmates are routinely subjected to violence, sexual harassment and assault, and similar negative treatments by both other inmates and guards (Jones & Pratt, 2008; Wolff et al., 2007a, b). This is not consistent with the notion of "desert." Further, it may in the long-term result in conditions in society upon inmate release that cause further harm to citizens, something that is also not consistent with social justice.

Conclusion

In this article, I laid out the main theories of social justice of John Rawls and David Miller. I then briefly identified the ways in which American criminal justice agencies help realize as well as interfere with achieving social justice. When evaluating criminal justice practice against the social justice theories of Rawls and Miller, we see that the ideals of American criminal justice are consistent with social justice while many actual practices of criminal justice agencies make achieving social justice impossible. That is, there is a significant gap between the ideals of criminal justice in the United States and the realities of criminal justice practice.

Of course, American criminal justice agencies may or may not even be about social justice (Arrigo, 1998). That is, one reason our "criminal justice system" may not achieve social justice is that it is not even aimed at doing so. This should change. In my opinion, criminal justice agencies should be set up to help achieve social justice, and should also be evaluated for their efforts to do so. This claim is based on the fact that citizens actually hold dear the principles of social justice laid out by Rawis and Miller (Miller, 2003).

Given that people actually hold values consistent with social justice, it logically follows that they would not agree to many of our criminal justice practices if they were aware of them. That is, if we defined our criminal justice policies behind a "veil of ignorance" and blind to our own personal preferences, then the problems we see in criminal justice practice today would not be present because they threaten our social justice values, as laid out in our criminal justice ideals.

References

Agnew, R. (2005). Pressured into crime: An overview of general strain theory. New York: Oxford University Press.

Alpert, G., Dunham, R., & Stroshine, M. (2005), Policing: Continuity and change. Long Grove, Illinois: Waveland.

American Civil Liberties Union. (2008). Prisoners' rights, Retrieved Dec 4, 2008, from http://www.aclu.org/prison/index.html.

Arrigo, B. (1998). Social justice, criminal justice. Beverly Hills, CA Wadsworth.

Ashworth, A. (1994). Justifying the grounds for mitigation. Criminal Justice Ethics, 13(1), 5.

Barak, G., Leighton, P., & Flavin, J. (2006). Class, race, gender, and crime: The social realities of justice, in America (2nd ed.). Lanham, MD: Rowman and Littlefield.

Baumer, E., & Gustafson, R. (2007). Social organization and instrumental crime: Assessing the empirical validity of classic and contemporary anomie theories. Criminology, 45(3), 617.

Beard, D. (1913). An economic interpretation of the constitution of the United States. New York: MacMillan.

Bell, J., Clow, K., & Ricciardelli, R. (2008). Causes of wrongful conviction: Looking at student knowledge. Journal of Criminal Justice Education, 19(1), 75.

Benavie, A. (2009). Drugs: America's holy war. New York: Routledge.

Berry, B. (2005). Why social justice matters. Cambridge, England: Polity Press.

Brewer, T. (2004). Race and jurors' receptivity to mitigation in capital cases: The effect of jurors' defendants' and victims' race in combination. Law and Human Behavior, 28(5), 529.

Brighouse, H. (2005). Justice,Cambridge, England: Polity Press.

Brown, B., & Jolivette, G. (2005). A primer: Three strikes ***The impact after more than a decade. Retrieved Sept 30, 2008, from http://www.lao.ca.eov/2005/3_Strikes_102005.htm.

Bureau of Justice Statistics, (2008). Indigent defense statistics. Retrieved Oct 9, 2008, from http://www.ojp/usdoj/gov/bjs.id.htm.

Clear, T., Cole, G, & Reisig, M. (2008). American corrections. Beverly Hills, CA: Wadsworth.

Davenport, A. (2008). Basic criminal law: The constitution, procedure, and crimes (2nd ed.). Upper Saddle River, NJ: Prentice Hall.

Feagin, J. (2001). Racist America New York: Routledge.

Fisher, G. (2003). Plea bargaining's triumph: A history of plea bargaining in America. Stanford, CA: Stanford University Press.

Harrigan, J. (2000). Empty dreams, empty pockets: Class and bias in American politics. New York: Addison-Wesley Longman.

International Association of Chiefs of Police. (2008). Law enforcement code of conduct, Retrieved Oct 9, 2008, from http://iacp.org/documents/index.cfm?document_id=94&document_type_id=4&fuseaction=document.

Jones, T., & Pratt, T. (2008). The prevalence of sexual violence in prison: The state of the knowledge base and implications for evidence-based correctional policy making. International Journal of Offender Therapy and Comparative Criminology, 52(3), 280.

Little, M., & Steinberg, L.(2006). Psychological correlates of adolescent drug dealing in the inner city: Potential roles of opportunity, conventional commitments, and maturity. Journal of Research in Crime and Delinqueney, 43(4), 357.

Loewen, J. (2007). Lies my teacher told me: Everything your American history textbook got wrong. New York: Touchstone.

Lurigio, A., & Loose, A. (2008). The disproportionate incarceration of African Americans for drug offenses: The national and Illinois perspective. Journal of Ethnicity in Criminal Justice, 6(3), 223.

Lynch, M., McGurrin, D., & Fenwick, M. (2004). Disappearing act: The representation of corporate crime research in criminological literature. Journal of Criminal Justice, 32(5), 389.

Lynch, M., Michalowski, R., & Groves, B. (2000). The new primer in radical criminology: Critical perspectives on crime, power and identity. Monsey, NY: Willow Tree Press.

Macallair, D., & Males, M. (1999). Striking out: The failure of California's "three strikes and you're out" law. Retrieved Oct 1, 2008, from http://www.cjcj.org/pubs/three_strikes/strikingout.html.

McGarrell, E., &. Flanagan, T. (1987). Measuring and explaining legislator crime control ideology. Journal of Research in Crime and Delinquency, 24(2), 102.

Meier, R., & Geis, G. (1997). Victimless crime? Prostitution, homosexuality, and abortion. New York: Oxford.

Merton, R. (1938). Social structure and anomie, American Sociological Review, 3, 672, 682.

Miller, D. (2003). Principles of social justice Boston, MA: Harvard University Press.

Miller, K. (2007). Racial profiling and postmodern society. Journal of Contemporary Criminal Justice, 23(1), 248.

National Association of Criminal Defense Lawyers. (2008). History of right to counsel. Retrieved Oct 1, 2008, from http://www.nlada.org/About/About_HistoryDefender.

Neubauer, D. (2007). America's courts and the criminal justice system. Beverly Hills, CA: Wadsworth.

New Century Foundation. (2005). The color of crime. Retrieved June 6, 2006, from http://www.colorofcrime.com/colorofcrime2005.pdf.

Omi, M. (1994). Racial formation in the United States. New York: Routledge.

Orth, J. (2007). Due process of law: A brief history. Lawrence, KS: University of Kansas Press.

Pad field, N. (2009). Shining the torch on plea-bargaining. The Cambridge Law Journal, 68(1), 11–15.

Rand Corporation. (2005). California's new three strikes law: Retrieved Oct 9, 2008, from http://www.rand.org/pubs/research_briefs/RB4009/index1.html.

Rawls, J. (2003). Justice as fairness: A restatement (2nd ed.). Boston, MA: Belknap Press.

Reiman, J. (2003). The rich get richer and the poor get prison: Ideology, class, and criminal justice (8th ed.). Boston, MA: Allyn & Bacon.

Ristroph, A. (2006). Desert, democracy, and sentencing reform. Journal of Criminal Law and Criminology, 96(4), 1293–1352.

Robinson, M. (2009). Justice blind? Ideals and realities of American criminal justice (3rd ed.). Upper Saddle River, NJ: Prentice Hall.

Robinson, M., & Murphy, D. (2008). Greed is good: Maximization and elite deviance in America. Lanham, MD: Rowman and Little field.

Ross, J., & Richards, S. (2002). Convict criminology. Beverly Hills, CA: Wadsworth.
Ross, J., & Rothe, D. (2007). Swimming upstream: Teaching state crime to students at American universities. Journal of Criminal Justice Education, 18(3), 460.
Rothe, D., & Friedrichs, D. (2006). The state of the criminology of crimes of the state. Social Justice, 33(1), 147–161.
Scherlen, A., & Robinson, M. (2008). Open access to criminal justice scholarship: A matter of social justice. Journal of Criminal Justice Education, 19(1), 54–74.
Sennott, C., & Galliher, J. (2006). Lifetime felony disenfranchisement in Florida, Texas, and Iowa: Symbolic and instrumental law. Social Justice, 33(1), 79–94.
Shelden, R. (2000). Controlling the dangerous classes: A critical introduction to the history of criminal justice. Boston, MA: Allyn & Bacon.
Sidanius, J., & Pratto., F. (2001). Social dominance: An intergroup theory of social hierarchy and oppression. New York: Cambridge University Press.
Siegel, A. (2005). Moving down the wedge of injustice: A proposal for a third generation of wrongful convictions scholarship and advocacy. American Criminal Law Renew, 42(4), 1219–1237.
Simon, D. (2007). Elite deviance (9th ed.). Boston. MA: Allyn & Bacon.
Simons, R., & Gray, P. (1989). Perceived blocked opportunity as an explanation of delinquency among lower-class black males: A research note Journal of Research in Crime and Delinquency, 26(1), 90.
Sourcebook of Criminal Justice Statistics. (2008). Table 4.1. Arrests by offense charged, age group, and race. United States, 2006. Retrieved Oct 1, 2008, from htip://www. albany.edu/sourcebook/pdf/t4102006.pdf.
Stuart, G. (2008). Miranda: The Story of America's right to remain silent. Tucson, AZ: University of Arizona Press.
Sykes, G., & Western, B. (2007). The society of captives: A study of a maximum security prison. Princeton, NJ: University of Princeton Press.
Walker, S. (2005). Sense and nonsense about crime and drugs: A policy guide (7th ed.). Belmont, CA: Wadsworth.
Walker, S., Spohn, C., & DeLone, M. (2007). The color of justice: Race, ethnicity, and crime in America (5th ed.). Belmont, CA: Wadsworth.
Wheelock, D. (2005). Collateral consequences and racial inequality: Felon status restrictions as a system of disadvantage. Journal of Contemporary Criminal Justice, 21(1), 82.
Withrow, B. (2005). Racial profiling: From rhetoric to reason. Upper Saddle River, NJ: Prentice Hall.
Wolff, N., Blitz, C., Shi, J., Siegel, J., & Bachman, R. (2007a). Physical violence inside prisons: Rates of victimization Criminal Justice and Behavior, 34(5), 588.
Wolff, N., Shi, J., Blitz, C., & Siegel, J. (2007b). Understanding sexual victimization inside prisons: Factors that predict risk. Crime and Public Policy, 6(3), 535.
Zinn, H. (2003). A people's history of the United States. New York: Harper Perennial.

Section II

Identifying Inequities in American Society

Introduction to Section II

Identifying Inequities in American Society

By Michelle Foster

This section incorporates readings illustrating the inequities that continue to persist in American society. A great variety of circumstances can contribute to disparities in a person's life. Geographic location, familial situations, health history, financial status, and living situations are just some of the factors that can lead to inequities. Minorities, specifically young black males, continue to be overrepresented in our prisons. The legal process is supposed to include fairness, justice, and equity at all stages of the criminal justice process. Interestingly, however, it appears that black males disproportionately receive tougher, longer sentences than white males. Moreover, it is believed that black offenders experience discrimination from jurors taxed with determining the accused's quilt or innocence. "Lady Justice" is portrayed as blind—blind to the offender's race, nationality, age, gender, and background—and a dispenser of justice with impartiality to all. But "Lady Justice" is not blind since it is not entirely possible to be so. Legal justice is achieved by applying the law. Those who apply the law, however, are still people—individuals with their own subjective understandings of information, circumstances, and legalese.

The following three chapters are provided to help provide the reader with a broader perspective on the sources of inequality and the mounting problems therefrom. Chapter 4 examines the personal experiences of individuals who were offenders as juveniles and through into adulthood. These offenders present accounts of their contacts with law enforcement, the legal system, and incarceration. Obtaining firsthand accounts from those subjected to the criminal justice system is valuable both for understanding problems from the accused's perspective, and also for developing practices and punishments that may be more appropriate for prevention, especially in the case of juveniles. During the interviews, the juveniles discuss their confusion with their personal rights—e.g., receiving bad advice by public defenders or being represented by ineffective counsel—and failings with the punishment they received that was intended to deter them from future crime.

The prison boom and the inequality that has arisen from it is the focus of Chapter 5. From the mid-1970s and into the 1990s, people were incarcerated at higher rates than ever before. Also, during these periods civil lawsuits against institutions and the government for civil rights and civil liberties violations were at an all-time high. An argument is presented that these lawsuits have contributed to the barriers that have existed and continue to persist from racial inequality. This interesting perspective aids in the understanding as to why there has been and continues to be such unequal treatment in the justice system.

The last part of this section, Chapter 6, demonstrates that racial inequalities still exist in the criminal justice process. Cynthia Jones identifies a source for the biases as being one of "discretionary power" on the part of law enforcement and the legal system. As an example, stop-and-frisk procedures by law enforcement have contributed to the rise in minorities entering the criminal justice system in New York City. A stop-and-frisk is a temporary "stop" or holding of an individual in situations where a law enforcement officer believes an individual may be engaging in or about to engage in some type of illegal activity, while the "frisk" is a pat down of the person's outer clothing. Stop-and-frisks are helpful during police patrols as a method of preventing and reducing criminal activity. In recent years, however, police departments have been *forcing* law enforcement officers to engage in stop-and-frisks in targeted areas in hopes of securing more arrests. If officers fail to increase their stop-and-frisk activities during patrols, those officers could fear reprimands. Given that there are large populations of minorities in inner-city areas such as in New York, and that New York City has increased its stop-and-frisk activities, then it is easy to assume that minorities will be arrested more for crimes. The use of a stop-and-frisk tactic by law enforcement is intended to be discretionary, but the NYPD is using this discretion as a source of power over individuals. For example, there's the case of Nicholas Peart, a young black male who was walking to the store. Two officers approached Mr. Peart from an unmarked car and forced him to lie on the ground. This was not the first time he was stopped by police, but the third time. His case is just one example of the misuse of discretionary power.[1]

1 For further reading about Nicholas Peart see an article published in the *New York Times* by Nicholas K. Peart, December 17, 2011, "Why is the N.Y.P.D. After Me?" http://www.nytimes.com/2011/12/18/opinion/sunday/young-black-and-frisked-by-the-nypd.html?_r=0.

Chapter Four

Rush to Judgment

Prisoners' Views on Juvenile Justice

By Frank Butler

Introduction

To fully appreciate the workings and outcomes of the juvenile justice system, it is valuable to understand the experiences of persons who have been processed through it. Having lived through the "system" first-hand, they are well positioned to comment on its operation. The present study was developed to hear the voices of former juvenile offenders, who have since become adult offenders, for the unique insights they can make to our understanding of how juvenile justice is received. This research focuses on the perceptions of adult male prisoners whom juvenile justice failed to prevent recidivating. Listening to these adult convicts' voices about what it means pragmatically to be processed as "delinquent" yields insights that can help to humanize juvenile justice, both by sensitizing juvenile justice practitioners to the backstage perceptions of delinquents, and by suggesting public policy reforms that might address some of the issues—particularly ethical ones—raised by the prisoners. Listening to their stories helps us to better understand the human condition (Waldram, 2007).

Review of the Literature

Major ethical issues of social inequity have inhered in juvenile justice in the United States since its inception. Platt's (1977) classic account of the Progressive "child savers," who crafted juvenile courts, details the class-based politics that led genteel reformers to couch intrusive control mechanisms for the financially poor as benign ministrations that would rescue them from evil and corruption. Rothman (2002) describes the conflict between moral conscience and bureaucratic convenience that ensnared the burgeoning juvenile system, with the latter ultimately triumphing.

Idealism continued to collide with reality during the first century of a formal juvenile justice "system." The grand rehabilitative rhetoric which draped its beginnings in the first half of the 20th century became increasingly tattered as socio-political forces in the latter half of the century reconstructed deviant youth as primarily depraved (Feld 1999). A focus on the behavioral malleability of wayward adolescents dimmed as dazzling visions of hardened proto-criminals, who threatened social stability, became politically ascendant.

In the mid-to-late 20th century, juvenile justice was increasingly politicized, resulting in what Feld (2003) describes as an "inversion" of juvenile jurisprudence and sentencing policy. Judicial discretion was supplanted by politically charged legislative and executive power, as goals like public safety and criminal punishment were substituted for more benign concepts like a youth's "amenability to treatment" and her "best interests." A spurious wave of juvenile violent crime in the late 1980s and 1990s, sensationalized by the mass media (Ruddell and Decker 2005), discredited the juvenile court and enabled the transfer of adolescents from juvenile adjudication to adult criminal processing and punishment (Beckett and Sasson 2004). The shift of power was from ostensibly impartial juvenile court judges to the politicized public prosecutor, whose discretion in both juvenile and adult cases is vast and primarily unregulated (Davis 2007). That transfer of power has been described as ripe with "injustice and irrationality" from a public policy standpoint (Bishop 2004).

More recently there appears to be some "softening" in juvenile justice. In 2005 the U.S. Supreme Court eliminated the death penalty for juveniles (*Roper v. Christopher Simmons*, 543 U.S. 551), and in 2010 it ruled that for non-homicide crimes, juveniles cannot be sentenced to life in prison without parole (*Terrance Graham v. Florida*, 130 S.Ct. 2011). Rates of transfer of juveniles to adult court have declined (Redding 2008). The number of juveniles in residential placement decreased from 105,055 in 1997 (a rate of 356 juveniles per 100,000 juveniles in the population) to 81,015 in 2008 (a rate of 263 per 100,000) (Hockenberry, Sickmund, and Sladky 2011; Sickmund 2010). The public—at least when presented with highly hypothetical vignettes–is willing to pay for early childhood delinquency-prevention programs and for rehabilitation, in lieu of incarceration, for youth charged with serious crimes (Nagin et al. 2006). Some states, such as Florida, favor transfer to adult court "[o]nly for youths accused of especially serious crimes and for those with a history of failing to reform" (Applegate, Davis, and Cullen 2009:70).

The raced nature of much of criminal justice has been lamented (Alexander 2010; Reiman and Leighton 2010; Sentencing Project 2008; Mauer and King 2007; Capers 2006). In the United States in 2006, of the nearly 93,000 youth in residential placement: 40 percent were Black, 35 percent were White, and an additional 20 percent were classified as Hispanic (Office of Juvenile Justice and Delinquency Prevention n.d). The targeting of illegal drugs since the 1980s has had markedly disparate impact on people of color, including youth of color who are brought into the juvenile and adult systems (Mauer 2006).

Detention had an especially pernicious effect in disadvantaging Black youth relative to White youth (Leiber and Fox 2005), and racial disparities intensify as one progresses through the juvenile process (Hoytt et al. 2002). In 2002, Blacks represented 16 percent of the juvenile population nationwide, but 29 percent of the delinquency caseload, with

Black youth constituting a disproportionate share of cases at all stages of case processing (referral, detention, petitioning, waiver, adjudication, residential placement, and formal probation) (Snyder and Sickmund 2006).

Other ethical issues regarding the experience of juvenile justice processes have also been studied. For example, Feld's (2006) research on police interrogation of juveniles concluded that youth who are fifteen and younger are generally incapable of exercising their *Miranda* rights. Institutionalization of juveniles in reform schools has been seen as iatrogenic in terms of promoting future criminality (Miller 1991). Unhealthy "paradoxes of treatment" have been identified in juvenile correctional facilities: encouraging emotional displays while also rigidly controlling such displays; exposing youth to competing frames of interpersonal misfortune and individualized deviant motivation as sources for their delinquency; and providing incentives for youth to game the system by simply "jumping through the hoops" (Abrams, Kim, and Anderson-Nathe 2005).

Against the ethical thicket that encompasses so much of what is done with juveniles, it is prudent to explore the experiences of those who have lived within juvenile institutions. Consistent with the tenets of many critical perspectives, the present study relates stories of the marginalized.

Relatively few studies in contemporary criminal justice have examined juvenile justice from the vantage points of those who have experienced it. First-hand perspectives on adult imprisonment have been explored (e.g., West-Smith, Pogrebin and Poole 2000; Toch 1992). Also, some research has been done with regard to perceptions of other important players in juvenile justice. For example, in a mail survey of 115 parents of youths involved in juvenile justice in a mid-western county, Benner, Mooney, and Epstein (2003) found that respondents felt their children's most important service need was responsible case management. Brubaker and Fox (2010) interviewed 20 service providers who worked with girls in juvenile justice and found providers were often overwhelmed by the panoply of serious social disadvantages faced by their clients. Additionally, there was a lack of structured collaboration among providers, as well as a dearth of gender-specific and culturally-specific programming, particularly for African-American girls.

Gaarder, Rodriguez and Zatz (2004) examined the perceptions of girls from the viewpoint of juvenile court practitioners, particularly probation officers. They found that "stereotypical images of girls outweighed any realities," with court practitioners commonly using gendered stereotypes that failed to perceive links between the girls' manipulative behaviors and their prior victimizations (2004:555). They concluded that "juvenile court staff often act based more on the perceptions they have of girls and their families than on the realities the girls face, including both individual and societal factors" (2004:572).

Corley, Bynum and Wordes (1995) also interviewed juvenile court personnel and found that decision-makers weighed family factors as particularly important in determinations about intake, processing, disposition, and placement. Leniency was more likely when parents exhibited what the court personnel perceived as acceptable levels of control over their families, and when they were seen as cooperative with the court.

Two-parent families were presumed to have better control than single-parent families, and such family variables effectively "became class and race surrogates" (1995:168).

A few studies have examined youths' perspectives shortly after discharge from juvenile institutions. In interviewing 35 youth in Massachusetts who had been in residential treatment, Hartwell et al. (2010) learned that the most difficult aspects of transitioning back to the community, according to the youths, involved the allure of former peers and the old environment, as well as the availability of drugs and lack of money. Abrams (2006) studied ten youths during the first few months post-release from a twelve-month therapeutic correctional institution in Minnesota, and found that financial support and "selective involvement" with old influences were important means to reduce the likelihood of recidivating. Mincey et al. (2008) interviewed nine graduates of juvenile residential programs in Miami, revealing the importance of supportive families during this time of transition, as well as the challenges of overcoming environmental factors like drugs, violence, and lack of income.

A few studies have examined the views of delinquents themselves. Huerter and Saltzman (1992) assessed the perceptions of 24 youths in residential placement in Colorado, with regard to their delinquency court processes. Participants generally had a negative view of the police, and only half of participants felt they understood what was happening when they were in court. Common suggestions by participants for improving the system included: treat juveniles separately from adults; have court personnel speak to and listen to juvenile defendants; and treat juveniles with patience, including allowing them time to question and comment in court.

Redding and Fuller (2004) studied 37 juveniles who had been automatically tried as adults under Georgia law. The participants had been unaware of the transfer law; they felt that they may have been deterred from their crime if they had been aware; and they believed it was unfair to be criminally processed as adults. Shannon and Abrams (2007) interviewed seven juvenile offenders who were fathers during their incarceration in Minnesota. They concluded that "fatherhood posits the potential for desistance from crime, yet these young men are in need of a structured intervention to actualize this possibility" (Shannon and Abrams 2007:189).

Bright, Ward, and Negi (2011:45) interviewed nine girls following juvenile court involvement, finding that "maltreatment and victimization, family problems, neighborhood-level poverty and crime, and a lack of support from larger-scale institutions such as income maintenance and school systems" were major factors perceived by participants as contributing to their delinquency. Veneziano, Veneziano, and Gill (2001) had 116 state prison inmates complete a questionnaire with regard to their perceptions of juvenile justice. They found that most participants who had been adjudicated found juvenile justice not especially helpful, nor did those participants feel that the system acted as a deterrent for other juveniles.

The present study focuses on convicted adult offenders' recollections and perceptions of juvenile justice system events that they experienced as youth. Though they are not necessarily accurate or complete descriptions in an "objective" sense, the perceived realities of juvenile justice processes by former juvenile offenders who are now adult offenders, are worthy of study, in order to assess the deep, human impacts that such processes can have, and in order to appreciate that subjective definitions of reality have very real consequences for individual actors (Thomas and Znaniecki, 1995 [1918]).

Method

The study sample was selected from the largest men's prison in a state located in the mid-Atlantic region of the United States. The prison held a variety of prisoners, classified at different levels of security, including maximum security. There is no reason to believe the inmates of this particular prison differed appreciably in terms of demographics, compared with inmates in other men's prisons throughout the state. Adults were interviewed, rather than juveniles, in order to obtain a retrospective on juvenile justice experiences held by men who had time to reflect on their youth and its impact on their adult lives.[1] Though the men's narratives do not necessarily portray present operations of juvenile justice, they do offer insights into the philosophies that prevailed in the system, especially the impacts on the lives of these adult offenders in their youth.

The prison in which the interviews were conducted did not possess information on which prisoners had been in placement as juveniles, but it did maintain a listing of all prisoners under age forty (n=183), which was initially chosen as the upper age limit for this study so that the participants' juvenile experiences would not be too remote from contemporary juvenile justice, and so that a meaningful sample could be obtained. The author was permitted access to the automated case summaries for each of these prisoners. For some, but not all, prisoners who had been considered for parole, the case summary contained a section on juvenile history and placement.[2] Sampling was limited to prisoners whose case summaries indicated at least one juvenile placement.

Twenty-eight participants were identified in this way. Each potential participant was initially issued a "call out" sheet by the prison's psychology department to report to the psychology treatment area at a particular time. There was no indication of the purpose of the visit. The author met with each man individually, explained the study and its purpose, and inquired whether the prisoner wished to participate.[3] It was made clear that the study concerned only the prisoner's juvenile experiences, not his adult criminality. The refusal rate at initial meeting was 21 percent (n=6). Additionally, three men, who agreed to participate, withdrew during the course of the study, for a variety of reasons.

The files on the participants that were accessible to the author contained only rudimentary information, sometimes incomplete, about the reasons for their current confinement. The available data indicate that these men's current incarceration was related primarily to aggravated assault, robbery, criminal homicide, or drug offenses.

In order also to understand the experiences of persons who had committed extremely serious crimes as youth, another eleven participants were identified from among the "juvenile lifers" at the prison. Those are men who were convicted of some form of criminal homicide committed when they were juveniles, and they were sentenced to "natural life" (with no possibility for parole in this state) in prison. Because the prison had no listing at all of who were juvenile-lifers, the author relied on the prison psychologists to identify juvenile-lifers, in large part, by a snowball method. An informal, hand-written list of juvenile lifers, prepared by some of the juvenile lifers themselves, was also consulted. These men were invited to participate in the same manner as described above for the men who were not juvenile-lifers.

The racial/ethnic composition of the participants (n=30, consisting of 19 non-juvenile-lifers and 11 juvenile-lifers) was: 50 percent African-American (n=15), 13 percent bi-racial (n=4), 20 percent White (n=6), 13 percent Latino (n=4), and 3 percent Asian (n=1). Among the juvenile-lifers alone, 64 percent were African-American (n=7), 27 percent bi-racial (n=3), and 9 percent Latino (n=1). The mean age of the juvenile lifer sample was 35 years (range 23 to 50; median 34); the mean age of the non-lifer sample was 29 years (range 21 to 38; median 30).

Semi-structured, open-ended interviews were used. Each prisoner was asked to describe his youth: his experiences of getting in trouble with the law as a youth (discussed chronologically), who or what was important to him, how he felt he was treated during the juvenile justice processes he experienced, his home and school experiences, his friends, and his dreams for the future. Finally, each was asked about his present views of juvenile justice, including what, if anything, he would like to see changed with the system. [Not all of these topics are part of the present analysis.]

All interviews were conducted by the author, working alone with the participant, in an office with a closed door. The setting for the interviews was the prison's psychology department, in whichever psychologist's, psychiatrist's, or nurse's office happened to be vacant. Interviews were conducted from November 2007 to January 2008. Each participant was interviewed at least twice, and each interview lasted approximately one hour. The interview topics had been pre-tested with a small group of juvenile-lifers at the prison.

The second interview with each participant was largely a validity check: the author summarized his understanding of what the participant had said during the first interview, asked for clarification and elaboration on issues that were unclear, and allowed the participant to add any new information that was relevant.

The prison prohibited any form of recording of interviews, other than hand-written notes, so the author manually recorded participants' statements, including participants' narratives during each interview, and these were transcribed shortly after the interview. Thus, the statements reported in this article are not verbatim quotes but rather the author's best recordation of what the participant said. Attempts were made to capture the participant's authentic phraseology as much as possible.

Data analysis was based primarily in grounded theory (Charmaz, 2006), starting with participants' own perspectives and meanings and recognizing that participants are experts with regard to their own experiences. A major goal is to understand the nature of a phenomenon, especially its key concepts, as it occurs across individuals. The inductive method yields theories that are contextual and local.[4]

Central Themes

The participants' earliest recollection of episodes of apprehension as juveniles involved their participation, primarily in theft (including shoplifting, bicycle theft, and car theft) and drug possession. Over half of participants had early histories of theft, and one third had early histories of drug possession. Nearly all participants received probation, rather than a more severe penalty, for their early juvenile cases.

Over three quarters of participants discussed at least one crime against the person as part of their juvenile history. (This includes twelve participants who described homicides, including all the juvenile-lifers). Excluding the homicides by the juvenile-lifers, crimes against the person tended to be either assault [usually of another youth] (sixteen participants) or robbery (ten participants). Another relatively common crime, described by nearly a quarter of participants as part of their juvenile history, is burglary.

A variety of themes surfaced from participants' discussions of their juvenile-justice experiences, which can be categorized chronologically as involving police, courts, and placement.

Police Unfairness

With regard to the police, the major theme expressed by participants related to police unfairness. One common aspect involved ***intimidation by the police, especially during interrogation***. Examples of comments follow.[5]

> ***GL***: They didn't give *Miranda* warnings because they said I wasn't under arrest. As a kid, I didn't think I could leave. I was there from 9 a.m. to 11 p.m.
>
> ***FF***: I wish I knew not to speak without a lawyer present. The detective had me thinking I'd just be a witness. The detective was the con man, and I took it.

A major purpose of the *Miranda* warnings is to communicate clearly to suspects that the police are not their friends or allies. However, some police officers and police departments have devised subtle ways to comply with the letter of *Miranda* but not its spirit. Teens' immaturity and impulsivity make them especially vulnerable to such duplicitous tactics.

The observations are primarily consistent with the literature. Feld (2006) found that juveniles under sixteen years of age generally lacked the ability to exercise *Miranda* rights. Grisso (2006) reported that 55 percent of delinquent youth misunderstood at least part of the *Miranda* warnings, compared with 23 percent of adults. Rogers et al. (2008:80) concluded that "[t]he synergistic effects of poor reading comprehension, low intelligence, and comorbid mental disorders are likely to have catastrophic effects on Miranda comprehension and subsequent reasoning."

Another theme regarding the police relates to ***street-level harassment, including the use of extra-legal violence.*** Examples are:

> ***AF***: The police would take us to a White neighbor-hood where there was a rival gang, and tell us to walk home.
>
> **TR**: I got my ass whooped by the police every time. When I wasn't arrested, I got smacked with a gun and harassed.

Experiencing abuses of power by the police can easily engender further disrespect for the law among youth, whose view of authority is often unfavorable to begin with, as part of the natural history of adolescence. Extra-legal imposition of official force against youth aggravates an already tenuous relationship, boding ill for long-term equanimity in police-community relationships. Brunson and Miller (2005) have identified common concerns among Black youth with regard to persistent harassment and disrespectful treatment by the police, undermining the legitimacy of the police. Huerter and Saltzman (1992) also found that adjudicated youth tended to have a low opinion of the police, due largely to perceived harassment and physical abuse of power.

Finally, it should be noted that one-third of study participants (and one-fourth of juvenile lifers) felt they were treated fairly by the police when they were juveniles.

Courtroom Alienation

Beyond the police stages of arrest and interrogation, participants tended to find their court experiences almost hostile. Indeed, the frequency of misgivings about the court far exceeded those about the police. The most common concern about court, expressed by at least two-thirds of participants (including all of the juvenile lifers), is ***lack of understanding of the juvenile and/or adult court processes*** in their cases. For example:

> ***PS***: I didn't understand what they were talking about. The words they was using I never heard before. I'm just agreeing even though I don't know what they talking about.
>
> ***DT***: While in juvenile detention before trial, I couldn't study the law. There was no law library. I wouldn't know where to start even if a law library was available. You need a guide to take you through anything at that age … I had no clue that life was actually life … I never got into life "without parole"; I took parole for granted.
>
> ***FD***: As a kid, you understand nothing. The whole process goes over your head … All the lawyer talk (like objections, cross-examination), I got none of that … You're sitting there, and everything around you is affecting you but you don't understand it … The process is like walking in the complete dark. You need somebody to set them down and explain; kids need to understand the process and get help with legal terminology. When at the detention facility pending trial, I had major charges over my head, but nobody explained them; it was just TV and card games.

AM: I didn't understand court. I found it was a lot different from the movies. I was nervous, shaking. The judge looks at you like you're guilty, prove your innocence. My lawyer tells me to be quiet… Everything is yak, yak, yak. You say you know because you don't want to look dumb.

A few participants noted that they understood court proceedings eventually, after having been through multiple, prior court processes. Finally, six participants felt that they comprehended what was going on in juvenile court.

Participants' non-comprehension of what was transpiring in court was very common. This occurred in juvenile court and was exacerbated when juveniles were prosecuted in adult court. It is difficult for juveniles to accept the basic fairness of a process directed at or against them when they cannot fathom how the outcome is derived. Indeed, Redding and Fuller (2004) found that none of the 37 juveniles who participated in their study had anticipated they would be tried as an adult for the particular crime they committed. In juvenile court it is ironic that that many youth cannot understand what is happening to them in what is theoretically a youth-centered jurisprudence (Rajack-Talley, Talley, and Tewksbury 2005).

Procedural due process would seem to require at least a basic comprehension of legal processes being used to remove one's liberty. A youth's ability to engage in crime is not necessarily correlated with his level of legal sophistication. What is striking is the naiveté and immaturity that many of these youth exhibited, often in the face of potentially major criminal punishments.

Aside from the inherent difficulties of the specialized jargon so typical of court processes, youth involved in juvenile justice commonly present with learning disabilities (Beyer 2006). The average IQ of youth in detention is approximately 85 (general range: 70 to 100), compared to a youth nation-wide average of 100 (general range: 85 to 115), and about sixty percent of youth in detention meet the criteria for at least one mental disorder, compared to about eighteen to twenty percent of youth in the general population (Grisso 2006). The combined effects of psycho-social immaturity, compromised mental faculties, and an environment steeped in esoteric terminology make comprehension of court procedures a genuine challenge for many youth.

Exacerbating these difficulties is another court-related theme: ***ineffectiveness and poor quality of defense counsel***. Nearly all the men were seriously dissatisfied with the legal representation they received when they were juveniles. In contrast, a few participants (including two juvenile-lifers) felt their lawyers did at least an adequate job, and a few participants who had multiple juvenile cases reported differing experiences (some good, some bad) with their lawyers.

Among the men who expressed concerns about legal representation, the most common issues related to the relatively little time spent with clients and shoddy representation. All of the illustrative quotes given here are from juvenile-lifers.

AD: I got a court-appointed lawyer. My mom was going to hire an attorney, but he convinced her he could handle the case by himself. I never seen him

> except when at court. He never discussed witnesses or strategy with me… I gave him a list of witnesses who was there; he tried to contact a couple of them the day of the defense and said they could be there at 3:00, but the judge wouldn't give a continuance… The lawyer skipped the defense, and we just went to closing argument.
>
> ***FD***: Based on what my court-appointed lawyer said, this isn't a complicated case. I only saw the lawyer twice before trial: at the preliminary hearing and at arraignment… There was no investigation by my lawyer, and no expert… My lawyer didn't put on a case: as soon as the prosecutor rested, he rested.
>
> ***VK***: My court-appointed lawyer had me believe I'd serve 10-15 years. She wanted me to plead guilty. My focus was on 10-15 years based on what my lawyer said, not "life." I didn't understand what "life" meant. Years later the lawyer said she made some mistakes early in her career.
>
> ***AF***: I had a court-appointed lawyer, who only talked to me at City Hall. My lawyer didn't explain the life sentence. Court-appointed lawyers, they be with the D.A… My lawyer tricked me into testifying, saying that if I don't get on the stand, he wouldn't put any of my witnesses on the stand. I was scared. I'm in adult court. I didn't want to testify.

It is axiomatic that government-appointed lawyers for indigent defendants rarely have much time to spend with those clients. Often viewed as a merely unfortunate issue in the background for adult defendants, it comes into much higher relief when the clients are adolescents who, from the outset, are more disadvantaged in that they are less likely to understand criminal processes and courtroom legalese.

Participants' generally poor experiences with their lawyers reflect serious issues with the role of counsel for youth. Drizin and Luloff (2007) suggest a number of problems with representation of youth in juvenile court: "poor investigation, infrequent use of motions, high caseloads, over-reliance on pleas, a juvenile court culture of wanting to 'help' juveniles, and a general lack of training among attorneys on youth and adolescence" (2007:289). Except for the juvenile court culture, all of these probably apply also for youth transferred to adult court.

Especially in cases of juveniles who were given "natural life" sentences, the quality of legal representation was often seriously lacking and sometimes seemed unethical. The minimal time spent with youth facing the prospect of the penultimate penalty, the lack of investigation of their cases, and the miscommunications about fundamental matters—all betray capitulation to almost a rush-to-guilt process. Youth who trust in their counsel to help guide them through very adult-type processes may ultimately find themselves embittered.

Independent of concerns with defense counsel, the perception of a ***compromise of judicial neutrality*** was evident in the narratives of some participants, again more pronounced among the juvenile-lifers. Twenty percent of participants discussed issues regarding perceived improper conduct by judges in their cases as juveniles. All of these raise the specter of judicial bias.

> **ST**: The judge doesn't listen to the kid or his lawyer; it's like a kangaroo court.
>
> **TR**: I caught another case for resisting arrest. The judge threw the file across the courtroom. He said, "You were supposed to be here." [I had absconded.] He said I was a menace to society. He told the D.A. and the public defender to shut up. He kicked everybody out of the courtroom. I was sentenced to three years at a maximum security juvenile facility.
>
> ***AD***: During the trial, the guys at the jail told me every day to go to the law library and study my case, but I trusted my lawyer. Everything my lawyer asked for, the judge would shoot him down. The judge was like a third D.A.... He was asleep during parts of my trial. My lawyer didn't want to embarrass the judge by objecting. I objected, saying clearly, "Your Honor, you can't be asleep during my trial." The record, though, just says there was an "excited inaudible outburst."
>
> ***GL***: They tricked me out of a jury trial. They said they'd go for the death penalty if I took a jury trial. It was a bench trial... The judge was running it like a well-oiled machine by the time we got to trial.

These perceptions, especially when viewed in combination with the other court-related themes, present images very much at odds with official rhetoric about how the courts are supposed to operate. Blatant compromises of judicial neutrality are supposed to elicit, at a minimum, strenuous objection from defense counsel. That such was not forthcoming is unsurprising if defense counsel were as deficient as many participants found them.

Dissatisfaction with the judicial role may in part reflect youth's anticipatory injustice: "Combined with immature psychosocial capacities that contribute to a foreshortened time perspective and reduced ability to take others' perspectives, adolescents may have a heightened attention to fairness in justice system procedures" (Woolard, Harvell, and Graham 2008:209). Such an emphasis on fairness, however, is not entirely misplaced: a society that schools youth on civics lessons about government and justice had best seek to deliver on those goods when youth find themselves enmeshed in "justice."

Juvenile-placement Ambivalence

Finally, reflecting upon the "corrections" aspect of their cases, nearly all participants who discussed time they had spent at a private, non-secure juvenile facility reported primarily favorably on that experience. The same applies for those who discussed treatment facilities and adolescent-shelter facilities.

Private, non-secure juvenile facilities were the most common form of placement. These included traditional residential, as well as farm and school, facilities. A peculiar form of social commentary, the major theme from participants was that these ***private, non-secure facilities were preferable to their home environments.***

> ***SS***: The private facility was better than home. There were van rides, three meals, snacks; you were allowed to smoke if your guardian agreed. I spent 15 months there.
>
> ***AD***: I was at the juvenile facility for 9½ months. I met guys from all over the city who were selling drugs, robbing, stealing cars… When I was 17, I thought that if I get caught, I'll do nine months at that beautiful facility or be with girls at the other private juvenile facility, and I'll get home passes.
>
> ***PS***: It made me feel comfortable, so it didn't help me; it was a nice juvenile placement. They should have been rougher (more rules); they should scare you. It shouldn't be like Candyland. It should be halfway like an adult prison… Only two staff members tried to help me; they talked with me on a daily basis. They felt bad when I lost my mom. Everybody else was a—holes.
>
> **TR**: I was at a private juvenile facility for nine months. It was like a college campus. The food was better than five-star restaurants. There were weekend hikes, swimming, pool, basketball. School was in the morning. I got home passes every month. When I heard about how good it was, I wondered, "Are they sending me to jail or college?" If this is punishment, I'm gonna do crime the rest of my life.

Though obviously lacking in deterrent effect, due to their contrast with the pathetically destitute home environments from which most of these youth came, the private placements would seem appropriate milieu for rehabilitative efforts. Participants' experiences also reflect the importance of continuation, and probably even expansion, of services post-confinement, when youth commonly return to impoverished communities that present them with few legitimate opportunities for success. The punitive side of juvenile justice is best complemented with an array of community and school resources that seeks to ameliorate the abject social conditions in which most of these youth find themselves.

The few men who had been sent to facilities specifically for treatment for substance abuse tended to have been sent there as young teens. Perhaps not surprisingly, the common theme was that the ***substance-abuse treatment was ineffective, largely related to the youth's immaturity***.

> **NL**: At 12 years old, I was sent to a 45-day rehab. It had one section for adults and another for juveniles… I didn't know nothing about rehab. I was too young to comprehend. I didn't think I had a problem with drinking or smoking weed.
>
> **HP**: At 15 I was sent to a rehab facility for juveniles. It had girls; that's what I looked forward to. I was tryin' to do the time and get right back home; I didn't

really hear that crap. I found out about PCP and said I wouldn't smoke that again; I just smoked marijuana after that... The placement was like camp, not like hard time.

For participants whose placements involved group homes there was no clear pattern: ***some group homes were viewed favorably, while others were deemed baleful.*** Such mixed findings are expected, in light of the great variability in milieu and resources among group homes. Nevertheless, it is easy to see how the lower strata among group homes can actually aggravate social and emotional conditions associated with delinquency and criminality.

> **GG**: When I was 14, the judge put me in foster care. About six kids lived in the foster home in a trailer park. All the kids had been in trouble. There were two foster parents and their son and his wife and their kids too. The foster parents took the money and used it on themselves. I just got one phone call, and no other contact, with my parents ... I skipped school every day when I was there. No one knew. I'd pretend I was going to school ... The foster mother would put my clothes in the dryer without washing them ... Then the judge put me in a halfway house for boys, with 10 to 15 kids. It was run by college interns. We cooked our own food and ran the house. The program was a joke. I had fun. There were fights all the time. We could do whatever we wanted... There was a fraternity house across the street and another one next door. As soon as the third shift came, he'd set the alarm clock and go to sleep. Then we would go to the fraternity house next door and party ... Where's the rehab? I faked it 'til I made it.
>
> **RL**: I was found delinquent and placed in a group home for juveniles and dependents. All were treated equally. It was co-ed. The group home was very helpful. I graduated from computer school and got a GED while there. They taught independent living skills; the group home was great.

In contrast to group-home experiences, participants who had spent time at secure juvenile facilities almost uniformly found that experience unhelpful. These unfavorable views were offset only in that ***school and sports programs at secure placements were often valued.*** Those seemingly rehabilitative components, however, had little long-term impact on participants' lives, especially when subsumed in the more depressing environment of secure placement itself.

> **SS**: I was 15 when I got locked up at the secure juvenile facility. There were drugs and stabbings there; it was like a penitentiary... They had an awesome school program; I did well. I got into the boxing program. They helped me with my dyslexia. I started to excel at academics, carpentry, welding, computers.
>
> **BL**: At the maximum-security juvenile facility there was no discipline in terms of how they ran the place. We pretty much did what we wanted, other

> than when they pressed charges. They feared us more than we feared them… The staff sometimes came to work drunk or high; they sit around and collect a paycheck.

Maximum-security juvenile facilities have been found to produce youth who "lost hope and opportunities without ever having much of either to begin with" (Inderbitzin 2005:19). Austin, Johnson, and Weitzer (2005) report that community-based programs produce outcomes at least as good as traditional training schools, in terms of recidivism and community adjustment. Such programs "reduce crowding, cut the costs of operating juvenile detention centers, shield offenders from the stigma of institutionalization, help offenders avoid associating with youth who have more serious delinquent histories, and maintain positive ties between the juvenile and his or her family and community" (Austin et al. 2005:3).

Adult-institution Perniciousness

Finally, for participants whose histories included placement in adult jail or prison, their experiences were recalled—not unexpectedly—as traumatizing by nearly everyone. Participants' narratives convey some of the ***terror of adolescent existence in the machismo of the adult institution***.

> ***DT***: At 16 I was sent to adult prison, separated from adult prisoners. When I turned 17, I was transferred to another adult prison where there was no separation. It was creepy; there were dim lights. That was when I first started seeing the violence and attitude and atmosphere of prison, like fights over crazy stuff. The first thing I did was got me a knife; I made it from the bottom of my chair… It was very, very taxing mentally… Fear gave me a heightened awareness of seriousness. I had to grow up but didn't have any experience growing up. A lot of things I had to figure out real fast… They put me out in general population after I turned 18.
>
> ***FF***: In jail, I didn't know what was going to happen. I looked for ammunition like soda cans to defend myself. I carved my name in my hand with a razor blade, to make people think I'm crazy. I was in the adult jail until my second statement, when I told the detective I was 15. At first I lied and told them I was 18, thinking I'd get bail, because juveniles don't get bail.
>
> ***RL***: At 16 I was in the New York adult jail for a couple days, until my mother bonded me out. I was just in the intake block. It shattered my idea that I was just a kid.

Participants' experiences with adult jails and prisons show that those facilities may instill fear but are otherwise emotionally—and often physically—dangerous for youth. Far more than secure juveniles facilities, these institutions approach Goffman's (1957) "total institutions" and entail the fundamental deprivations of life that Sykes (1958) termed "pains of imprisonment." Unless the goal is to produce "state-raised convicts" who learn predation rather than cooperation (Abbott 1981), containment of adolescents in such institutions appears contraindicated. Redding and Fuller (2004) suggest that incarceration in adult facilities may have a brutalizing effect on youth, as they learn the acceptability of violence and also harbor a deep sense of having been treated unfairly.

Hope for Reform

Aside from an opportunity to tell their stories, a major appeal of the study for most participants was the ability to suggest ways in which juvenile justice might be improved for kids in the future. Perhaps participants saw some redemptive value in this discussion; even the relatively reticent tended to become garrulous on this topic. One-third of participants suggested ideas that hearken back to original ***individualized and rehabilitative ideals*** that underlay the formation of a separate juvenile apparatus.

> **RH:** Don't rush to judgment about what type of person you are… You get a label. They too quick to label you… At camp, most of the staff were there for the paycheck. Just a few counselors took an interest. You need to sit down and talk with kids, give them a chance to open up.
>
> **ST:** Probation officers should stop treating kids like future felons, instead of like a kid in trouble. Don't treat kids like they must be failures as adults.
>
> **PP:** Cops and courts need to listen. Don't assume you're lying. We might not actually be lying. Don't just assume you've heard that line before.
>
> **NL:** Don't certify juveniles as adults. You're saying there's no room for growth and development.

The tendency to pre-judge and stereotype young people is perhaps strongest when the youth are in trouble with the law. Based on the views of participants (which are fairly consistent with the tenets of labeling theory in criminology [e.g., Becker 1963; Lemert 1951]), treating youth as failures exacerbates their alienation and may actually be criminogenic.

Mincey et al's (2008) study of the perceptions of adjudicated delinquents also found marked concern with unfair treatment in juvenile justice. Similar to the present findings, Huerter and Saltzman (1992) noted that adjudicated youths' suggestions for improving juvenile justice stressed having court personnel speak with them and listen to them, seeing them as "much more than a piece of paper" (1992: 355).

The tendency for decision-makers to minimize youths' voices can create a system in which the "justice" that prevails is rooted in a reality devoid of particular details that do not fit well with decision-makers' own lives and experiences. It is especially easy to downplay the perspectives of youth who are most different from decision-makers:

> The tendency in law to separate reason and objectivity from feelings and subjectivity, thereby reifying abstraction over context, has resulted in a legal

> system that ignores individual stories situated within specific contexts and governed by the facts of particular lives. The result is that, in many instances, individuals subjected to, restricted, and defined by norms based on the characteristics of people who share no similarities with them cannot avoid future interactions with a legal system that ignores the realities of their lives while forcing the individual to comply with a norm that simply does not fit. (Michaelis, 2001:306)

Over one-quarter of participants discussed ideas that centered on the theme of ***mentoring and other safe havens***. Here the emphasis was on mentoring that expands a youth's horizons, provides models for lawful living, and gives hope. Such desiderata might also be considered valuable for schools in their social mission of fostering civility among youth.

> **RW:** Children need to be shown love; they need to know that somebody cares about them. Mentoring shouldn't just be geared to sports. Talk about money and your own business or vocational skills. Take kids out of their environment and give them hands-on experience with different cultures.
>
> ***DT***: Kids need exposure to positive influences; they need to be around people they respect. They should be able to see that doing something good is cool too. Let kids see that I got plenty of money and am not doing anything illegal. Give kids hope, rather than having them think that respect is gained by hitting (like father hitting mother) or by having a gun.
>
> ***AD***: When they started closing the rec centers down, we roamed the streets after school to 6:30, looking for drug dealers. Kids need safe havens, rather than get into mischief, especially when their parents are at work. Summer camps are important too.
>
> **HG:** We need to help kids stay in school, rather than not go to school because of fear of bullying or getting shot.

Discussion and Policy Implications

When adult prisoners reflect upon their own experiences as juveniles, a variety of ethical discrepancies in the operation of justice systems becomes apparent. As the clay which the juvenile justice apparatus sought to mold into more law-abiding citizens, these men raise issues about the reality of juvenile processes, which they have known first-hand, as it differs significantly from what the jurisprudence of juvenile justice proposes ought to be. This includes experiences of juvenile exclusion from traditional processes in favor of removal to adult criminal processes. The sample used in this study (adult prisoners who were in some form of placement as juveniles) is particularly helpful in understanding the deficiencies of juvenile justice.

The ease of overreaching in interrogations (e.g., Rogers et al. 2008; Scott-Hayward 2007); the less-than-zealous advocacy by counsel (e.g., Drizin and Luloff 2007); the psychological trauma, learning disabilities, and immature thinking, identity, and moral reasoning that are common in these youth (e.g., Beyer 2006; Scott and Steinberg 2003); the substantial racial differences in the processing of Black youth (e.g., Lieber and Johnson 2008; Snyder and Sickmund 2006); the welcome nature of juvenile placement as a respite from poverty and family dysfunction juxtaposed against the terror of placement in adult jails and prisons (e.g., Ashkar and Kenny 2008; Equal Justice Initiative 2007)—individually and in concert these phenomena present serious ethical challenges for juvenile justice. Though the sample in the present study is inherently biased in that it consists of juvenile justice "failures," an important consideration is that the general sense of injustice with regard to juvenile processes—including the "rush to judgment"—may further alienate troubled youth from non-criminal self-concepts (Redding 2008).

The tableau that emerges from participants' lived reality is of a heavily bureaucratic juvenile justice that is much more focused on efficient processing or removal of cases, than on the youths themselves. The bureaucracy can be self-serving in employing vast numbers of practitioners, with the youths themselves as ancillary considerations. In keeping with bureaucratic interests, there tends to be a "rush to judgment" with concomitant incentives to "cut corners" with regard to adolescents' legal and personal interests.

Ethical problems in the operation of juvenile justice are patent. The deontological ethics and rights-based ethics upon which ostensibly juvenile justice is founded are sometimes substantially compromised in the interests of bureaucratic goals. Perhaps an approach based in feminist ethics, with its emphasis on moral sentiments like compassion and sympathy, could engender reform that reflects some of the nobler original theoretical underpinnings of juvenile justice.

Many of the changes recommended by the study's participants are highly consistent with feminist ethical approaches and with restorative justice approaches. Participants suggested that rather than largely pre-judging youth and increasingly ostracizing them from juvenile justice processes, juvenile justice should pay greater attention to listening to youth and taking an interest in them. Ideas of participants emphasized mentoring and showing youth that people care about them. Those kinds of approaches may go much further in reducing juvenile crime than the more common scheme of rapid judgment and official ostracism.

Exploratory research of this nature contains a number of limitations. Though participants' experiences of juvenile justice spanned a few states, the fact remains that the study involved a small sample from one prison. Also, sampling was limited to the relatively small proportion of inmates whose juvenile histories were accessible through prison records. As commonly occurs in qualitative research, the findings are not intended as widely generalizable. Rather, they provide rich information on the particular experiences of a set of men who are relatively difficult to access, yielding insights that are not adequately disclosed in less personalized approaches.

Additionally, though the author took pains to write notes, using the actual language of participants as much as possible, the inability to tape-record the interviews affects the ability to understand precisely what participants said. The observations and insights of the prisoners themselves may be inaccurate, due partly to the passage of time and the influence of subsequent experiences, such as incarceration in a maximum-security facility. From a phenomenological perspective, though, everything about the stories is significant in that each participant "is speaking a form of truth—his own truth—constructed according to what is meaningful for him" (Skrapec 2001:54). Finally, the juvenile experiences of participants occurred primarily in the 1990s, during times of moral panic over youth violence, so they may not reflect precisely how youths in juvenile justice are treated today.

In spite of these limitations, the experiences and perceptions of persons for whom juvenile justice has not "succeeded" raise important policy concerns. Indeed, these tend to be the youth with whom the "system" has not done a good job, both in terms of juvenile processes and in terms of their multiple socioeconomic disadvantages. Rather than transforming juvenile offenders into productive citizens, juvenile justice interventions paradoxically can be iatrogenic, doing further violence to their possibilities and beings.

These men's experiences militate against heavy investment in juvenile justice as a type of "crime control industry," or "prison-industrial complex," that provides financial security for a host of criminal-justice practitioners, agencies, and institutions, while offering little in terms of guiding youth toward non-criminal futures. Processing youth as faceless "delinquents" through arcane legal machinations they do not understand, embittering them with hypocrisy about "rights," and placing them in juvenile facilities of marginal rehabilitative value (or worse, in adult facilities where they know psychological terror)—such do not seem proper ingredients in a recipe for long-term reductions in youth criminality. Rather, consistent with the suggestions of participants who have lived through the failures of the system, it is much more prudent at least to attempt to address the enervating net of social pathologies that so commonly encompasses their lives, including poverty, joblessness, disrupted families, substance use, and alienation from school.

Consistent with the noblest ideals of juvenile justice, troubled youth are still malleable to ministrations that can change their lives for the better: mentors who take a sincere and enduring interest in them; safe havens from the social and emotional storms they confront so often; programs that alleviate abject poverty and its attendant disadvantages; schools that provide hope for meaningful futures. These efforts are apt to do far more to reduce serious delinquency than wholesale processing of stereotypical youth through impersonal, degrading, and primarily punitive processes.

Endnotes

1. This is in contrast to juveniles, who would be assessing their experiences *in medias res* and who presumably lack some of the maturity and insight that are supposed to accompany adulthood.

2. More likely than not, the computerized file contained no information at all about juvenile history or placement. If a prisoner had not been considered for parole or had not recently been admitted to the prison, there likely was no juvenile information.
3. The study protocol, including the consent form, was approved by an Institutional Review Board after full review, which included affirmation from a long-time prisoner advocate that in her view the protocol posed no potential for harm to the prisoners.
4. The sizable quantity of textual data obtained from the interviews was analyzed for recurring themes with the aid of software (NVivo 8) for coding and organizing text. All interview transcripts were loaded as source documents. Themes and patterns were sought via the coding process, initially using "free" coding and then batching similar codes as "tree" coding.
5. Throughout this article, pseudonymous initials are used to identify participants; the initials for juvenile-lifer participants are shown in boldface italic type.

References

Abbott, Jack Henry. 1981. *In the Belly of the Beast: Letters from Prison.* NY: Random House.

Abrams, Laura S. 2006. "From Corrections to Community: Youth Offenders' Perceptions of the Challenges of Transition." *Journal of Offender Rehabilitation* 44(2/3):31–53.

Abrams, Laura S., Kyoungho Kim, and Ben Anderson-Nathe. 2005. "Paradoxes of Treatment in Juvenile Corrections." *Child and Youth Care Forum* 34:7–25.

Alexander, Michelle. 2010. *The New Jim Crow: Mass Incarceration in the Age of Colorblindness.* NY: New Press.

Applegate, Brandon K., Robin K. Davis, and Francis T. Cullen. 2009. "Reconsidering Child Saving: The Extent and Correlates of Public Support for Excluding Youths from the Juvenile Court." *Crime and Delinquency* 55:51–77.

Ashkar, Peter J., and Dianna T. Kenny. 2008. "Views from the Inside: Young Offenders' Subjective Experiences of Incarceration." *International Journal of Offender Therapy and Comparative Criminology* 52:584–597.

Austin, James, Kelly D. Johnson and Ronald Weitzer. 2005. Alternatives to the Secure Detention and Confinement of Juvenile Offenders. Washington, DC: Office of Juvenile Justice and Delinquency Prevention.

Becker, Howard S. 1963. *Outsiders: Studies in the Sociology of Deviance.* NY: Free Press.

Beckett, Katherine, and Theodore Sasson. 2004. *The Politics of Injustice: Crime and Punishment in America* (2nd Ed.). Thousand Oaks, CA: Sage.

Benner, Gregory J., Paul Mooney, and Michael H. Epstein. 2003. "The Impact of Time on Parent Perspectives on the Barriers to Services and the Service Needs of Youths in the Juvenile Justice System." *Juvenile and Family Court Journal* 54(2):41–49.

Beyer, Marty. 2006. "Fifty Delinquents in Juvenile and Adult Court." *American Journal of Orthopsychiatry* 76:206–214.

Bishop, Donna M. 2004. "Injustice and Irrationality in Contemporary Youth Policy." *Criminology and Public Policy* 3:633–644.

Bright, Charlotte L., Sara K. Ward, and Nalini J. Negi. 2011. "'The Chain has to Be Broken': A Qualitative Investigation of the Experiences of Young Women Following Juvenile Court Involvement." *Feminist Criminology* 6(1):32–53.

Brubaker, Sarah J., and Kristan C. Fox. 2010. "Urban African American Girls at Risk: An Exploratory Study of Service Needs and Provision." *Youth Violence and Juvenile Justice*, 8(3):250–265.

Brunson, Rod K., and Jody Miller. 2005. "Young Black Men and Urban Policing in the United States." *British Journal of Criminology* 46:613–640.

Capers, I. Bennett. 2006. "On Justitia, Race, Gender, and Blindness." *Michigan Journal of Race and Law* 12:203–233.

Charmaz, Kathy. 2006. *Constructing Grounded Theory: A Practical Guide Through Qualitative Analysis*. Los Angeles, CA: Sage.

Corley, Charles J., Timothy S. Bynum, and Madeline Wordes. 1995. "Conceptions of Family and Juvenile Court Processes: A Qualitative Assessment." *Justice System Journal* 18(2):157–172.

Davis, Angela J. 2007. *Arbitrary Justice: The Power of the American Prosecutor.* NY: Oxford University Press.

Drizen, Steven A., and Greg Luloff. 2007. "Are Juvenile Courts a Breeding Ground for Wrongful Convictions?" *Northern Kentucky Law Review* 34:257–322.

Equal Justice Initiative. 2007. Cruel and Unusual: Sentencing 13- and 14-Year-Old Children to Die in Prison. Montgomery, AL: Equal Justice Initiative.

Feld, Barry C. 2006. "Police Interrogation of Juveniles: An Empirical Study of Policy and Practice." *Journal of Criminal Law and Criminology* 97:219–316.

Feld, Barry C. 2003. "The Politics of Race and Juvenile Justice: The 'Due Process Revolution' and the Conservative Reaction." *Justice Quarterly* 20:765–800.

Feld, Barry C. 1999. "The Honest Politician's Guide to Juvenile Justice in the Twenty-First Century." *Annals, AAPSS* 564:10–27.

Gaarder, Emily, Nancy Rodriguez, and Marjorie S. Zatz. 2004. "Criers, Liars, and Manipulators: Probation Officers' Views of Girls." *Justice Quarterly* 21(3):547–578.

Goffman, Erving. 1957. Characteristics of Total Institutions. Symposium on Preventive and Social Psychiatry. Washington, DC: Walter Reed Army Institute of Research.

Grisso, Thomas. 2006. "Adolescents' Decision Making: A Developmental Perspective on Constitutional Provisions in Delinquency Cases." *New England Journal on Criminal and Civil Confinement* 32:3–14.

Hartwell, Stephanie, Robert McMackin, Robert Tansi, and Nozomi Bartlett. 2010. "'I Grew Up Too Fast for My Age:' Postdischarge Issues and Experiences of Male Juvenile Offenders." *Journal of Offender Rehabilitation* 49:495–515.

Hockenberry, Melissa, Melissa Sickmund, and Anthony Sladky. 2011. "Juvenile Residential Facility Census, 2008: Selected Findings" (U.S. Department of Justice). Retrieved October 2, 2011: (https://www.ncjrs.gov/pdffiles1/ojjdp/231683.pdf).

Huerter, Regina M., and Bonnie E. Saltzman. 1992. "What Do 'They' Think? The Delinquency Court Process in Colorado as Viewed by the Youth." *Denver University Law Review* 69(3):345–358.

Hoytt, Eleanor H., Vincent Schiraldi, Brenda V. Smith, and Jason Ziedenberg. 2002. Reducing Racial Disparities in Juvenile Detention: Pathways to Juvenile Detention Reform. Baltimore, MD: Annie E. Casey Foundation.

Inderbitzin, Michelle. 2005. "Growing Up Behind Bars: An Ethnographic Study of Adolescent Inmates in a Cottage for Violent Offenders." *Journal of Offender Rehabilitation* 42:1–22.

Lemert, Edwin M. 1951. *Social Pathology: Systematic Approaches to the Study of Sociopathic Behavior*. New York: McGraw-Hill.

Lieber, Michael J., and Kristan C. Fox. 2005. "Race and the Impact of Detention on Juvenile Justice Decision Making." *Crime and Delinquency* 51:470–497.

Lieber, Michael J., and Joseph D. Johnson. 2008. "Being Young and Black: What Are Their Effects on Juvenile Justice Decision Making?" *Crime and Delinquency* 54:560–581.

Mauer, Marc. 2006. *Race to Incarcerate*, Revised and Updated. NY: New Press.

Mauer, Marc, and Ryan S. King. 2007. A 25-year Quagmire: The War on Drugs and Its Impact on American Society. Washington, DC: The Sentencing Project.

Michaelis, Karen L. 2001. "School Violence: The Call for a Critical Theory of Juvenile Justice." *Brigham Young University Education and Law Journal* 2:299–326.

Miller, Jerome G. 1991. *Last One Over the Wall: The Massachusetts Experiment in Closing Reform Schools*. Columbus, OH: Ohio State University Press.

Mincey, Barrett, Nancy Maldonado, Candace H. Lacey, and Steve D. Thompson. 2008. "Perceptions of Successful Graduates of Juvenile Residential Programs: Reflections and Suggestions for Success." *Journal of Correctional Education* 59(1):8–31.

Nagin, Daniel S., Alex R. Piquero, Elizabeth S. Scott, and Laurence Steinberg. 2006. "Public Preferences for Rehabilitation Versus Incarceration of Juvenile Offenders: Evidence from a Contingent Validation Survey." *Criminology and Public Policy* 5:627–651.

Office of Juvenile Justice and Delinquency Prevention. n.d. Census of Juveniles in Residential Placement: 1997–2007. Retrieved October 9, 2011 (http://www.ojjdp.gov/ojstatbb/ezacjrp).

Platt, Anthony M. 1977. *The Child Savers: The Invention of Delinquency* (2nd Ed., Enlarged). Chicago: University of Chicago Press.

Rajack-Talley, Theresa, Clarence R. Talley, and Richard Tewksbury. 2005. "The Knowledge of Detained Juveniles about the Juvenile Justice System." *Juvenile and Family Court Journal* 56:29–39.

Redding, Richard E. 2008. Juvenile Transfer Laws: An Effective Deterrent to Delinquency? Washington, DC: Office of Juvenile Justice and Delinquency Prevention.

Redding, Richard E., and Elizabeth J. Fuller. 2004. "What Do Juvenile Offenders Know about Being Tried as Adults? Implications for Deterrence." *Juvenile and Family Court Journal* 55(3):35–44.

Reiman, Jeffrey, and Paul Leighton. 2010. *The Rich Get Richer and the Poor Get Prison: Ideology, Class, and Criminal Justice*, 9th Ed. Boston, MA: Allyn and Bacon.

Rogers, Richard, Lisa L. Hazelwood, Kenneth W. Sewell, Daniel W. Shuman, and Hayley L. Blackwood. 2008. "The Comprehensibility and Content of Juvenile Miranda Warnings." *Psychology, Public Policy and Law* 14:63–87.

Rothman, David J. 2002. *Conscience and Convenience: The Asylum and its Alternatives in Progressive America* (Revised Ed.). Edison, NJ: Transaction.

Ruddell, Rick, and Scott H. Decker. 2005. "Kids and Assault Weapons: Social Problem or Social Construction?" *Criminal Justice Review* 30:45–63.

Scott, Elizabeth S., and Laurence Steinberg. 2003. "Blaming Youth." *Texas Law Review* 81(3):799–840.

Scott-Hayward, Christine S. 2007. "Explaining Juvenile False Confessions: Adolescent Development and Police Interrogation." *Law and Psychology Review* 31:53–76.
Sentencing Project 2008. Reducing Racial Disparity in the Criminal Justice System: A Manual for Practitioners and Policymakers. Washington, DC: The Sentencing Project.
Shannon, Sarah K.S., and Laura S. Abrams. 2007. "Juvenile Offenders as Fathers: Perceptions of Fatherhood, Crime, and Becoming an Adult." *Families in Society* 88(2):183–191.
Sickmund, Melissa. 2010. Juveniles in Residential Placement, 1997–2008 (U.S. Department of Justice). Retrieved October 2, 2011 (https://www.ncjrs.gov/pdffiles1/ojjdp/229379.pdf).
Skrapec, Candice A. 2001. "Phenomenology and Serial Murder." *Homicide Studies* 5(1):46-63.
Snyder, Howard N., and Melissa Sickmund. 2006. Juvenile Offenders and Victims: 2006 National Report. Washington, DC: National Center for Juvenile Justice.
Sykes, Gresham M. 1958. *The Society of Captives: A Study of a Maximum Security Prison*. Princeton, NJ: Princeton University Press.
Thomas, William I., and Florian Znaniecki. 1995 [1918]. *The Polish Peasant in Europe and America*. Champaign, IL: University of Illinois Press.
Toch, Hans. 1992. *Mosaic of Despair: Human Breakdowns in Prison* (Revised Ed.). Washington, DC: American Psychological Association.
Veneziano, Carol, Louis Veneziano, and Allen Gill. 2001. "Perceptions of the Juvenile Justice System among Adult Prison Inmates." *Journal of Offender Rehabilitation* 32(3):53–61
Waldram, James B. 2007. "Everybody Has a Story: Listening to Imprisoned Sexual Offenders." *Qualitative Health Research* 17(7):963–970.
West-Smith, Mary, Mark R. Pogrebin, and Eric D. Poole. 2000. "Denial of Parole: An Inmate Perspective." *Federal Probation* 64:3–10.
Woolard, Jennifer L., Samantha Harvell, and Sandra Graham. 2008. "Anticipatory Injustice among Adolescents: Age and Racial/Ethnic Differences in Perceived Unfairness of the Justice System." *Behavioral Sciences and the Law* 26:207–226.

Cases Cited

Roper v. Christopher Simmons, 543 U.S. 551 (2005)
Terrance Graham v. Florida, 130 S.Ct. 2011 (2010)

Chapter Five

Mass Incarceration and the Paradox of Prison Conditions Litigation

By Heather Schoenfeld

In this article I examine how prison conditions litigation in the 1970s, as an outgrowth of the civil rights movement, inadvertently contributed to the rise of mass incarceration in the United States. Using Florida as a case study, I detail how prison conditions litigation that aimed to reduce incarceration was translated in the political arena as a court order to build prisons. Drawing on insights from historical institutionalist scholarship, I argue that this paradox can be explained by considering the different historical and political contexts of the initial legal framing and the final compliance with the court order. In addition, I demonstrate how the choices made by policy makers around court compliance created policy feedback effects that further expanded the coercive capacity of the state and transformed political calculations around crime control. The findings suggest how "successful" court challenges for institutional change can have long-term outcomes that are contrary to social justice goals. The paradox of prison litigation is especially compelling because inmates' lawyers were specifically concerned about racial injustice, yet mass incarceration is arguably the greatest obstacle to racial equality in the twenty-first century.

In the late 1960s, prison inmates in the United States drew inspiration and resources from the movement for black civil rights in order to challenge prison conditions and practices through the federal courts (Cummins 1994; Jacobs 1980; Strum 1993). The civil rights lawyers who represented them not only sought to extend hard-fought "rights" to prisoners, but they also "had extraordinary high hopes that ... [prison conditions] litigation, and in particular overcrowding litigation" would reduce states' reliance on incarceration (Schlanger 2006:560). Prisoners and their lawyers throughout the 1970s and 1980s were largely successful: By 1993, 40 states were under court order to reduce overcrowding and/or eliminate unconstitutional conditions of confinement (Sturm 1993). Yet despite the noted "success" of prison litigation, the decarceration goals of lawyers were never realized.[1] In fact, just the opposite occurred: Since 1973, the incarceration rate in the United States has grown by 700 percent (Western 2006:13).

In this article I ask how prison conditions litigation intended to reduce the state's reliance on incarceration eventually contributed to unprecedented prison growth. This question is important because despite recent restrictions on litigation by inmates, "the civil rights injunction is more alive in the prison and jail setting than the conventional wisdom recognizes" (Schlanger 2006:555). In addition, this question complicates explanations of the new "culture of control" or "law-and-order" politics that foreground the *backlash to* the civil rights movement (Beckett 1997; Garland 2001; Weaver 2007) by suggesting that mass incarceration is also a result of policies that *complied with* civil rights litigation. Finally, the paradox of prison litigation in the United States is especially compelling because inmates' lawyers were motivated by concerns for racial justice: Particularly in the South, prison reform litigation targeted historical racial inequities in the prison system (Feeley & Rubin 1998; Yackle 1989). Yet the growth of incarceration over the last 30 years has been disproportionately concentrated on poor black communities and has arguably reinscribed second-class citizenship on black Americans since the civil rights movement (Wacquant 2002; Western 2006).[2]

Although some existing scholarship characterizes prison litigation as a "double-edged sword," it has not systematically examined how specific prison litigation contributed to the rise of mass incarceration at the state level (Feeley & Swearingen 2004:466; Schlanger 1999). Using Florida as a case study, I demonstrate how the legal challenge to the grossly inadequate condition of state prisons, *Costello v. Wainwright* (1975) (hereinafter "*Costello*"), was a product of developments in civil rights law and legal activists' concerns for racial justice. Given the liberalization of racial politics in Florida, the national consensus on rehabilitation (and less secure confinement for offenders), and the state's widespread efforts at reform, inmates' lawyers hoped that the litigation would force Florida state policy makers to rethink their conservative penal policy. Yet between the negotiation of the court order in the late 1970s and its enforcement in the late 1980s, the political context had changed from reform to retrenchment (Pierson 1994). Increasingly, the dominant political discourse depicted black citizens as drains on the state rather than rightful claimants of equal opportunity (MacLean 2006), and criminal offenders as objects of "risk" rather than rehabilitation (Feeley & Simon 1992). In this new context, policy makers began to understand the problem as not too many people in prison but the risk of too many people being released from prison. Thus, state policy makers *translated* the court order on overcrowding as an order to *build prisons*. In the long run, compliance with the court order increased the state's capacity and willingness to incarcerate, leading to the further expansion of incarceration throughout the 1990s in ways that continued to disproportionately impact black Americans (see Figure 5.1).

---

1 On the success of prison litigation see Feeley and Rubin (1998) and Feeley and Swearingen (2004). See Crouch and Marquart (1989), Filter (1996), and Taggart (1989) for a more circumspect take on the impact of prison litigation.

2 In the United States, 1 in 15 adult black men versus 1 in 106 white men are in prison (Pew Center on the States 2008:34).

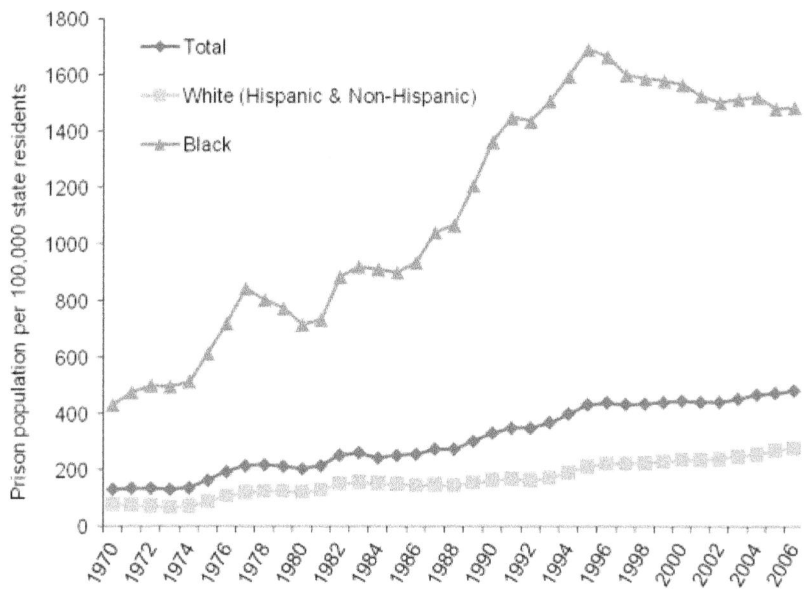

Figure 5.1. Incarceration Rates by Race, Florida, 1970–2006.

Source: Compiled by author from Florida Department of Corrections Annual Reports and Bureau of the Census.

To explain how policy makers translated compliance with prison litigation as an order to build prisons, I present a chronological "strategic narrative" of *Costello* (Pedriana & Stryker 2004; Stryker 1996). The narrative details the translation of *Costello* across a changing political and social context between its origins in 1973 and final compliance with the court order in 1993.[3] To do this I draw on a variety of primary data, including state records, court documents, newspaper articles, and 54 formal interviews with key actors (see Methods Appendix for details). Throughout the narrative I highlight the key decisions that directed the course of the litigation and its implementation in social policy in ways that put the state on the path toward mass incarceration.

Note that my findings highlight a previously unconsidered explanatory factor in the rise of mass incarceration: the role of prison conditions litigation. Specifically, I find that prison conditions litigation was a mediating factor in the politicization of punishment. Politicians' interpretation of the litigation created a platform by which they could draw on cultural distrust of the state (Zimring et al. 2001; see also Lynch 2010) and racialized fears of criminals (Russell-Brown 2008) for their political advantage. Consequently, the translation of prison litigation in the political arena can help explain some of the contemporary features of "governing through crime," such as its bipartisan support, the zero-sum game between criminals and victims (Garland 2001), and the value of prison "capacity" regardless of prisons' ability to lower the crime rate (Simon 2007).

3 *Costello* covered medical care, overcrowding, and food service in the Florida prisons. My narrative does not cover the medical care or food services portion of the litigation.

More broadly, my findings point to new reasons that positive legal outcomes for the disadvantaged may not be sufficient for reducing inequality in the long term. Beyond those detailed in other scholarship, such as the "myth of rights," the need for congruent political mobilization, the presence of symbolic victories, and the limits of court enforcement, I argue that research should examine how "progressive" court orders are "translated" into social policy by lawmakers. Specifically, I find that the contingencies of timing and the broader political and social context over which litigation unfolds can cause unintentional and unfavorable terms of compliance. In addition, I argue that researchers need to consider how the translation process can produce "feedback effects" that ultimately bring about consequences that are quite opposed to the spirit of the initial legal mobilization.

Timing and the Translation of Compliance

This article builds on understandings of "legal translation" (White 1990, 1996), or how narrative and rhetoric underpin legal claims. I conceive legal translation as happening on both the front end and back end of litigation. On the front end, legal translation is "how reformers translate their moral values and political goals into ... plausible legal claims and arguments" (i.e., legal framing) (Paris 2001:640). On the back end, it is how the language and content of court decisions is understood for the purposes of implementation. Research on legal translation is important because on the front end, legal framing shapes court opinions that, on the back end, can "powerfully shape the language of politics" and the current and future "agenda of contention" (Paris 2006:1028; citing ideas in Brigham 1987). In particular, this article considers the ways in which *timing* influences how legal framing impacts the translation of compliance. This insight about timing, gleaned from historical institutionalist scholarship on social policy and institutional change, helps explain how legal "successes" in court can have detrimental impacts over the long run.

Contemporary scholarship in sociolegal studies examines not only the success or failure of court decisions, but also the contingencies and conditions that affect courts' ability to bring about social change (McCann 2006; Stryker 2007). Important for the case of institutional reform litigation, this scholarship finds that court procedure, which requires lawyers to choose one particular legal argument, can lead to a narrow reframing of disputes and narrow definitions of social problems (Bumiller 1988; Coglianese 2001; McCann 1992). In the case of civil rights litigation, the focus on liberal notions of freedom, i.e., "negative rights" or freedom from coercion, gives way to a remedy that "merely neutralizes the inappropriate conduct of the perpetrator," rather than positively affirming the self-determination of the victim (Freeman 1995:29; Frymer 2005; Roberts 1995). The construction of prisoners' rights fell squarely into this negative rights tradition, as the courts ruled that Florida inmates had a right to be free from immediate physical violence brought about by overcrowding and inadequate medical attention. This framing precluded consideration of whether those in prison should have been there in the first place-even though this was part of the larger critique waged by the prisoners' movement (see Jackson 1972).

In a recent article, Paris (2006) imagines new realms of research analyzing change agents' conscious or unconscious choices about how to frame their claims in the legal arena. While this research agenda is important, it neglects an essential part of the processes by which law brings about social change. Instead, this article focuses on legal translation on the back end-the conscious or unconscious choices by those responsible for implementing court decisions. The contention that "law is a language into which other languages must be continuously translated" holds true in reverse: implementation requires the translation of the language of law into other languages, including the language of compliance, social policy, and politics (White 1996:55, cited by Paris 2006:1026). This is not to say that prison reformers' early choices for framing legal claims did not matter-they certainly did. But researchers need to better understand how the language of the court is ultimately understood in the political arena by those responsible for compliance.

Scholarship on legal framing has also recognized that the convergence of social movement strategy and legal discourse can help account for the "success" of some reform litigation (McCann 2006; Paris 2001). Numerous empirical case studies have demonstrated that court decisions are more likely to lead to change in policy (on the books and on the ground) when complemented by active political pressure from below (McCann 1994; Melnick 1994; Paris 2006; Pedriana 2006; Pedriana & Stryker 2004; Ziv 2001). However, the effect of timing on the convergence between legal framing and political strategy has often been overlooked. In addition, legal scholarship has not sufficiently considered the impact of timing on the convergence between political context, policy implementation, and court enforcement—generally thought to be the weakness of courts (McCann 2006:32). Yet historical institutionalist scholars have created multiple theoretical models that elucidate how the timing of policy initiatives influences future practices and institutional development (Pierson 2004; Thelen 1999). This work can be applied to legal initiatives in ways that demonstrate how the lasting impact of court decisions depends on the timing of legal translation.

For example, advocates of "path-dependent" explanations hypothesize that timing and the substance of decisions have independent causal effects on social outcomes:

> Specific patterns of timing and sequence matter; starting from similar conditions, a wide range of social outcomes may be possible; large consequences may result from relatively "small" or contingent events; particular courses of action, once introduced, can be virtually impossible to reverse (Pierson 2000:251).

In law, path dependency occurs when the "ideational constraints of liberal legal doctrine" (Paris 2001:637) restrict the content of judicial decisions, which in turn "block one path of development while encouraging another" (Stone Sweet 2002:119); or when the system of legal precedent creates a branching quality to the law as "each step in one direction increases the likelihood of additional steps in the same direction" (Hathaway 2001:628; see also Cunningham 2006; Gillette 1998; Posner 2000).

In explaining policy outcomes historical institutionalist scholarship points out that the *when* of policy innovation can be as important as the *what* of policy ideas (Weir 1992). Or in the case of legal outcomes, the timing of litigation with historical and political context can be more important than the legal arguments themselves. Similar to scholarship that recognizes courts' inability to control the temporal order of cases that come before them (Stone Sweet 2002), the case of prison litigation in Florida demonstrates that plaintiffs do not control the speed of the court process. As a result, while the initial framing by legal activists may be congruent with their goals in one political context, the actual period of compliance can take place in a different historical and political context that undermines litigators' original goals.

The contingencies of legal translation can have long-term "policy feedback" effects. Policy feedback is the idea that past policy shapes politics or the language and capacity of interest groups to frame and enact subsequent policy (Orloff 1993). Policy decisions will have significant feedback effects when they create large institutions, organize beneficiary groups, or are embedded into economic and social structures (Hacker 2002). The same can be said for legal decisions that become embedded in social policy. In the case of prison litigation in Florida, the framework of the consent order became institutionalized in state law in ways that structured political contention and limited the options for court compliance. In turn, the translation of compliance created new resources, incentives, and opportunities that changed political and policy calculations around crime control.

Legal Translation on the Front End

The Foundations of Prison Litigation in Florida

Similar to other prison litigation across the country in the 1970s, the prison conditions litigation in Florida was a product of the personal biographies of civil rights lawyers, specific developments in civil rights law itself, and newly available resources for legal challenges to civil rights violations (Smith 1974; see generally Greenberg 2004; Thomas 1988). The case study of Florida supports Schlanger's (1999) contention that the source of prison litigation is best described not just by the actions of activist judges (Feeley & Rubin 1998), but by "looking, instead, at the interaction between sympathetic judges and a set of advocates who saw a potential for urging change by lawsuit and had both resources to bring case after case and expertise to work effectively within the legal frameworks governing both contested and settled orders" (Schlanger 1999:2030).

The plaintiffs in *Costello* were represented by Tobias Simon, a local veteran civil rights attorney who had defended Dr. Martin Luther King Jr. and supporters in St. Augustine, Florida, during one of the more violent clashes of the civil rights movement (Associated Press 1964). In the late 1960s, Simon, motivated by the racial disparities in death sentences, turned his attention to death penalty cases in Florida (Greenberg [1985]2004:479). Simon's trips to death row exposed him to the brutal conditions at Florida State Prison, where cells designed for two housed 10, and inmate "medics" provided medical "treatment" to other inmates. Looking for an opportunity to address overcrowding, in 1972 Simon agreed to represent two inmates who had filed a complaint in the United States District Court for the Middle District of Florida about inadequate medical care at Florida State Prison.[4] District Judge Charles R. Scott, one of the active pro–civil rights judges in the South, knew Simon well and had previously signaled his respect for the "advantages of the class device" in Simon's work on the death penalty (*Adderly v. Wainwright* 1972:400). Within a few months, Simon had added overcrowding to the complaint, and Judge Scott certified it as a class action on February 22, 1973. Extending the successful framework from death penalty lawsuits, the amended complaint sued Louie Wainwright, the director of the Florida Division of Corrections (later renamed the Florida Department of Corrections [hereafter "FDOC"]), for relief from overcrowding and inadequate medical care that caused "substantial harm to inmates in violation of the Eighth Amendment prohibition against cruel and unusual punishment." Specifically, Simon asked the court to compel state officials to "re-distribute" or "reduce" the prison population in one of three ways: "either stem the influx of inmates ...; accelerate the discharge of qualified inmates ...; or allocate adequate funds and facilities to care for the ever-expanding inmate population" (Amended complaint, 2 Jan. 1973).[5]

While the lawsuit did not specifically challenge racial injustice—as deplorable prison conditions equally impacted black and white inmates—it addressed racial inequality in at least three regards. First, as mentioned above, the key actors initiating the case—Simon and Judge Scott—were themselves motivated by concerns about racial inequality. And in directing the course of *Costello*, they drew on their civil rights litigation experience and doctrinal and procedural precedents established in desegregation and other civil rights cases.[6] Second, at the time racial inequality pervaded all state institutions in Florida, including the penal system (V. Miller n.d.). In their court filings, the plaintiffs repeatedly blamed the overcrowding on "governmental neglect," which was due to the

4 Earlier, as a staff attorney for the ACLU, Simon had volunteered to represent Clarence Earl Gideon, whose petition to the Supreme Court became the basis of the right to counsel (*Gideon v. Wainwright* 1963). Although Gideon eventually refused the ACLU's help, Simon later wrote of that experience in terms that pointed to the logic of his commitment to protecting the rights of prisoners: "It has become almost axiomatic that the great rights which are secured for all of us by the Bill of Rights are constantly tested and retested in the courts by the people who live in the bottom of society's barrel. ... Upon the shoulders of such persons are our great rights carried" (quoted in Lewis 1964:239).

5 Legal documents referred to in the text are on file with the author.

6 For example, citing *Carter v. West Feliciana School Board* (1970), Judge Scott ordered the defendants to cooperate with a comprehensive survey of FDOC medical care by a Special Master (*Costello v. Wainwright* 1973). In addition, he assigned the United States as amicus curiae in order to tap the resources of the Civil Rights Division of the Department of Justice (see also Yackle 1989). Judge Scott also gave the U.S. Department of Justice rights of a party, which allowed it to participate actively in discovery, cross-examination, and oral arguments on behalf of the plaintiffs (*Costello v. Wainwright* 1972). Simon drew on his relationship with and the resources of the Legal Defense Fund and the ACLU's National Prison Project.

legacy of racialized penal servitude in Florida (DuBois 1901; Mancini 1996) and the dominance of Northern rural segregationist legislators, who opposed spending money on black prisoners (Schoenfeld 2009). In a nod to the legacy of slavery, in his first order Judge Scott reproached the defendants that "a free democratic society cannot ... stack [inmates] like chattels in a warehouse" (*Costello v. Wainwright* 1975:38). Finally, this same legacy contributed to Florida's "highly conservative criminal justice policy," which relied on "excessive use of imprisonment by the courts" (Ohmart & Bradley 1972:A-1). As Simon's statements later indicated, he hoped that the lawsuit would force state legislators to amend Florida's penal culture, beginning by releasing nonviolent offenders and reforming sentencing in order to divert offenders from prison (Interview, Elisabeth DuFresne, inmate lawyer, 21 Sept. 2009). And similar to the eradication of the death penalty and the provision of social services for the poor (Davis 1995; Greenberg 2004), these measures stood to disproportionately benefit black offenders, who at the time made up more than 55 percent of the prison population in Florida (compared to the less than 15 percent black population of the state; Florida Division of Corrections 1973:54; U.S. Bureau of the Census 1970: Table 24).

At the time, Simon's hope that the state would reduce the prison population was understandable. First, there was a national move *away* from secure confinement. The National Advisory Commission on Criminal Justice Standards and Goals (1973) recommended halting prison construction and using community sanctions instead of prison sentences for all but the worst offenders. Second, Floridians had recently elected a "reform" governor, Reubin Askew, and court-ordered legislative reapportionment had brought a new cohort of more progressive policy makers to the state capitol, many of whom realized that recent federal court decisions on prison conditions meant they "would have to do something different" (Interview, Jim Tillman, former Florida State House Representative, 10 May 2007).[7] In addition, the Attica prison riot in 1971 and subsequent riots across the country's prisons, including in Florida, sparked legislators' concern about prison violence:

> We had three and four people staying in a cell made for one person at the main prison. So overcrowded conditions and the fact that correctional officers were terribly underpaid and qualifications were if you had a broad back and a weak mind and could hit somebody over the head with a baton, you qualified to be a prison guard ... our correctional system was just a boiling pot ready to explode (Interview, Jim Tillman, former Florida State House Representative, 10 May 2007).

Finally, administrators at the FDOC *embraced* the lawsuit. As overcrowding threatened to jeopardize the progress Wainwright had made "modernizing" the prison system, he welcomed the chance to use the court as leverage with state legislators (Interview, Louie

7 In 1971, the Eighth Circuit Court of Appeals affirmed the decision in *Holt v. Sarver* (1970) that the whole prison system in Arkansas constituted cruel and unusual punishment. Other early prison litigation cases include *Taylor v. Perini* (1972) (entering a consent decree for the Ohio prison system) and *Battle v. Anderson* (1974) (finding that several conditions in the Oklahoma prison system violated the Constitution).

Wainwright, 17 April 2007; Florida Division of Corrections 1973:45). In fact, in spring 1973, when Simon asked the court to restrict the FDOC from accepting more inmates into the system, Wainwright took it upon himself to do so. In addition, he signed a pretrial stipulation agreeing to "gross systemic deficiencies in the delivery of adequate medical care to inmates" and "severe overcrowding" in the prison system (Pretrial stipulation, 6 Dec. 1974).

The *Costello* Injunction

By 1975, the legislature had still not appropriated adequate resources for the prison system, and Governor Askew, facing a tough re-election campaign, had strictly forbade more system closures, so Simon refiled the application for preliminary injunction. Granted by Judge Scott, the injunction became both the legal and political cornerstone of the events that unfolded around *Costello*. As it met with the political reality on the ground, it guided both sides' interpretation of the case and the resulting consent decree. In particular, three aspects of the injunctive order were important, including the definition of the problem, the substantive framework of the order, and the assumption of responsibility for relief.

First, the language of the injunction defined the problem as the immediate possibility of violence in overcrowded prisons. In his published decision, Judge Scott cited several medical experts and Wainwright, who all testified that the overcrowding created unsanitary, unhealthy, and dangerous living conditions for the inmates. In addition, a fair amount of attention during the testimony, and in the reasoning for the court, involved the mental health of inmates, including the suggestion that crowded conditions put black and white inmates too close to each other and that this could lead to physical violence (*Costello v. Wainwright* 1975:12–14). By interpreting the problem as such, Judge Scott's decision precluded a discussion of the underlying purpose and use of the prison system.

Second, in establishing the framework for relief, Judge Scott selectively relied on a report by the American Justice Institute (the "AJI report") submitted in Simon's application for injunction. He chose to use its concept of "prison capacity"—ordering the defendants to "reduce the overall inmate population" in five stages over one year to "emergency capacity," defined as "the population beyond which the institution must be considered critically, and quite probably, dangerously overcrowded," and in 18 months to "normal capacity," defined as "that population which an institution can properly accommodate on an average daily basis" (*Costello v. Wainwright* 1975:34).[8] Judge Scott

8 As fully defined by the American Justice Institute:

> "Normal capacity" [is] that population which an institution can properly accommodate on an average daily basis. It represents that population which best utilizes the resources currently available. It should include some vacant beds, to accommodate population surges, and to allow for different classifications of inmates within institutional totals.
>
> "Maximal capacity" [is] the fullest possible use of the plant, given virtually unlimited program and staff resources.

specifically stated that the order was based on the nebulous concept of "capacity" rather than a fixed number, in order to motivate the "Division of Corrections to maintain its pertinacious program of developing further innovations to increase the capacity of the Florida penal system" (*Costello v. Wainwright* 1975:35).

It is important to note that Judge Scott chose not to point to some very specific remedies suggested by the AJI report that would have *reduced admissions* to the prison system, including increasing the age of youth that could be sent to prison, developing short-term incarceration options for minor offenders, or establishing a pre-commitment diagnostic service to the courts that had been shown to "divert a significant number away from the prison system" (Ohmart & Bradley 1972:B12–14). Thus by focusing the relief on "capacity" rather than a reduction of the prison population as originally asked for by the plaintiffs, Judge Scott's order left open the possibility of compliance by prison growth.

Third, the decision placed the primary responsibility for reducing the population to "normal capacity" on the FDOC. However, in elucidating the ways to reduce overcrowding, Judge Scott touched on a number of means that required the cooperation of other institutional actors. For example, he suggested that the Florida Parole and Probation Commission could accelerate granting of parole, that courts could increase their use of pretrial intervention programs, or that the State of Florida could "simply construct or lease additional facilities" (*Costello v. Wainwright* 1975:39). However, by himself, Wainwright only had the authority to find ways to house inmates temporarily, or to award inmates between five and 15 days per month of "gain-time" (reductions to original prison sentences for good behavior, participation in programming, or other positive activity).[9] Consequently, by placing responsibility for compliance on Wainwright, rather than the governor or legislature, Judge Scott's order empowered the FDOC to direct the translation of compliance in ways that did not divert people from prison.

The Initial Reaction by Lawmakers: Delay and Limited Reform

The injunction hit state lawmakers like a "bombshell" (Interview, William Sherrill, former attorney for the Florida Department of Legal Affairs, 4 Feb. 2008). However, because of the legacy of *Brown v. Board of Education* (1954), instead of prompting

---

> "Emergency capacity" [is] the population beyond which the institution must be considered *critically, and quite probably, dangerously overcrowded*. It includes every bed in the institution which it is judged can safely be occupied at times of peak populations either due to intermittent and unpredictable population surges or to emergency and temporary circumstances (Ohmart & Bradley 1972:C-6; emphasis added).

9 At the time, it was common practice by state corrections agencies to award "gaintime," or "good time." Florida had a history of controlling the prison population via gain-time. The first gain-time laws came about as part of the large overhaul of the Division of Corrections in 1957 (Fla. Laws 1957, ch. 57–121, sec. 25). At the time, gain-time credits were given to inmates at the discretion of the individual warden or prison supervisor. In 1963, the legislature spelled out a more generous, but uniform, schedule of gain-time credits, awarding each inmate a certain number of days' credit for each month served depending on the length of the original sentence (Fla. Laws 1963, ch. 63–243).

legislators to "do something," it prompted invectives against federal court interference. As one House Representative wrote to the Florida Sheriffs Association:

> I want you to know that I am in complete agreement with your position. … The Federal Courts have stepped in to legislate conditions in our jails and once again the rights of criminals are vastly superior to those of honest, hard-working, taxpaying, law obeying citizens … we might as well sign a contract with the Hilton Hotel to come in and build and operate our penal system (if you can call it one) (Letter to Rayman Hamlin, President, Florida Sheriffs Association, 5 Feb. 1975).

Yet the state could not appeal the case on factual grounds because the FDOC had repeatedly conceded to the basic facts. Therefore, state attorneys appealed on the procedural grounds that because the injunction required Wainwright to violate the state law (by closing the prison system to new entrants), the case needed to be heard by a three-judge panel (Interview, William Sherrill, former attorney for the Florida Department of Legal Affairs, 4 Feb. 2008). The delay tactic worked, and over the next two years the case went all the way to the Supreme Court.[10]

When the injunction was reinstated in May 1977, legislators responded ambiguously with lofty mandates, small reforms, and relatively little in the way of funding. As a result, FDOC administrators spent most of their time trying to figure out where to put newly arriving inmates:

> In those days … much of our time and energy went to finding bed space for the people who were being sent in. They [the legislature] hadn't yet figured out that when you send someone to prison you have to have a bed and a place for them to stay. In the early days, it was our problem. I mean I heard legislators say in open meetings, "What are you going to do with your prisoners?" Those are actually the words [they used]. I told them, "These are the state of Florida's prisoners" (Interview, Dave Bachman, former deputy director, FDOC, 28 March 2007).

Given the historical underfunding of the Florida penal system by the state legislature and the realization that the FDOC had no ability to stem the flow of inmates but would be held responsible anyway, FDOC administrators advocated changes to the gain-time laws for more leeway in releasing inmates (Fla. Laws 1978, ch. 78–304). Despite this new discretion, the FDOC still estimated that it would need 7,000 new prison beds because commitments to prison continued to increase (see Figure 5.2). In response, the state

---

10 *Costello v. Wainwright*, 525 F 2d. 1239 (Crt. of App. 5th Cir. 1976, affirmed), 539 F 2d. 547 (en banc), reversed and remanded, 430 U.S. 325 (1977). Relying almost completely on the lack of challenge to the constitutionality of the law in question, the Court clarified that the "temporary suspension of an otherwise valid state statute" in order to comply with court-ordered relief is *not* "equivalent to finding that statute unconstitutional" *(Costello v. Wainwright* 1977:328).

Figure 5.2. Increase in Annual Commitments to Florida Prisons, 1960–1980.
SOURCE: Florida Department of Corrections Annual Reports; additional information available from the author.

conducted a survey that relied on the same concepts of "capacity" as the injunctive order but labeled them "design capacity" and "maximum capacity" in order to arrive at different numbers-reducing the FDOC's estimated need to 3,400 beds (Florida Department of Offender Rehabilitation, Bureau of Planning Research and Staff Development, 8 July 1976). The concepts of design and maximum capacity then became the framework for a settlement agreement reached almost two years later.

Legal Translation on the Back End

Sensing that the federal courts were turning against broad intervention in prison conditions cases, Simon worked with state lawyers on a compromise between his demand for a prison system based on "design capacity" and the state's desire to maintain prisons at "maximum capacity" (Interview, Elisabeth DuFresne, inmate lawyer, 21 Sept. 2009).[11] The result, the Overcrowding Settlement Agreement (OSA), approved in February 1980, stipulated that no individual prison could exceed maximum capacity (and could only be at maximum capacity for five days) and, most important, that the inmate population of the entire system could not exceed "design capacity" plus one-third. It defined

11 In May 1979, the Supreme Court held that lower courts should defer to the expertise of correction officials and that double-celling was not a violation of the Eighth Amendment *(Bell v. Wollfish* 1979). The Court's subsequent rulings trended away from a broad interpretation of prisoners' rights and comprehensive federal court intervention (Schlanger 2006).

"design capacity" as 40 to 90 square feet for inmates in individual cells and no less than 55 square feet per inmate in dorms; and "maximum capacity" as approximately 33 percent less space per inmate (40 to 60 square feet for cells and 37.5 square feet for dormitories), with double bunking allowed along outer walls (*Costello v. Wainwright* 1980). In addition, the FDOC agreed to no longer use three deteriorating buildings for housing inmates. In exchange, the plaintiffs agreed to drop any liability claims and gave the FDOC five and a half years to comply with the consent decree.

Unlike the injunctive order, the Court emphasized the responsibility of not only Wainwright, but the governor and the legislature as well. In fact, although the U.S. Department of Justice and some national reformers felt that a settlement agreement was "premature," Simon may have been more optimistic about state compliance because of the election of Bob Graham as governor (Personal communication, former law partner of Toby Simon, 20 March 2007). Having pledged to "exercise" his "authority and leadership" to implement the terms of the OSA, Governor Bob Graham appointed Simon and the state's legal representative to a Governor's Advisory Committee on Corrections charged with developing legislative mechanisms for compliance (Press release, governor's office, 12 Nov. 1980).

The Institutionalization of the *Costello* Consent Decree in State Law

Notwithstanding the work of the Governor's Advisory Committee, the OSA was only incorporated into state law after the state experienced a "prison overcrowding crisis" in spring 1982. In 1980, Wainwright had lobbied the governor for more prison beds, insisting that the FDOC had "no control over the growth of the system and the cost of providing care and supervision for the increasing number of inmates" (Letter to Governor Graham, 13 Jan. 1981). However, Governor Graham and the legislature, wanting to direct state funds elsewhere, were not forthcoming with additional resources (Florida House of Representatives 1996). Responding to ongoing revelations of brutality in the prisons, Judge Scott ordered an immediate status report, which revealed that 19 of the FDOC's 25 institutions were operating above maximum capacity and that the FDOC had built temporary wooden housing in order to count 1,640 additional bed spaces (Report to the Court Pursuant to the Order of May 12, 1982).[12] William Sheppard, who took over as lead counsel for the plaintiffs after Simon died of cancer, argued that the "plywood tents" were potential fire hazards and as such were an immediate threat to the inmates (Hearing on violation of settlement agreement, 6 July 1982). Although Judge Scott allowed them, he warned that "further recalcitrance in building adequate permanent facilities to house state prisoners will breed further woes for the defendants" (Order, 14 July 1982, pp. 8–9).

The legislature responded by appropriating money for 2,000 more prison beds and convening a bipartisan task force to recommend solutions to the overcrowding crisis.

---

12 According to Richard Dugger, the warden of Florida State Prison at the time, the temporary structures were not used to house inmates but were constructed in order to count the space when determining "maximum capacity" (Interview, Richard Dugger, former secretary of the FDOC, 22 March 2007).

Although the task force recognized public concern over crime, it also noted the fiscal consequences of a crime policy that relied too heavily on confinement (Corrections Overcrowding Task Force 1983). A similar sentiment was expressed by some members of the public:

> Florida simply cannot afford to build more and more prisons. … But Florida, as many other states, is under a federal court order to reduce its prison population or provide more space. This pressure is valid because the courts have recognized the rights of inmates not to be treated as animals *(The Evening Independent,* 17 March 1983, Editorial, n.p.).

And indeed, the task force's recommendations, codified in the Corrections Reform Act of 1983, included the implementation of sentencing guidelines and policies to stem the flow of offenders into prison through alternative court dispositions (including drug treatment and a stricter form of probation). The task force hoped that guidelines would "regulate the type of offenders who require incarceration … reduce their average length of stay … [and] foster greater public and professional confidence due to the honesty of the new system" (Corrections Overcrowding Task Force 1983:iii). The law even included an official goal to lower the state's incarceration rate (Fla. Laws 1983, ch. 83–131).

Yet lawmakers also understood that guidelines and goals, in and of themselves, would not necessarily keep the prison population under maximum capacity—making additional statutory release mechanisms necessary. Thus, the 1983 reforms included new retroactive gain-time rules that shortened sentences by up to 50 percent and an emergency release gain-time mechanism to deal with "crisis overcrowding." The latter, developed by the *Costello* lawyers in their earlier capacity as members of the Governor's Advisory Commission on Corrections, required the FDOC to reward additional gain-time of up to 30 days, in five-day increments, to all inmates eligible to receive gain-time when the prison population reached within two percentage points of "system maximum capacity" (Fla. Laws 1983, ch. 83–131).

The decision to institutionalize the *Costello* consent decree through gain-time laws had significant feedback effects on the translation of compliance. While FDOC administrators could not compel prosecutors and judges to use the sentencing alternatives in the 1983 reforms, they could use the gain-time laws to compel legislators to fund more prisons. An FDOC administrator explained,

> [The Overcrowding Agreement] helped us tremendously, because we finally had some standards. We wanted that. … So we developed through that, housing standards—"maximum capacity" beyond which we wouldn't be able to go without violating the *Costello* Agreement. That then gave us the hammer we needed to go to the legislature and say "look, we are within two percentage points of being in contempt of court, we have got to build more beds, or we are going to have to trigger this release mechanism"—and nobody wanted to

do that, so they said, "We'll give you money for more beds" (Interview, Dave Bachman, former deputy director, FDOC, 28 March 2007).

The Timing of Final Compliance

Despite a temporary reduction in the prison population in 1984 (Dykstra 1986), by 1985 the prison system was still overcrowded and the FDOC was scheduled to lose an additional 1,367 beds when it closed two units under the terms of the consent decree. In anticipation of noncompliance, and concerned about the safety of the FDOC's temporary wooden housing, lead counsel Sheppard began filing notices of violation (e.g., Notice of Violation of Overcrowding Settlement Agreement and Motion for Order to Show Cause, 27 March 1985). Judge Scott's successor, Judge Susan H. Black, reacting to the state's slow response, appointed a Special Master and Monitor in order to significantly increase the court's day-to-day monitoring of the prison system (Opinion and Order Preamble, 22 Aug. 1985). When coupled with the advent of the crack cocaine epidemic and a conservative shift in state politics, the timing of this pressure from the court marked a critical juncture that led to state officials' decision to comply by building more prison beds.

Although President Ronald Reagan had declared a "war on drugs" in 1982, arrests for drug offenses in Florida grew only slightly before 1985. But in summer 1986, the media discovered crack cocaine, and Florida law enforcement and politicians committed new resources to the "fight" against drugs (Drummond 1988; Petchel 1987; Ritchie & Gallagher 1988). In the second half of 1986, arrests for sale and possession of cocaine in Florida jumped by 30 percent. The increased prosecution of cocaine offenses led to a spike in prison admissions: Between fiscal year 1986 and 1987, prison admissions

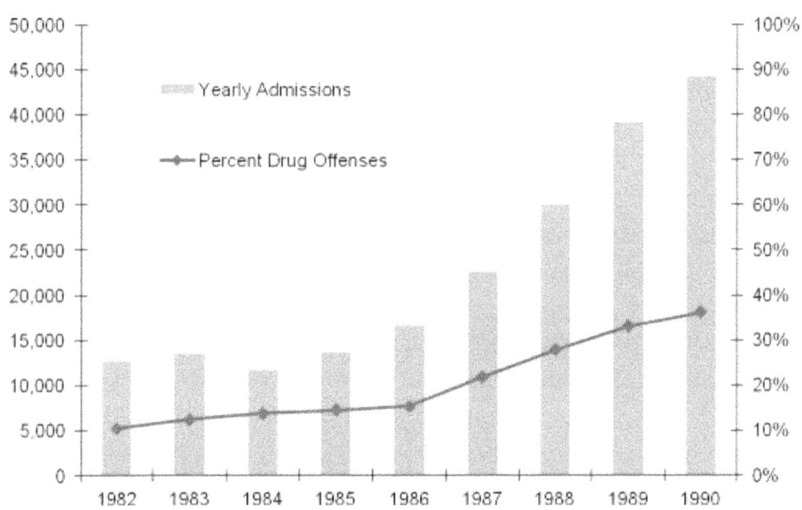

Figure 5.3. Prison Admissions for Drugs as a Percentage of Total, 1980–1990.
SOURCE: Florida Department of Corrections Annual Reports; additional information available from the author.

increased by 7,400 offenders (or 33 percent). Forty-six percent of this increase was due to the increase in admissions for drug crimes (see Figure 5.3; FDOC 1987:38; 1988:28, 41). As others have noted, the increase in drug offender admissions had a disproportionate impact on black offenders (Mauer 1999; Tonry 1995): Between 1986 and 1990, the number of black offenders admitted to prison for drug crimes increased by 850 percent, while admissions for white drug offenders increased by 210 percent (statistical information from FDOC annual reports 1986–1990; available upon request).

The unprecedented number of prison admissions led to another overcrowding crisis that perfectly coincided with the arrival of a new Republican governor and a more conservative legislature. In January 1987, the new Secretary of Corrections, Richard Dugger, warned Governor Bob Martinez that the prison population was about to exceed 99 percent of design capacity. Realizing that Judge Black was "rapidly losing patience," Governor Martinez quickly called a special legislative session to enact measures that could immediately reduce the emergency overcrowding, including new gain-time rules that gave additional discretion to the FDOC (State of Florida, Journal of the House: First Special Session "A", 1987). However, the crack cocaine scare also prompted legislators to restrict gain-time for drug and habitual offenders.[13] The legislature funded contracted jail beds, tent beds, and beds in converted industry buildings (Fla. Laws 1987, ch. 87–1). However, the court's increased monitoring had made clear that "temporary" housing was an "unacceptable" long-term solution (Dahl 1987a), forcing the Martinez administration to develop a permanent solution to overcrowding and the *Costello* lawsuit.

As Governor Martinez had campaigned in the mold of President Reagan, he was predisposed to support aggressive policing and the use of prison (Nordheimer 1986). Former Governors Askew's and Graham's previous decisions to accelerate the release of inmates further guided Governor Martinez's understanding of the state's options under *Costello*. Consequently, the Martinez administration believed that "under the terms of the federal court order, inmates must be released early when a population cap is reached" (*St. Petersburg Times*, 19 Dec. 1986, Editorial, n.p.). Eager to reverse the "mistakes" of his predecessors, and under pressure from district attorneys and county sheriffs strongly opposed to "releasing inmates through the back door" (Interview, Ed Austin, former president, Florida Prosecuting Attorney's Association, 21 Sept. 2008), Governor Martinez and Dugger began to advocate a new large-scale prison construction program. As Lieutenant Governor Bobby Brantley, who headed the initiative for Governor Martinez, explained,

> It is a hard thing [funding prisons] because … you've got educational needs and [the public] don't want to … spend all this money on prisoners, because the public, they'll tell you real quick [*sic*], "Oh yeah do what Governor Graham did, put 'em in tents." I mean they'd bury 'em all if it was up to the public. But

13 When the prison population reached 98 percent of capacity, instead of *requiring* the FDOC to credit *all* inmates with five-day increments of gain-time, the new administrative gain-time mechanism *allowed* the FDOC to grant up to 60 days of administrative gain-time to all inmates with positive work evaluations, program participation, and/or behavior adjustment, except those serving mandatory minimum terms for drug crimes, firearm possession, and capital offenses. Sex offenders who had not received "treatment" and those sentenced as "habitual offenders" were also ineligible (Fla. Laws 1987, ch. 87–2).

> *yeah we had to do it* ... there's just not a whole lot more that anybody's been able to come up with ... other than lock 'em up (Interview, former Lieutenant Governor Bobby Brantley, 12 April 2007; emphasis added).[14]

In order to overcome the public's and legislators' resistance to prison construction, the Martinez administration used the threat of "early releases." For example, the governor's office sent state legislators (and local officials) lists of offenders from their districts who would be released if the state did not build more prisons: "I mean we actually did this, 'Here's a list of the people that are ... going to be appearing in the neighborhood near you'" (Interview, former Lieutenant Governor Bobby Brantley, 12 April 2007). While some Democrats argued that Florida relied too heavily on incarceration and that the state budget lacked resources for drug treatment programs, they were also concerned that the new release mechanism would overwhelm their urban districts with prison releasees (Dahl & Nickens 1987). Thus, according to Jon Mills, the former Democratic Speaker of the House from relatively liberal Gainesville, Democrats also felt the urgency of the moment:

> I think there was some looking ahead, but it was more viewed as this is what we have to do and *there really are no other options* and trying to work with the Department and work with the Governor and others to meet what was a situation that had backed up (Interview, Jon Mills, former Florida State House Representative, 26 April 2007; emphasis added).

Of course, the legislature did have other options, but none were as guaranteed to end the overcrowding. Lawyers from the Florida Justice Institute, for example, argued that the state should redouble its 1983 reform efforts and expand alternatives such as probation, restitution, community control, community service, and work release (Berg 1987). This argument, however, did not "hold water" with many legislators because "if somebody gets killed because you don't have a [prison] bed ... [or] the Federal Court tells you to release [a criminal offender] and they kill someone the next night, that's not very good" (Interview, Robert Trammell, former Florida State House Representative, 1 May 2007).

This interpretation of the lack of options was compounded by the media's coverage of the release program: Newspaper articles quoted judges, prosecutors, and defense attorneys worried about offenders returning to the community faster than expected (Dahl 1987b). Rightly or wrongly, the media blamed the early release mechanisms on the legislature, which then blamed the federal courts: "I don't like letting them out on administrative gain time at all, but we've got to go by the federal guidelines until we build enough prisons to hold them" (former State Senator Wayne Hollingsworth (D) Lake

14 Brantley's recollection of his perception that the public opposed spending money on prisons was probably accurate for the time period. A poll commissioned by one of Governor Martinez's political opponents found that only 15 percent of respondents favored the construction of new prisons (*St. Petersburg Times*, 20 May 1988, 6B). This perception changed by the mid-1990s when legislators repeatedly stated that the public wanted to lock up offenders "whatever it cost."

City, quoted in Dahl 1987b). Despite new restrictions on potential releasees, in winter 1988 a repeat offender named Charlie Street, who had served only half of his prison sentence, killed two Miami police officers. Calling the incident "Florida's Willie Horton," the *Miami Herald* reported the crime in a tone meant to capitalize on racial fears:

> NUMBNESS is the first reaction to the murders of Metro Police Officers Richard Boles and David Strzalkowski. Then, as the story unfolds, the shock gives way to rage. Screaming rage. Rage that cracks the veneer of civilization from one end of urban South Florida to the other. How could these two fine, dedicated police officers be dead, allegedly at the hands of a career criminal, an attempted murderer just 10 days out of state prison ... ("Florida's 'Willie Horton,'" *Miami Herald*, 30 Nov. 1988, p. 24A).

Although it is not uncommon for released inmates to re-offend, because of the media attention and the national politicization of prisoner releases, legislators felt the need to express their outrage by vowing to "build more prisons to make room for more criminals" (Dahl 1989:D1).

As a consequence of this series of decisions, legislators approved what would later be called "an aggressive prison construction program" (Florida House of Representatives 1996:13). Between 1987 and 1991, the legislature appropriated 27,087 "prison bedspaces" (or 20 major correctional institutions)—six times what had been appropriated in the previous five years (Florida House of Representatives 1996:13). Yet despite these new measures, because of increasing prison admissions and gain-time restrictions on drug offenders, the FDOC had to continue granting early release to inmates. In fact, by the end of the decade Florida prisons had gained national attention, with the *New York Times* reporting that for every prisoner the FDOC accepted, it had to release one (Malcolm 1989).

The Final Settlement

The prison building program and the accelerated releases finally brought the state into compliance 21 years after Michael Costello's original complaint. In May 1991, the parties to *Costello* entered into an agreement with the governor and the state legislature that stipulated four points. The first three concerned the stability, independence, and power of a newly created medical oversight agency (the Correctional Medical Authority [CMA]), and the fourth required that the legislature enact a law to maintain the prison system population at or below design capacity plus one-third.[15] Although Sheppard "didn't have faith in the system," he had successfully forced the FDOC to stop using tents and wooden facilities and was "satisfied that we had done everything that we could."

---

15 In 1986, at the urging of the Special Master, the legislature created the Correctional Medical Authority (CMA) to replace the monitoring functions of the court (Fla. Laws 1986, ch. 86–183). Funded by the state but politically independent, the CMA was staffed by professionals who had the authority to compel the FDOC to fix deficiencies. The CMA also indirectly monitored overcrowding through its oversight of FDOC's Office of Health Services, which was tasked with certifying housing occupancy.

> When they said, we will put it in the statute, I said, fine, put it in the statute and when you get it done come back and talk to me, and they did that. I guess I was more hopeful that it would last (Interview, William Sheppard, 21 Feb. 2008).[16]

The Special Master's final report agreed that Dugger's actions as secretary of the FDOC supported a "conclusion of a good faith effort to comply":

> These actions include not only removal from bed inventory of questionable actual housing units and of certain jail and other beds which did not exist but also the promulgation ... of criteria by which the Department will determine bed capacity (Special Master's Report and Recommendation on Case Closure, 9 Oct. 1992, p. 7).

The report further cited that compliance had been "maintained long enough" that future noncompliance was unlikely (p. 49).

On March 30, 1993, after hearing direct assurances of the state's commitment from Lieutenant Governor Kenneth "Buddy" MacKay and the new Secretary of Corrections, Harry Singletary, Judge Black issued her opinion and order granting final judgment (*Costello v. Wainwright* 1993). Expressing confidence that the CMA would faithfully monitor health care delivery and act as a "check on unconstitutional levels of overcrowding" (1993:15), Judge Black found it an adequate mechanism to "assure continued compliance with the orders entered" (1993:18). As the future would confirm, however, Sheppard's reluctance was justified: In 1995, the state legislature modified the prison capacity law to allow for design capacity plus one-half (Fla. Laws 1995, ch. 95–251). Yet his reservation that the state would not maintain safe and adequate housing and medical care for inmates did not foresee the long-term effects of the prison litigation—which were only just becoming clear.

The Path of *Costello*: Policy Feedback and Future Prison Growth

By 1993, when *Costello* was finally settled, 50,000 people were incarcerated in Florida's state prisons—up from just below 20,000 in 1980. In the next 15 years, the state prison population grew by another 50,000 (see Figure 5.4; FDOC 1981, 1994, 2008). Although unintended and unanticipated, the ways in which *Costello* was understood in the political arena and translated into social policy had feedback effects that increased the state's capacity and willingness to build prisons. In turn, this new capacity and willingness paved the way for the "tough justice" laws of the 1990s, which guaranteed increasing incarceration rates for years to come and the persistence of racial inequality.

---

16 The prison capacity requirement was codified in state law in 1992 (Fla. Stat. § 944.023, 1993).

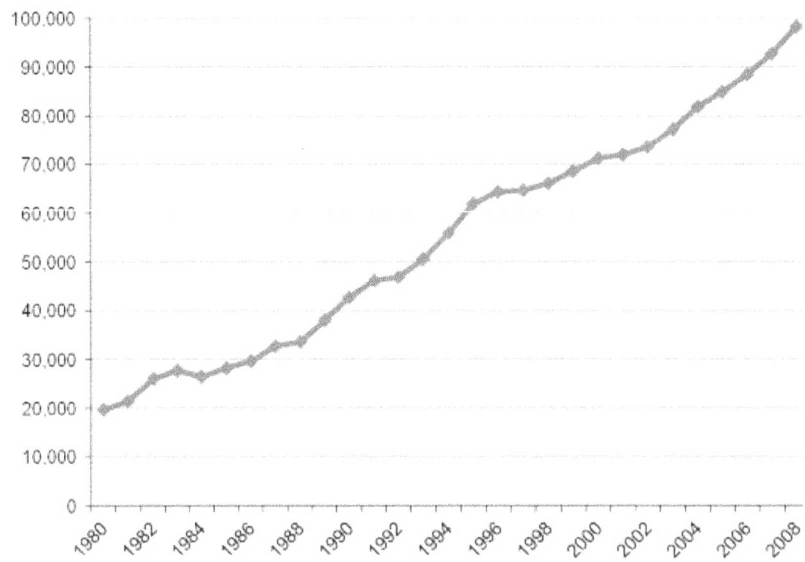

Figure 5.4. Prison Population Growth in Florida, 1980–2008.
SOURCE: Florida Department of Corrections Annual Reports; additional information available from the author.

First, the decisions that brought the FDOC into compliance in the crucial period from 1987 to 1991 increased the state's capacity to build going forward. In order to comply with the court order, Dugger took responsibility for "building prisons in the quickest, least expensive way possible" (Interview, Richard Dugger, former secretary of the FDOC, 22 March 2007). To find the cheapest land on which to build prisons, the FDOC abandoned efforts to put prisons in the southern half of the state, close to the homes of most inmates (FDOC 1990). Instead it ran advertisements in North Florida local newspapers and developed glossy brochures on the economic benefit of prisons for rural communities (Florida Department of Corrections brochure: "Siting of New Correctional Facilities," 1990). The FDOC then built prisons in the counties that provided free land and ready-made infrastructure. This policy created new incentives for state lawmakers to support prisons. As one North Florida state legislator stated,

> Well, [the state] needed a prison and I figured if it was going to be somewhere we ought to get some advantage out of it. … [It] was always recognized [as] a good clean industry, no smokestacks, employed a lot of people. [Later] the Chamber [of Commerce] saw it as economic development (Interview, Samuel Bell, former Florida State House Representative, 30 May 2007).

Of the 20 new prisons built between 1987 and 1993, 13 were located in North Florida, five in Central Florida, and only two in South Florida.

In order to build cheaply, the FDOC also abandoned ongoing efforts to expand smaller "community-based" institutions and instead used in-house architects and engineers to develop a "quick construction," dormitory-style institution that could be built almost entirely with inmate and staff labor (FDOC 1988). In the early 1990s, the FDOC improved its inmate-built prison prototype, making it even faster to build, and more secure (Rhine 1998). The litigation and dynamic release policies also forced the FDOC and the state to create internal mechanisms that strengthened policy makers' capacity to enhance criminal sentences in the future, including a nonpartisan statutory system to predict prison populations and an in-house corrections data processing system to calculate inmate release dates.

Second, the decision to comply with *Costello* through early releases and prison growth had feedback effects that reduced the perceived costs and increased the political benefits of incarceration as a crime control strategy—resulting in a new willingness to build prisons. In the 1970s and early 1980s, legislators were loath to build prisons for a variety of reasons: some ideological (the state should treat, rather than warehouse), some fiscal (state budget dollars should be spent elsewhere), some political (voters would punish politicians who spent state money on prisoners). But in the late 1980s, these concerns were tempered by the conservative shift in state politics, the perceived financial benefit of prisons for rural communities, and the absence of a negative public response to the building program into the early 1990s. These developments reinforced state legislators' calculation that they could spend money on prisons (as a trade-off with transportation, education, or health care) without any political cost (Klas 1991). Furthermore, organized interests that could have highlighted the costs of prison growth did not appear. Traditional civil rights organizations, black legislators, and urban Democrats who were concerned about over-incarceration and racial disparities did not enter into the debate because they served constituents who were the most impacted by crime (Burgos 1988; Marques 1988). Thus even in more liberal districts, as long as prisons stayed out of the news (i.e., no more egregious brutality or conditions scandals), legislators did not lose voters' support by funding prison expansion (Interview, Jon Mills, former Florida State House Representative, 26 April 2007).

The events of the late 1980s also marked the ascent of the political use of crime in Florida. When new sensational crimes occurred, as in the case of Charlie Street, legislators felt compelled to enhance criminal penalties and place further restrictions on who was eligible for gain-time (Fla. Laws 1988, ch. 88–131).[17] However, because they did this while the state was still under court order, they had to continue the early-release program. With fewer people eligible for early release, the time served by eligible offenders decreased even further, such that by the early 1990s, average time served was less than 35 percent of court-imposed sentences (Task Force for the Review of the Criminal

17 Similar to the Willie Horton episode and the defeat of Michael Dukakis, Florida state lawmakers still remember the name "Charlie Street" and the lesson that releasing offenders can have negative political consequences.

Justice and Corrections Systems 1994:14).[18] The liberal gain-time policies galvanized the law enforcement community, who used the opposition to early release policies to lobby legislators, organize victims' groups, and provide the media with juicy sound bites (Schoenfeld 2009). In the early 1990s, the perceived public backlash to the release policies created new incentives for lawmakers to expand prison capacity.[19] Thus in 1994, legislators funded another 14,000 prison beds in order to end the early release program (including beds in three private prison facilities). And in 1995, they passed one of the first "truth-in-sentencing" laws in the country, which required all future inmates to serve 85 percent of their court-imposed sentence (Fla. Laws 1995, ch. 95–294).

Since then, having realized both the physical capacity and the political willingness to build prisons, state lawmakers have continually used crime and prison resources to enhance their political capital (Garland 2001; Simon 2007; Wacquant 2009). For example, in 1995, Florida emblematically "reintroduced" chain gangs due to the initiative of State Senator Charlie Crist, who came to be known as "Chain Gang Charlie" and is now the current governor of Florida (Fla. Laws 1995, ch. 95–283). In 1999, Governor Jeb Bush campaigned on the slogan "10-20-LIFE," promising mandatory sentences for those who carried guns during the commission of a crime (Fla. Laws 1999, ch. 99–12). His initiative passed despite the fact that the violent crime rate in Florida had been decreasing an average of 4 percent per year since 1990 (Florida Department of Law Enforcement 2008: n.p.). Most recently, in response to "the horrendous murders of children like Adam Walsh, Carlie Brucia, Jessica Lunsford, [and] Sarah Lunde," Governor Crist passed the Anti-Murder Act, which stipulates zero tolerance for probation violators (Florida Governor's Office 2007: n.p.). Passed unanimously by the legislature, the large potential fiscal impact of the law (estimated at more than $20 million per year) was hardly considered by legislators during the committee hearings before its passage.

To accommodate the growth in the prison population that accompanied tough justice laws, the FDOC built an additional 32 institutions between 1995 and 2007 at an average cost per bed of $12,000 to $30,000 (FDOC 1996:13, 2007b). In 2007, Florida spent one in every 11 budget dollars on corrections, a total of $2.7 billion (Pew Center on the States 2008:30). Similar to many other states with oversized prison populations, in 2009 Florida faced a deficit of $2.4 billion and began cutting back on state services (Cave 2009). In addition, if the prison population continues to grow at this pace, the

---

18 In 1988, the legislature replaced administrative gain-time with "provisional credits," which allowed for up to 90 days to be subtracted from the sentence of eligible inmates when the prison population reached 97.5 percent of capacity. It became so common it was referred to as "computer release" (Interview, Assistant Bureau Chief of Sentence Structure, FDOC, 30 March 2007).

19 The backlash to early releases even impacted national politicians in Florida (Nurse 1993). Congressmen Charles Canady (12th District) and Bill McCollum (8th District), with the support of their respective county sheriffs, introduced the Prison Litigation Relief Act in summer 1993. The Act aimed to "limit judicial interference in the management of the nation's prisons and jails" (H. R. 2354, introduced in the 103rd Cong.). Their proposed bill was eventually incorporated into the Prison Litigation Reform Act of 1995, which has drastically reduced the number of federal claims filed by prisoners and has conceivably prevented legitimate claims from being heard (Schlanger & Shay 2007).

FDOC will need to add another 16,500 beds over the next five years (Pew Center on the States 2008:10).

It is important to note that this growth in incarceration continues to disproportionately impact black Americans and contribute to racial inequality. New crime initiatives, like those passed in the late 1980s, have disparate consequences: For example, of the almost 4,000 inmates currently imprisoned under "10-20-LIFE," more than 63 percent are black (non-Hispanic) (FsDOC 2007a:6). As when the *Costello* litigation began, the percentage of black inmates in the FDOC is still more than 50 percent, and the ratio of black to white incarceration is approximately 5.5 to 1 (FDOC 2007b:38).

Conclusion and Discussion

The story of prison litigation in the United States presents a paradox: How could legal mobilization aimed at decreasing incarceration and improving prison conditions have been successful, yet contribute to unprecedented levels of incarceration in the long run? This paradox is exemplified in a statement by Simon, the original lawyer for the inmates in *Costello*, during the hearings for the OSA in 1979:

> My own hope is that once the Federal Court enters a non-appealable order we will see the last of the new prisons built in this state. The system will begin to look at other remedies ... because we know that if the prisons get overcrowded again ... they will have to begin spending considerable sums of dollars for the construction of prisons. *And the legislature for the first time will be forced to make that choice.* For that reason, your honor ... we have signed it (Transcript, hearing on OSA, 23 Oct. 1979; emphasis added).

Yet less than 10 years later, the legislature chose to comply with the order through a massive prison building initiative. As Mills, the Speaker of the Florida House of Representatives in 1987, later recalled, legislators did not feel like they had a choice:

> The corrections situation was unchangeable and immutable and you had to deal with it. *It really ... wasn't a discretionary issue*; not dealing with it had ... public safety consequences. So it wasn't a matter of joyfully pushing for more funding for corrections. It was a fact of life and a fact of the circumstances of that period of time (Interview, Jon Mills, former Florida State House Representative, 26 April 2007; emphasis added).

The case study of Florida prison litigation suggests that the discrepancy between Simon's and Mills's understanding of the state's options can be explained by considering the congruence and timing of legal translation on both the front and back end and how decisions around legal translation constrained or enabled future possibilities for compliance.

Prisoners' rights lawyers and activists in the early 1970s were concerned about the overreliance on confinement, the overrepresentation of black Americans in the criminal justice system, and negligible treatment of inmates. Given the historical context, litigating these issues meant translating them into a problem of constitutional "rights" (Scheingold 2004). While reformers' decarceration goals seem profoundly misplaced in today's political climate, at that time they were in sync with national criminal justice experts who were promoting the ideal of rehabilitation and a future with fewer prisons (American Friends Service Committee 1971; Blumstein & Cohen 1973). However, the "rights" framing of prison litigation limited the ideation of the problem to the "immediate dangerous conditions" instead of, for example, the overuse of incarceration for low-level offenses.

Had the framework of the initial preliminary injunction required the state to *reduce* the prison population using specific measures designed to permanently decrease commitments to prison, the idea of regulating "prison capacity" may not have taken on such central importance. As it was, the capacity framework guided negotiations over a consent decree. Similarly, the injunction left space for FDOC administrators, as the "target population," to interpret the court's decision based on their own needs and understandings (Horowitz 1977). In their view, the court order was an opportunity to finally extract sufficient resources from the state. Yet during the first part of the 1980s legislators opposed spending more money on corrections, so instead they attempted to reduce the prison population through sentencing reform. In addition, legislators opted to regulate immediate overcrowding crises, as defined by *Costello*, by releasing inmates before the end of their sentences.

Together, the 1983 reforms offered the best chance for compliance along the terms envisioned by Simon and other prisoners' rights attorneys. However, the reforms were stymied because legislators did not create new infrastructure or incentives to force district attorneys and judges to utilize alternatives to state prison. In addition, because of the timing of court intervention, the reforms were given less than two years to work. As a consequence, the prison system remained overcrowded and the FDOC was forced to create temporary housing. The attorney for the inmates used the potential danger of temporary housing to uncover the state's unwillingness to enact permanent remedies, prompting the court to increase its monitoring of the prison system.

Having already "experimented" with reform, state officials were left with two options that could *guarantee* a long-term solution to overcrowding: release offenders, or build more prisons. Timed with the beginning of the first Republican administration in 20 years and the crack cocaine scare, releasing offenders became politically untenable—thus legislators' belief that building prisons was their *only* option. Yet increased drug offense enforcement forced the FDOC to continue to grant accelerated gain-time to inmates in order to stabilize the prison population. The governor, law enforcement, and the media all used the "early releases" for strategic advantage, conflating the legislative release mechanism with the court order to end overcrowding and reinforcing the notion that *Costello* required the state to build new prisons.

As historical institutionalist scholarship suggests, the case study of Florida prison litigation highlights how the contingencies of timing can affect the court's ability to bring about social change. The temporal separation between the translation of a problem into a lawsuit on the front end and the translation of the court order into public policy on the back end creates the possibility that legal outcomes will diverge from legal activists' original intentions. Even when a court order favors the aggrieved party and aims to reduce inequality or remedy injustice, the process by which it is translated over time, with all its contingencies, can produce "compliance" that is unintended or unfavorable.[20] Thus scholars of law and social change should consider the ongoing political and historical contexts "in which courts do their work" (Paris 2001), from the initial interpretation of the legal issues at stake, to the legal remedy, to compliance efforts by responsible parties.

The case of Florida prison litigation also points to limits of traditional grassroots mobilization in expanding the progressive possibilities of court decisions. Although a grassroots prison reform movement did not exist in Florida during the *Costello* litigation, it seems unlikely that it could have focused the translation of compliance toward reducing incarceration in the long run. Traditional civil rights organizations did not see it in their interest to advocate on behalf of criminal offenders. And even if they had, in the 1970s civil rights organizations were marginalized in Florida state politics. Most important, inmates' lawyers could not have predicted the mobilization of law enforcement, and victims' groups in support of incarceration. With the advantage of hindsight and unlimited resources, inmates' lawyers could have countered this mobilization by organizing educators and public welfare activists to maintain political support for the 1983 reforms.

In addition, the case of prison litigation in Florida highlights the role of policy feedback in the long-term evaluation of social change efforts through the courts. In Florida, the choices made by policy makers around court compliance, including where and how to build prisons, created policy feedback effects that further expanded the coercive capacity of the state and transformed political calculations around crime control. Thus scholarship on law and social change needs to look beyond one-dimensional "measures" of court success (Stryker 2007:74) (such as the implementation of law "on the books" and "on the ground") and instead follow how legal translation generates new constituencies, molds new languages of contention, and constrains and enables the definition of new "problems."

The framework of policy feedback can also help researchers better understand some features of the "law-and-order" politics of the 1990s. By translating the court order into a statutory release mechanism, legislators effectively increased the discrepancy between nominal and actual prison sentence lengths. In turn, this discrepancy created a potent symbol for politicians and interest groups looking to capitalize on the public's distrust of the state (Zimring et al. 2001). While there may have been valid reasons to shorten prison sentences, politicians in the early 1990s could claim that the "forced release"

20 Others have made the argument that civil rights litigation, and in particular *Brown v. Board of Education* (1954), did not ultimately bring about the racial equality that plaintiffs envisioned (Bell 2004). One can argue that in *Brown*, the meaning of "compliance" was formally rewritten by the Court as the political context changed, rendering "compliance" insufficient to achieve educational equality.

of offenders before the end of their “true” sentences was a substantial harm to public safety and a “risk” not worth taking. This claim then reinforced the racialized “fear that government authorities [would] serve the interests of criminals” over law-abiding citizens (Zimring et al. 2001:231). In this sense, while unintentional, the prison conditions litigation created a means by which state legislators and district attorneys could attack judicial discretion, expand mandatory minimums, and abolish sentencing guidelines. The political backlash to “early releases” thus allowed politicians to strengthen their own political authority by building new prisons and enacting new policy meant to keep more criminals behind bars for longer periods of time (Simon 2007).

The finding that prison litigation contributed to mass incarceration in Florida supports the “double-edged” sword scholarship about prison conditions litigation (Feeley & Swearingen 2004:466) and substantiates the concern that “by promoting the comforting idea of the ‘lawful prison,’ the litigation movement may have smoothed the way for ever-harsher sentences and criminal policies” (Schlanger 1999:2036, commenting on Feeley & Rubin 1998: note 19). Yet the findings run counter to the idea that prisoner rights litigation engendered a backlash within prisons that drew corrections administrators toward a “custody orientation” (Gottschalk 2006; Irwin 1980; Lynch 2010). To the contrary, Florida prison officials embraced prison conditions litigation, using it as a chance to pry needed resources from the state legislature (see also Carroll 1998). The story of prison litigation in Florida also extends new scholarship that finds counterintuitive explanations for mass incarceration. As Gottschalk (2006) has carefully detailed, we should consider how “not the usual suspects,” but rather women’s rights groups and other “liberal” organizations, contributed to policies of mass incarceration. In this case, concerns about racial justice ultimately helped create incentives to expand the penal state, which now ensnares 1 in 11 black adults (in prison or jail or under probation or parole supervision) (Pew Center on the States 2009:1).

Finally, the story of Florida demonstrates how detailed, in-depth accounts of prison growth in one particular state can offer new theoretical insights to explanations of mass incarceration. As most scholarship on the growth in incarceration has focused on the national level (Beckett 1997; Garland 2001; Murakawa 2005; Simon 2007), scholars of punishment have only begun to examine the unique paths to mass incarceration at the state level (Campbell 2009; Lynch 2010; L. Miller 2008; Page n.d.). I believe that more scholarship in this vein will demonstrate that prison litigation had similarly nonintuitive effects in other states. Future scholarship, therefore, should examine other states’ growth in prison capacity, the state-level politics of punishment, and the specific ways in which race has shaped the penal States of America.

Methods Appendix

The data for this article are drawn from a larger case study of prison growth in Florida between 1950 and 2000 (Schoenfeld 2009). The case study incorporated the analysis of a variety of primary data, including archival records, court records, and formal interviews. These sources are supplemented by secondary accounts of Florida’s political history,

Perspective	1970–1986	1987–2000	Total Number of People Interviewed
FDOC Personnel	12	8	12
State Legislators (Democrats)	6	3	7
State Legislators (Republicans)	4	4	7
Gubernatorial/Legislative Staff	4	7	7
Lawyers (Prisoners)	6	4	6
Lawyers (State)	1	1	2
Other Legal	1	0	1
Special Interests/Other	6	12	12

newspaper articles, and crime and law enforcement data. In addition, my understanding of Florida's politics and its prison system was also informed by numerous informal conversations and field visits to a representative sample of Florida's correctional institutions.

I created a historical record of key decisions concerning Florida's system of punishment between 1950 and 2000 with archival data from the Florida State Archives and Library, the Florida Legislative Library, the Florida Supreme Court Library, and the FDOC. I reconstructed the *Costello* case using publicly available court decisions and filings and hearing transcripts, pleadings, correspondence, and monitoring and other reports from the private files of William Sheppard, Esq., in Jacksonville, Florida. Documents referred to in the text are on file with the author.

From the documentary evidence I identified key actors involved in promoting or opposing key legislation and/or administrative changes from a variety of perspectives, including elected state officials, bureaucrats, legal and other activists, and representatives of special interest groups. I reached out to 75 potential interviewees, being careful to include people from each time period, both Republicans and Democrats and people who were less formally involved in the policy process. I was able to conduct 54 formal interviews between March 2007 and September 2009. Where I could not speak directly to key people, I relied on the archival data and newspaper accounts of their positions, statements, and actions. For the most part I was able to conduct interviews in person and digitally record and transcribe them (I asked permission to record interviews and only three people declined). Interviews lasted anywhere from 45 minutes to 2 ½ hours. Since interviewees are elected or appointed public officials, or lawyers asked about their professional decisions and duties, I was granted an exemption by the IRB to receive oral consent. Where relevant I use interviewees' real names. The following table lists the number of interviewees by perspective and time period:

I generated separate interview schedules for each of the 54 interviewees depending on the time period, the decisions made during the time period, and his or her involvement. In general, I asked interviewees about their role in the decisionmaking process, their goals, their choices, what information they used to guide their decisions, who supported their decisions and opposed their decisions, and their understandings of the consequences of their decisions. I asked interviewees who did not directly make policy decisions about the process by which decisions were made, the information available to decision makers, or other administrative processes. As interviewees were often speaking of events that happened years in the past, my detailed questions helped jog their memories. When their answers conflicted or were circumspect, I triangulated the information with available documentary evidence or newspaper articles from the time.

References

American Friends Service Committee (1971) *Struggle for Justice: A Report on Crime and Punishment in America*. New York: Hill & Wang.

Associated Press (1964) "King Seized in Florida Cafe Protest: Aide, 12 Others Also Jailed After Integration Try," *Los Angeles Times*, 12 June, p. 3.

Beckett, Katherine (1997) *Making Crime Pay: Law and Order in Contemporary American Politics*. New York: Oxford Univ. Press.

Bell, Derrick (2004) *Silent Covenants: Brown v. Board of Education and the Unfulfilled Hopes for Racial Reform*. New York: Oxford Univ. Press.

Berg, Randall C. (1987) *Florida Does Not Need More Prisons*. Florida Forum, Tallahassee.

Blumstein, Alfred, & Jacqueline Cohen (1973) "A Theory of the Stability of Punishment,"63 *J. of Criminal Law, Criminology and Political Science* 198–207.

Brigham, John (1987) *The Cult of the Court. Philadelphia*: Temple Univ. Press.

Bumiller, Kristin (1988) *The Civil Rights Society: The Social Construction of Victims*. Baltimore: John Hopkins Univ. Press.

Burgos, Frank (1988) "Lawmakers Ready to Battle Crime, Drugs," *The Miami Herald*, 3 April, p. 10.

Campbell, Michael (2009) "Agents of Change: Law Enforcement, Prisons, and Politics in Texas and California." Ph.D. diss., Department of Criminology, Law and Society, University of California, Irvine.

Carroll, Leo (1998) *Lawful Order: A Case Study of Correctional Crisis and Reform*. New York: Garland Publishing.

Cave, Damien (2009) "Budget Woes Expose Rifts over Tobacco Money," *The New York Times*, 14 Jan., p. A16.

Coglianese, Cary (2001) "Social Movements, Law and Society: The Institutionalization of the Environmental Law Movement," 150 *University of Pennsylvania Law Rev*. 85.

Corrections Overcrowding Task Force (1983) *Final Report and Recommendations*. State of Florida, Tallahassee.

Crouch, Ben, & James W. Marquart (1989) *An Appeal to Justice: Litigated Reform of Texas Prisons*. Austin: Univ. of Texas Press.

Cummins, Eric (1994) *The Rise and Fall of California's Radical Prison Movement*. Stanford, CA: Stanford Univ. Press.

Cunningham, Lawrence A. (2006) "The Common Law as an Iterative Process," 81 Notre *Dame Law Rev*. 747–82.

Dahl, David (1987a) "Martinez Will Seek Special Legislative Session on Prisons," *St. Petersburg Times*, 30 Jan., p. B1.

——(1987b) "Prison Time Dips to 20% of Sentence," *St. Petersburg Times*,4Nov., p. B1.

——(1989) "The Prison Crisis Series: For a Better Florida," *St. Petersburg Times*, 5 March, p. D1.

Dahl, David, & Tim Nickens (1987) "Plan Approved to Release Inmates to Ease Crowding," *St. Petersburg Times*, 5 Feb., p. B2.

Davis, Martha F. (1995) *Brutal Need: Lawyers and the Welfare Rights Movement*, 1960–1973. New Haven, CT: Yale Univ. Press.

Drummond, Tammerlin (1988) "Police Deaths on Rise in Florida, Officials Blame Transients, Drugs, Gun Law for Increase," *St. Petersburg Times*, 11 Jan., p. B1.

DuBois, W. E. B. (1901) "The Spawn of Slavery: The Convict Lease System in the South," 24 *Missionary Rev. of the World* 737–45.

Dykstra, Mark (1986) "Apart from the Crowd: Florida's New Prison Release Program," 14 *Florida State Univ. Law Rev.* 799–810.

Feeley, Malcolm, & Edward L. Rubin (1998) *s. Judicial Policy Making and the Modern State.* Cambridge, UK: Cambridge Univ. Press.

Feeley, Malcolm, & Jonathan Simon (1992) "The New Penology: Note on the Emerging Strategy of Corrections and Its Implications," 30 *Criminology* 449–74.

Feeley, Malcolm, & Van Swearingen (2004) "The Prison Conditions Cases and the Bureaucratization of American Corrections: Influences, Impacts and Implications," 24 *Pace Law Rev.* 433–75.

Filter, John (1996) "Another Look at the Judicial Power of the Purse: Courts, Corrections, and State Budgets in the 1980's," 30 *Law & Society Rev.* 399–414.

Florida Department of Corrections (1981) 1980–1981 *Annual Report.* Florida Department of Corrections, Tallahassee.

Florida Department of Corrections (1987) 1986–1987 *Annual Report.* Florida Department of Corrections, Tallahassee.

Florida Department of Corrections (1988) 1987–1988 *Annual Report.* Florida Department of Corrections, Tallahassee.

Florida Department of Corrections (1990) 1989–1990 *Annual Report.* Florida Department of Corrections, Tallahassee.

Florida Department of Corrections (1994) 1993–1994 *Annual Report.* Florida Department of Corrections, Tallahassee.

Florida Department of Corrections (1996) 1995–1996 *Annual Report.* Florida Department of Corrections, Tallahassee.

Florida Department of Corrections (2007a) "10-20-Life Criminals Sentenced to Florida's Prisons," http://www.dc.state.fl.us/pub/10-20-life/index.html (accessed 29 Jan. 2009).

Florida Department of Corrections (2007b) *2006–2007 Annual Report.* Florida Department of Corrections, Tallahassee. Florida Department of Corrections (2008) 2007–2008 Annual Report. Florida Department of Corrections, Tallahassee.

Florida Department of Law Enforcement (2008) "Total Violent Crime for Florida, 1989–2007," Florida Statistical Analysis Center, http://www.fdle.state.fl.us/Content/ getdoc/d0209ed2-68c4-4878-b8ca-c3129409bf3a/1989_fwd_violent.aspx (accessed 29 Jan. 2009).

Florida Division of Corrections (1973) *Ninth Biennial Report: July 1, 1971 to June 30, 1973.* Florida Division of Corrections, Tallahassee.

Florida House of Representatives (1996) *Corrections Issues Orientation Package.* Report, Committee on Corrections, Tallahassee.

Florida Governor's Office (2007) "Governor Crist Signs Anti-Murder Act," Press release, State of Florida, http://www.flgov.com/release/8709 (accessed Jan. 2009).

Freeman, Alan David (1995) "Legitimizing Racial Discrimination Through Antidiscrimination Law: A Critical Review of Supreme Court Doctrine," in K. Crenshaw et al., eds., *Critical Race Theory: The Key Writings That Formed the Movement.* New York: The New Press.

Frymer, Paul (2005) "Racism Revised: Courts, Labor Law, and the Institutional Construction of Racial Animus," 99 *American Political Science Rev.* 373–87.

Garland, David (2001) *Culture of Control: Crime and Social Order in Contemporary Society.* Chicago: Univ. of Chicago Press.

Gillette, Clayton P. (1998) "Lock-in Effects in Law and Norms," 78 *Bosten Univ. Law Rev.* 813.

Gottschalk, Marie (2006) *The Prison and the Gallows: The Politics of Mass Incarceration in America.* New York: Cambridge Univ. Press.

Greenberg, Jack (2004) *Crusaders in the Courts: Legal Battles of the Civil Rights Movement.* New York: Twelve Tables Press.

Hacker, Jacob S. (2002) *The Divided Welfare State: The Battle over Public and Private Social Benefits in the United States.* Cambridge, UK: Cambridge Univ. Press.

Hathaway, Oona A. (2001) "Path Dependence in the Law: The Course and Pattern of Legal Change in a Common Law System," 86 *Iowa Law Rev.* 601.

Horowitz, Donald (1977) *The Courts and Social Policy.* Washington, DC: Brookings Institution.

Irwin, John (1980) *Prisons in Turmoil.* Boston: Little, Brown.

Jackson, George (1972) *Blood in My Eye.* New York: Random House.

Jacobs, James B. (1980) "The Prisoners Rights Movement & Its Impacts," in N. Morris & M. Tonry, eds., *Crime and Justice: An Annual Review of Research.* Chicago: Univ. of Chicago Press.

Klas, Mary Ellen (1991) "Staff Readies $270 Million Budget Cuts," *The Palm Beach Post,* 9 Jan., p. 6A.

Lewis, Anthony (1964) *Gideon's Trumpet.* New York: Vintage Books.

Lynch, Mona (2010) *Sunbelt Justice: Arizona and the Transformation of American Punishment.* Palo Alto, CA: Stanford Law Books.

MacLean, Nancy (2006) *Freedom Is Not Enough: The Opening of the American Workplace.* New York: Russell Sage Foundation.

Malcolm, Andrew H. (1989) "Florida's Jammed Prisons, More in Means More Out," *The New York Times,* 3 July, p. 1.

Mancini, Matthew (1996) *One Dies Get Another: Convict Leasing in the American South.* Columbia, SC: Univ. of South Carolina Press.

Marques, Aminda (1988) "Neighbors," *The Miami Herald,* 16 June, p. 6.

Mauer, Marc (1999) *Race to Incarcerate.* New York: The Sentencing Project.

McCann, Michael W. (1992) "Reform Litigation on Trial," 17 *Law & Social Inquiry* 15–43.

—— (1994) *Rights at Work: Pay Equity and the Politics of Legal Mobilization.* Chicago: Univ. of Chicago Press.

—— (2006) "Law and Social Movements: Contemporary Perspectives," 2 *Annual Rev. of Law and Social Science* 17–38.
Melnick, R. Shep (1994) *Between the Lines: Interpreting Welfare Rights*. Washington, DC: Brookings Institution.
Miller, Lisa L. (2008) *The Perils of Federalism: Race, Poverty, and the Politics of Crime Control*. Oxford: Oxford Univ. Press.
Miller, Vivien (n.d.) *Life and Labor in Florida's Sunshine Prison*. Gainesville, FL: Univ. Press of Florida, forthcoming.
Murakawa, Naomi (2005) "Electing to Punish: Congress, Race and the American Criminal Justice State." Ph.D. diss., Department of Political Science, Yale University, New Haven, Connecticut.
National Advisory Commission on Criminal Justice Standards and Goals (1973) *Corrections*. Washington, DC: U.S. Department of Justice.
Nordheimer, Jon (1986) "Florida Race Underscores Changes," *The New York Times*, 2 Sept., p. D16.
Nurse, Doug (1993) "Canday Urges Limiting Judges' Power over Prisons," *The Tampa Tribune*, 3 June, p. 10A.
Ohmart, Howard, & Harold Bradley (1972) *Overcrowding in the Florida Prison System: A Technical Assistance Report*. Washington, DC: American Justice Institute.
Orloff, Ann Shola (1993) *The Politics of Pensions: A Comparative Analysis of Britain, Canada and the United States*. Madison: Univ. of Wisconsin Press.
Page, Joshua (n.d.) *The "Toughest Beat": Politics, Punishment, and the Prison Officers' Union in California*. Oxford: Oxford Univ. Press, forthcoming.
Paris, Michael (2001) "Legal Mobilization and the Politics of Reform: Lessons From School Finance Litigation in Kentucky, 1984–1995," 26 *Law & Social Inquiry* 631–84.
—— (2006) "The Politics of Rights: Then and Now," 31 *Law & Social Inquiry* 999–1034.
Pedriana, Nicholas (2006) "From Protective to Equal Treatment: Legal Framing Processes and Transformation of the Women's Movement in the 1960's," 111 *American J. of Sociology* 1718–61.
Pedriana, Nicholas, & Robin Stryker (2004) "The Strength of a Weak Agency: Enforcement of Title Vii of the 1964 Civil Rights Act and the Expansion of State Capacity, 1965–1971," 110 *American J. of Sociology* 709–60.
Petchel, Jacquee (1987) "Mother's Nightmare: Innocent Daughter Killed in Drug Fight," *The Miami Herald*, 30 Aug., p. 1BR.
Pew Center on the States (2008) *One in 100: Behind Bars in America 2008*. Washington, DC: The Pew Charitable Trusts.
Pew Center on the States (2009) *One in 31: The Long Reach of American Corrections*. Washington, DC: The Pew Charitable Trusts.
Pierson, Paul (1994) *Dismantling the Welfare State? Reagan, Thatcher and the Politics of Retrenchment*. Cambridge, UK: Cambridge Univ. Press.
—— (2000) "Increasing Returns, Path Dependence and the Study of Politics," 94 American Political Science Rev. 251–67.

—— (2004) Politics in Time: History, Institutions, and Social Analysis. Princeton, NJ: Princeton Univ. Press.

Posner, Richard (2000) "Path-Dependency, Pragmatism, and a Critique of History in Adjudication and Legal Scholarship," 67 *Univ. of Chicago Law Rev.* 573.

Rhine, Edward (1998) "Prison Design for the Future: Precast Concrete," in E. Rhine, ed., *Excellence in Corrections*—Best Practices. Alexandria, VA: American Correctional Association.

Ritchie, Lauren, & Kristen Gallagher (1988) "Drug Buy Becomes Deadly Deal: Woman Was Victim of Rising Cocaine Violence in Orlando," *The Orlando Sentinel*, 26 June, p. B1.

Roberts, Dorothy (1995) "Punishing Drug Addicts Who Have Babies: Women of Color, Equality, and the Right of Privacy," in K. Crenshaw et al., eds., *Critical Race Theory: The Key Writings That Formed the Movement.* New York: The New Press.

Russell-Brown, Katheryn (2008) *The Color of Crime (Second Edition): Racial Hoaxes, White Fear, Black Protectionism, Police Harassment, and Other Macroaggressions.* New York: New York Univ. Press.

Scheingold, Stuart A. (2004) *The Politics of Rights: Lawyers, Public Policy and Political Change*, 2d ed. Ann Arbor: Univ. of Michigan Press.

Schlanger, Margo (1999) "The Courts: Beyond the Hero Judge: Institutional Reform Litigation as Litigation," 97 *Michigan Law Rev.* 1994–2036.

—— (2006) "Civil Rights Injunctions Over Time: A Case Study of Jail and Prison Court Orders," 81 New York Univ. Law Rev. 550–628.

Schlanger, Margo, & Giovanna Shay (2007) *Preserving the Rule of Law in America's Prisons: The Case for Amending the Prison Litigation Reform Act.* American Constitution Society for Law and Policy, Washington, DC.

Schoenfeld, Heather (2009) "The Politics of Prison Growth: From Chain Gangs to Work Release Centers and Supermax Prisons, Florida, 1955–2000." PhD. diss., Department of Sociology, Northwestern University, Evanston, Illinois.

Simon, Jonathan (2007) *Governing Through Crime: How the War on Crime Transformed American Democracy and Created a Culture of Fear.* New York: Oxford Univ. Press.

Smith, Chesterfield (1974) "Development of Florida Legal Services, Inc.," 48 *Florida Bar J.* 733.

Stone Sweet, Alec (2002) "Path Dependence, Precedent, and Judicial Power," in A. Stone Sweet & M. Shapiro, eds., *On Law, Politics and Judicialization.* Oxford: Oxford Univ. Press.

Stryker, Robin (1996) "Beyond History vs. Theory: Strategic Narrative and Sociological Explanation," 24 *Sociological Methods and Research* 304–52.

—— (2007) "Half Empty, Half Full, or Neither: Law, Inequality, and Social Change in Capitalist Democracies," *3 Annual Rev. of Law and Social Science* 69–97.

Sturm, Susan P. (1993) "The Legacy and Future of Corrections Litigation," 142 *University of Pennsylvania Law Rev.* 639.

Taggart, William A. (1989) "Predefining the Power of the Federal Judiciary: The Impact of Court-Ordered Prison Reform on State Expenditures for Corrections," 23 *Law & Society Rev.* 241–71.

Task Force for the Review of the Criminal Justice and Corrections Systems (1994) *Interim Report.* State of Florida, Tallahassee.

Thelen, Kathleen (1999) "Historical Institutionalism in Comparative Politics," 2 *Annual Rev. of Political Science* 369–404.
Thomas, Jim (1988) *Prisoner Litigation: The Paradox of the Jailhouse Lawyer*. Lanham, MD: Rowman & Littlefield Publishers.
Tonry, Michael (1995) *Malign Neglect: Race, Crime and Punishment in America*. New York: Oxford Univ. Press.
U.S. Bureau of the Census (1970) "Historical Census Statistics on Population Totals by Race, 1790 to 1990, and by Hispanic Origin, 1970 to 1990, for the United States, Regions, Divisions, and States," Table 24, http://www.census.gov/population/www/ documentation/twps0056/twps0056.html.
Wacquant, Loic (2002) "From Slavery to Mass Incarceration," 13 New Left Rev. 41–60.
—— (2009) *Punishing the Poor: The New Government of Social Insecurity*. Chapel Hill, NC: Duke Univ. Press.
Weaver, Vesla M. (2007) "Frontlash: Race and the Development of Punitive Crime Policy," 21 *Studies in American Political Development* 230–65.
Weir, Margaret (1992) "Ideas and the Politics of Bounded Innovation," in S. Steinmo et al., eds., *Structuring Politics: Historical Institutionalism in Comparative Analysis*. New York: Cambridge Univ. Press.
Western, Bruce (2006) *Punishment and Inequality in America*. New York: Russell Sage Foundation.
White, James Boyd (1990) *Justice as Translation*: An Essay in Cultural and Legal Criticism. Chicago: Univ. of Chicago Press.
—— (1996) "Imagining the Law," in A. Sarat & T. Kearns, eds., *The Rhetoric of Law*. Ann Arbor: Univ. of Michigan Press.
Yackle, Larry W. (1989) *Reform and Regret: The Story of Federal Judicial Involvement in the Alabama Prison System*. New York: Oxford Univ. Press.
Zimring, Franklin E., et al. (2001) *Punishment and Democracy: Three Strikes You're Out in California*. Oxford: Oxford Univ. Press.
Ziv, Neta (2001) "Cause Lawyers, Clients, and the State," in A. Sarat & S. Scheingold, eds., *Cause Lawyering and the State in a Global Era*. Oxford: Oxford Univ. Press.

Cases Cited

*Adderly v. Wainwrigh*t, 58 F.R.D. 389 (M.D. Fla. 1972).
Battle v. Anderson, 376 F. Supp. 402 (E.D. Okla. 1974).
Bell v. Wollfish, 441 U.S. 520 (1979).
Brown v. Board of Education of Topeka, 347 U.S. 483 (1954).
Carter v. West Feliciana School Board, 396 U.S. 290 (1970).
Costello v. Wainwright, 353 F. Supp. 1324 (M.D. Fla. 1972)
Costello v. Wainwright, 387 F. Supp. 324 (M.D. Fla. 1973).
Costello v. Wainwright, 397 F. Supp. 20 (M.D. Fla. 1975).
Costello v. Wainwright, 525 F. 2d. 1239 (5th Cir. 1976).
Costello v. Wainwright, 539 F. 2d. 547 (5th Cir. 1976).
Costello v. Wainwright, 430 U.S. 325 (1977).

Costello v. Wainwright, 489 F. Supp. 1100 (M.D. Fla. 1980).
Costello v. Wainwright, 147 F.R.D. 258 (M.D. Fla. 1993).
Costello v. Wainwright, 372 U.S. 335 (1963).
Holt v. Sarver, 309 F. Supp. 362 (E.D. Ark. 1970).
Taylor v. Perini, 365 F. Supp. 557 (N.D. Ohio 1972).

Statutes Cited

Fla. Laws 1957, ch. 57–121, sec. 25.
Fla. Laws 1963, ch. 63–243.
Fla. Laws 1978, ch. 78–304.
Corrections Reform Act of 1983, Fla. Laws 1983, ch. 83–131.
Fla. Laws 1986, ch. 86–183.
Fla. Laws 1987, chs. 87–1, 87–2.
Fla. Laws 1988, ch. 88–131.
Fla. Stat. ¤944.023, 1993.
Fla. Laws 1995, chs. 95–251, 95–283, 95–294.
Fla. Laws 1999, ch. 99–12.
Prison Litigation Reform Act of 1995, Pub. L. No. 104-134 (codified as amended in scattered titles and sections of the U.S.C.); see also H.R. 3019, 104th Cong. (1996).

Chapter Six

Confronting Race in the Criminal Justice System

The ABA's Racial Justice Improvement Project

By Cynthia Jones

The criminal justice system in the United States is not post-racial. Across the country, African Americans, Latinos, and other minorities are overrepresented at each stage in the adjudication process. It is not uncommon for some to dismiss these disparities with oversimplified explanations, such as *"Minorities just commit a disproportionate amount of crimes,"* or *"The cops, prosecutors, and judges are racist and treat minorities more harshly."* Neither of these sentiments reflects the complexity of the problem of racial disparities in the criminal justice system. While minorities have a higher rate of criminal activity in some crime categories, this does not explain why minority defendants who commit the same crimes and have the same criminal history as white defendants are more likely to be denied pretrial release and are sentenced more harshly. Likewise, while there are some bad actors in the criminal justice system whose professional judgment is infected by racial bias, "race neutral" laws that are fairly and evenly enforced across all racial groups can still have a disparate impact on minority defendants.

To the extent there is a single cause of racial disparities in the criminal justice system, the culprit is likely discretionary power—who has it and how they use it to administer the criminal laws. Most criminal justice officials have wide latitude to make discretionary decisions that affect everything from whether a person will be stopped, frisked, arrested, or strip searched to discretionary determinations about whether a defendant will be charged with a serious felony, offered a plea bargain, detained prior to trial, or placed in a diversion program. Even during the posttrial stage, there are discretionary decisions made by judges, corrections officials, and community supervision officers regarding the conditions of probation, the location of confinement, and whether a parolee will be sent back to prison for a very minor technical violation.

Most agree that the goal of "achieving justice" necessitates criminal justice officials having flexibility to take into account the special circumstances in a particular case. Thus, discretionary authority is not undesirable when the actors engage in fair, bias-free decision making, applying policies and practices that do not have a disparate impact on minority communities. Therein lies the problem; many of the critical discretionary decisions that fuel the criminal adjudication process are made pursuant to informal (and often unwritten) policies and practices, and there is usually no entity inside or outside the criminal justice system charged with examining these discretionary decisions to determine whether they produce a pattern of racial disparities.

In this article, I briefly explore some of the legal barriers that prevent defendants from presenting evidence of racial disparities as a means of seeking relief from government action in criminal cases. I will also discuss the innovative work of the Racial Justice Improvement Project, a Criminal Justice Section initiative designed to reform policies and practices that produce racial disparities in local criminal justice systems.

Litigating Racial Disparities as a Defense to Criminal Charges

The most direct route to attacking racial disparities in the criminal adjudication process is for individual defendants who are adversely affected by a pattern of racial disparities to challenge the practice in their case (i.e., move to dismiss the indictment or suppress the evidence). This would shed much needed light on the problem and could serve as the impetus for critical systemic reforms in the way criminal justice officials use their discretion to administer the criminal laws. Under the current state of the law, however, even if a criminal defendant could access data and prove that he or she is in a class of minority defendants adversely (and disproportionately) affected by a policy or practice, it is unlikely that the defendant could successfully use the existence of the racial disparity as grounds for relief from the government's actions. For example, a Latino parolee who is arrested on a new charge is unlikely to prevail in halting a parole revocation proceeding by arguing (and proving) that the parole office either has not instituted revocation proceedings against similarly situated white parolees who were arrested, or that parole revocation is sought at a significantly higher rate against Latinos.

Despite the fact that there is a wealth of research showing racial disparities in the state and federal adjudication process from pretrial to postconviction, and notwithstanding a constitutional prohibition against the selective enforcement of the criminal laws based on race, a criminal defendant faces significant hurdles in attempting to assert a constitutional challenge to the government's discretionary decisions in criminal cases. Such claims, rooted in (and restricted to) the equal protection clause of the Fifth and Fourteenth Amendments to the United States Constitution, are extremely difficult to litigate.

If a minority defendant is stopped by the local police for a minor traffic infraction and wants to allege that he or she is the victim of racial profiling because the local police department disproportionately stops and searches minority motorists during routine traffic stops, even if true, the defendant would not likely prevail in challenging the actions of the police. In *Whren v. United States*, 517 U.S. 806 (1996), the defendant, an African-American motorist, claimed that the traffic stop by the police was pretextual, and that the police used their observation of a relatively minor traffic infraction as a basis to stop the defendant's vehicle to investigate unrelated crimes. In rejecting the defendant's claim that the traffic stop was an unreasonable seizure in violation of the Fourth Amendment, the Supreme Court held that, as long as the officer has probable cause to believe there is a traffic violation, however minor, the individual officer's "subjective intentions play no role" in the Fourth Amendment analysis. In so doing, the Supreme Court effectively placed the pervasive problem of racial profiling beyond the reach of the Fourth Amendment. Post-*Whren*, even if the defendant could show that the officers used their discretionary authority to stop a vehicle because the driver is a Muslim, as long as the police officer can point to some minor traffic infraction as the basis for the traffic stop, the actions of the police do not violate the Fourth Amendment.

Significantly, the *Whren* court stated that "the constitutional basis for objecting to intentionally discriminatory application of laws is the Equal Protection Clause." The court made this statement, however, with full knowledge that one month before *Whren*, in *United States v. Armstrong*, 517 U.S. 456 (1996), the court imposed a significant restraint on the ability of defendants seeking to raise such equal protection challenges to the discretionary authority of criminal justice officials. In *Armstrong*, the defendant sought discovery and/or dismissal of federal drug charges and claimed that, because he is black, the government chose to indict him in federal court (where he faced stiffer penalties) as opposed to state court. To prove his race-based selective prosecution claim, the defendant filed a discovery motion seeking information in the government's possession regarding the race of others prosecuted under the same federal drug statute. In support of the motion, the defendant provided information that all others prosecuted under the federal drug laws were black. The Supreme Court overruled the district court's order for the government to produce discovery on the race of those prosecuted and the criteria used by the government for prosecuting certain drug cases in federal court. As in *Whren*, the court stated, "so long as the prosecutor has probable cause to believe that the accused committed an offense defined by statute, the decision whether or not to prosecute, and what charge to file or bring before a grand jury, generally rests entirely in [the prosecutor's] discretion."

Although the *Armstrong* court acknowledged that prosecutorial discretion is subject to Fifth Amendment equal protection restraints and cannot be exercised "based on ... race, religion, or other arbitrary classification," *Armstrong* is troubling because the court did not reach the merits of the selective prosecution claim. Instead, the court denied the defendant the right to obtain the discovery needed to prove there was even merit to his claim. The court ruled that before a criminal defendant may even obtain discovery on a selective prosecution claim, the defendant must produce credible evidence that similarly situated defendants of other races could have been prosecuted, but were not prosecuted. As many scholars have noted, because this information is almost always exclusively in the possession of the government, the burden imposed by the court in *Armstrong* unduly restricts the ability of defendants to use the equal protection clause to obtain relief for claims of discriminatory application of the criminal laws. (*See generally* Angela J. Davis, Arbitrary Justice: the Power of the American Prosecutor 102–03 (Oxford 2007).) Not surprisingly, the holding in *Armstrong* has proved virtu-ally insurmountable. (*See* United States v. Venable, 666 F.3d 893 (4th Cir. 2012) (holding African-American defendant's evidence that two white defendants were not prosecuted in federal court under Project Exile for weapons-related offenses and evidence of a pattern of African Americans subjected to federal prosecution insufficient to obtain discovery in support of selective prosecution claim).)

Defendants face similar barriers to presenting evidence of racial bias and patterns of racial disparities in death penalty cases. In *McCleskey v. Kemp*, 481 U.S. 279 (1987), the court found no equal protection violation, despite the uncontroverted evidence that the death penalty was sought more frequently in cases where the victim is white and the defendant is black. In upholding the death sentence, the court reasoned that Mc-Cleskey failed to prove that there was discrimination by the government against him in seeking the death penalty. In 2012, however, 25 years after McCleskey, a condemned prisoner was able to get his death sentence overturned by using a state statute, North Carolina's Racial Justice Act, to prove, among other things, that "race was a significant factor in decisions to seek or impose the death sentence" (*See* State v. Robinson, No. 91 CRS 23143 (N.C. Super. Ct. Apr. 20, 2012).)

In sum, direct litigation to challenge the discretionary authority of police and prosecutors is generally not a viable strategy for addressing racial disparities in the criminal justice system. As discussed below, a collaboration among criminal justice officials is more likely to produce systemic changes that will ultimately reduce racial disparities in the adjudication process.

The Racial Justice Improvement Project

In fall 2010, the ABA Criminal Justice Section, in collaboration with the Bureau of Justice Assistance, launched the Racial Justice Improvement Project. The purpose of this two-year project is to work with officials in state and local criminal justice systems to identify the discretionary decision points in the adjudication process where policies and practices have an adverse impact on minorities and to develop evidence-based policy reforms to correct these racial disparities. The four jurisdictions chosen for the project are the state of Delaware; Saint Louis County, Minnesota; Kings County (Brooklyn), New York; and New Orleans, Louisiana. The task force in each jurisdiction received training, technical support, and oversight by the ABA, and a total of $24,000 to assist them in developing and implementing their racial justice reform. The ABA also advocated for (and frequently received) supplemental funding to assist each task force with training programs and other services needed along the way to develop their reform initiatives.

An essential component of this policy reform initiative is having the work of each task force developed and implemented under the watchful eye of the top criminal justice officials in each jurisdiction, all of whom have the ability to make and change policies and practices, and the expertise needed to successfully implement reforms. Thus, the composition of each task force was required to consist of the district attorney, the chief public defender, the police chief, the chief judge of the criminal court, and a representative from a community organization that focuses on criminal justice reform.

At the outset, we placed several restrictions on the work of each task force. First, each task force was cautioned that purely legal reforms that require legislative action or a litigation strategy to reverse binding precedent are outside the scope of this project. Second, broad, long-range reforms that cannot be implemented during the two-year grant period are not well-suited to the goals of the project. Also, to avoid the inevitable tension, finger-pointing, and defensiveness that often accompanies discussions of race and racial disparities, all policy reforms of the project must be supported by research and data collected from the various agencies within the local criminal justice system. This evidence-based approach also provides a baseline to measure the success of the reform post-implementation.

Within these parameters, each task force was charged with applying their considerable collective knowledge to identify a racial disparity in their local criminal justice system that was caused by (and could be redressed by) a discretionary policy or practice. In the first year, each task force formulated a "working hypothesis" regarding the exact cause of the disparity and collected and analyzed data to confirm the hypothesis and document the extent of the racial disparity. Currently, during the second year of the project, each task force is actively developing and implementing a specific racial justice reform.

Minnesota

Saint Louis County, Minnesota, spans over 170 miles across the northeastern border of Minnesota and sits within the Sixth Judicial District of the state court system. There are approximately 226,000 people who reside in Saint Louis County, which is overwhelmingly (93 percent) Caucasian, with a small (1 percent) African-American population, a slightly larger (2 percent) Native-American population, and a very small Latino population. Both Native Americans and African Americans are overrepresented in the county criminal justice system. The task force chose to focus its work on racial disparities in pretrial detention and began collaborating with the criminal justice entities that oversee arraignments and bail determinations.

Current Practices

Under Minnesota law, judges have wide latitude in making pretrial release decisions. Rule 6.02 of the Minnesota criminal procedure statute states that in making bond decisions, the court should consider factors such as community safety, the nature and circumstances of the offense, family ties, employment, financial resources, residence, criminal convictions, and prior history of appearing in court. In practice, however, not much of this information is actually known by the arraignment court judge when the bail determination is made. The judge usually knows only the name of the arrestee, the current charge, and the arrestee's prior criminal history in the state of Minnesota. The probation office prepares pretrial release reports and provides community supervision to the arrestees if released by the court. Pretrial release reports are prepared when requested by the judge, but reports are not prepared in every case. Moreover, Rule 6.02 states that the "court must set money bail ... on which the defendant may be released" in every case, but there are no specific guidelines on the amount of bail that should be imposed. As a result, many defendants are held in jail while awaiting trial because they cannot afford the bail imposed, and not because the court has sufficient information to determine whether they are a flight risk or pose a threat to community safety. The problem of overincarceration of the pretrial population is so severe that, for the last few years, Saint Louis County spends approximately $1 million to house its detainees (most of whom are pretrial) in jails in neighboring counties in the state.

Proposed Racial Justice Reform

The task force used a portion of its grant funds to hire a criminal justice research expert from the University of Minnesota to review and analyze pretrial release data obtained from the court. The expert's examination of felony cases in 2009 and 2010 showed that Caucasians were at least twice as likely as other racial categories to be released on their own recognizance, and minority defendants were more likely to have bail set, even after accounting for offense severity level and number of felony charges. Even Caucasians arrested while on probation were twice as likely to be released on their own recognizance than were similarly situated minority arrestees.

Over the course of the last year, the task force has been working with the judges and probation officers involved in the arraignment process to determine the reasons for the racial disparities in pretrial detention and how they can be corrected. One factor explored by the task force is whether the geographical distance that the arrestee lives from the courthouse is a factor used by arraignment judges and probation officers when evaluating an arrestee's suitability for release. If so, this race-neutral factor could have a disparate impact on many Native-American arrestees who live on distant reservations in the county. Another potential factor is the courtroom culture during arraignment proceedings. Judges are very deferential to the release/detention recommendations of the probation officers, and if probation officers do not recommend supervised release, that recommendation is generally honored by the court.

To date, the task force has taken several steps to address racial disparities in pretrial detention. First, the task force has met with every trial judge in the county, attended training on best practices and national standards for pretrial release, and consulted with the Washington, D.C.–based Pretrial Justice Institute on its pretrial detention practices. The task force plans to work with the court and probation office to shift and redefine the role of the judges and the probation officers during arraignment. Specifically, the task force plans to try to limit the role of probation to collecting and verifying the background information on arrestees that the arraignment judge is required to consider under Rule 6.02. This would empower the judge to make an informed and independent determination regarding pretrial release. Likewise, the task force hopes to work with the court to ensure that arraignment court judges have pretrial release investigations in each case before ordering pretrial detention, and expand the use of supervised release. Finally, the task force plans to work with judges to decrease reliance on money bonds that have effectively become a form of preventive detention for poor and minority arrestees. Finally, over the course of the year, the task force plans to host training sessions for probation officers and judges on pretrial release, implicit bias, and bias-free decision making. This training is a critical component of reforming how both groups exercise their discretion in evaluating minorities for pretrial release.

Delaware

The Delaware Racial Justice Task Force is the only group in the project that covers an entire state—all 1,954 square miles. The population of Delaware is approximately 65 percent Caucasian (non-Hispanic), 21 percent African American, and 8 percent Latino, but African Americans and Latinos are overrepresented throughout the Delaware criminal justice system. The task force decided to focus on racial disparities in probation revocation practices, and received enthusiastic support and cooperation from the director of Delaware Probation and Parole.

Current Practices

While there are Delaware statutes governing the authority of probation officers, Delaware law gives probation officers broad discretion in determining how to supervise probationers and when to seek revocation, as opposed to the imposition of less drastic community-based sanctions. The Delaware Department of Corrections oversees probation, parole, and the state detention facilities. The Delaware probation authority supervises approximately 20,000 probationers and has six probation offices located throughout the state. A 2012 preliminary study showed that 39 percent of admissions to Delaware prisons were probation violators, a substantial number due to missed appointments, curfew violations, or positive drug tests. In addition, probation data from 2009–2011 showed that, across all three years, there were racial disparities in probation revocation. Specifically, African-American probationers were revoked at a higher rate than Caucasian probationers.

Proposed Racial Justice Reform

The main focus of the task force reforms will be to work with the probation officials to develop policies and standards to guide the discretion of probation officers in the supervision of probationers. The task force has already taken specific steps to address how race might be influencing the discretionary decisions of probation officers. The task force sponsored a day-long training on implicit bias and bias-free decision making for all supervisory probation officers. Implicit bias training has now been incorporated into the mandatory training that all new probation officers receive, and the Department of Probation and Parole professional conduct policy was amended to expressly prohibit discriminatory decisions by probation officers. Beyond these initial steps taken during the first year of the project, the task force is actively planning training programs on implicit bias for all probation officers, public defenders, and judges in Delaware. The task force also met with officials in the District of Columbia to examine their approach to addressing probation violations with graduated sanctions. This model could prove effective in providing probation officers with alternatives to seeking revocation for probation violators. The task force plans to monitor these and other reforms and track their impact on racial disparities in probation revocation rates.

New Orleans

Unlike the other jurisdictions in the project, the overwhelming majority of the residents of New Orleans are African American. Post-Katrina, there is also a growing number of Latinos in the city. This racial composition is, of course, reflected throughout the local criminal justice system. While there are areas of racial disparities in the New Orleans criminal justice system, many of the reforms needed to address these disparities have been initiated by other reform projects or the reforms did not fit within the limited parameters of this project. The task force, therefore, decided to focus its energy on increasing the capacity of their criminal justice system to address an unmet need of minorities in the New Orleans criminal justice system. Specifically, the task force proposed an expansion of the diversion program run by the Orleans Parish District Attorney's Office. The task force felt the diversion program was too restrictive to accommodate the many nonviolent defendants who should be able to participate in diversion and avoid prosecution for low-level criminal conduct.

Current Practices

For the past few years, the Orleans Parish District Attorney's Office has run a drug treatment-based pretrial diversion program. Unlike many other diversion programs across the country, this diversion program is not governed by any statute or court rule, and the program was not developed or implemented in collaboration with the court or any other entity in the local criminal justice system. The DA's office has complete discretion to select and reject participants for the program. Moreover, there were no readily available written materials explaining the eligibility criteria for the program or setting forth the requirements for participants to complete the program. As a result, little was known about the operation of the diversion program outside of the DA's office. This lack of information generated both suspicion and resentment in the community and throughout the local criminal justice system. To further complicate matters, criminal court judges were not kept informed about the status or progress of diversion participants whose cases languished for months on their court dockets. Although the expert hired by the task force examined extensive data and did not identify any racial disparities in the diversion program, the DA's office and the task force joined forces to implement numerous reforms to improve the program.

Proposed Racial Justice Reform

The DA's office is quite proud of the overall success of its diversion program in providing drug treatment and related services, and was initially reluctant to open the program to task force scrutiny. Over time, top officials in the office welcomed the efforts of the task force to try to identify more nonviolent offenders for diversion, which would, in turn, allow the DA's office to devote its prosecution resources to the most violent offenders. In addition, the DA's office expressed interest in working with the task force to improve program participation by women with a history of prostitution-related offenses, and to get assistance with resources needed to better serve the growing population of Spanish speakers who, due to language barriers, could not fully participate in the diversion program.

Once all of the pertinent information regarding the diversion program was compiled, the task force and the DA's office produced a set of written materials that fully explain the eligibility criteria and program requirements for the diversion program. The task force then had the materials translated and reproduced in Spanish. In addition, the task force brokered a partnership between the diversion program staff and a local support group for women sex workers, and is currently working to arrange an onsite training with a Baltimore-based prostitution diversion program.

Prior to tackling the onerous task of proposing substantive changes to the diversion program, the task force hired an expert in pretrial diversion to provide critical guidance on "best practices" and national diversion standards. The task force also hosted a training program in New Orleans with representatives from several successful diversion programs across the country, and several members of the task force attended diversion training programs at a national conference. Armed with this wealth of knowledge and technical assistance, the task force began a productive collaboration with the DA's office to create a new, supplemental diversion program that will serve an additional population of defendants who do not need the intensive services and drug treatment required in the existing diversion program. Over the next year, the task force hopes to continue working with the DA's office to finalize and launch the new diversion program and track the progress of the participants.

New York

Kings County (Brooklyn), New York, encompasses over 71 square miles and is home to over 2.5 million people. The population of Brooklyn is incredibly diverse. More than 30 percent are African American, 19 percent are Hispanic, over 7 percent are Asian, slightly more than 40 percent are Caucasian, and others identify themselves as mixed-race. Brooklyn is also home to a wide range of immigrants from around the world. In fact, in many Brooklyn neighborhoods, English is not the predominate language spoken. The task force was initially formed and housed in the district attorney's office. Despite the initial vigor and enthusiasm of the task force, its reform efforts were hampered from the start. First, the task force was unable to gain the participation of the local police. Thus, regardless of the policy reform the task force initiated, it could not be a reform that would require coordination with the police department. Second, the task force did not have the active participation of a judge from the local trial court. While the task force was staffed by a very capable court representative, a supervising court attorney, proceeding without a trial judge meant that any racial justice reform agreed to by the task force could not be guided by the wisdom and insight of a member of the bench. In addition to the court representative, the core members of the task force are top level officials in the district attorney's office, the chief of the Brooklyn Defender Services office, and a very engaged community representative from the 88th Precinct Community Council, an organization that facilitates communication between the police and the community to address public safety issues in the local neighborhoods.

The task force decided to focus its reform efforts on DUI offenses. They operated on the premise that DUI was likely an "equal opportunity offense" committed by all racial groups at or about the same rate and, therefore, racial disparities in the adjudication of DUI offenses at any point from arrest to sentencing warranted closer scrutiny by the task force. The expert selected and hired by the task force examined a representative sample of DUI cases from 2009. The data compilation for the DUI study was onerous and involved manual examination of files by the research team. Although the initial report prepared by the researcher identified a pattern of racial disparities in sentencing misdemeanor DUI offenders, the report failed to take into account many key factors, such as new arrests, immigration detainers, parole violations, and probation violations, all of which explained the apparent racial disparity. That is, once the full criminal history of the DUI defendants was taken into account in the analysis, the researcher concluded that there was no racial disparity in the sentencing patterns in DUI cases. Upon receiving this final report, the DUI-focused racial justice reform was abandoned and the work of the task force shifted to other areas, including drug treatment for immigrants and increased access to alternative sentences for DUI offenses. The task force hopes to forge ahead in the coming months with a new reform initiative that can be implemented over the course of the next year.

Conclusion

The work of the Racial Justice Improvement Project is promising, and the racial justice reform process developed and implemented in the project has already yielded success in very diverse jurisdictions. While many jurisdictions have formed criminal justice coordinating committees to facilitate collaboration among criminal justice officials on criminal justice reform, few (if any) have been created to focus solely on addressing racial disparities. The creation of a standing racial justice task force is one way that local jurisdictions can make a sustained institutional commitment to racial justice reform.

Section III

Policy and Social Justice

Introduction to Section III

Policy and Social Justice

By Michelle Foster and Christopher Bellas

How we treat others who may appear less fortunate than ourselves says something about our nation. The United States has come a long way legislatively in recognizing that all citizens are equal. Beginning with the Civil Rights Act in the 1960s and expanding to the Americans with Disabilities Act (ADA) of the 1990s, America has taken great strides in making sure its citizens are treated equally. There are times, however, when we are reminded that legislation such as the ADA is necessary to dismiss any notion of inferiority. For example, in January 2013 the United States Department of Education cautioned a Tennessee school district that it must make reasonable accommodations for students with disabilities who want to participate in athletic events. Students must have "equitable access" to health and social benefits.

As demonstrated in the forthcoming chapter on the historical nature of those with disabilities, exclusion of those who are different because of their impairment has been an unfortunate circumstance in the history of our schools. Also, consider military personnel who have fought for our country only to come home "broken"—physically and psychologically. Post-traumatic stress disorder (PTSD) is quite common among returning veterans. PTSD is a real disability and not always treated as such; the end result is disastrous and leads to numerous problems such as homelessness, suicide, and violations of the law. Society then suffers from these acts.

Similarly, politics can also pose barriers. Political and legal decisions have great implications on social justice. The three chapters that follow address only several such social justice concerns. Chapter 7 illustrates how the infamous *Gideon v. Wainwright* (1963) case still raises issues involving the providing of an attorney for indigent individuals. Under the Sixth Amendment to the Constitution, if someone is accused of a criminal violation an attorney must be provided for that person if he or she cannot afford the representation. But concerns over effective counsel and jury perception are raised when an indigent individual uses a public defender. Public defenders are overworked and often underpaid, and sometimes public defenders do not have the resources to devote unlimited manpower and office funds to a case. Also, a public defender may be called to represent an indigent client without being provided adequate time to prepare or to educate themselves about the individual and the circumstances of the case, let alone to develop case strategies. As such, even though the court systems abide by the Sixth Amendment's provision for right to counsel, just how fully effective that representation actually is raises concerns for many.

Jones and *Katz*, the cases cited in Chapter 8, demonstrate the necessity for laws to be updated given the current needs of society. When cell phones first came on the scene they were large and cumbersome. Now we can use our cell phones like mini-computers. Because of these advancements in technology, legal issues have arisen surrounding the admissibility of e-mails and text messages in court; whether obtaining data from cell phones requires a warrant; whether tracking an individual or a vehicle by GPS is permissible, etc. Unfortunately, the only cases that law enforcement and the courts have for guidance are *Katz v. United States* (1967) and *United States v. Jones* (2012). Neither case fully addresses whether data on smartphones is open to a warrantless search. Using Katz as a standard, a person has a reasonable expectation of privacy. But because people are so willing to share their personal information, location, and the like on social media and social networking sites, how then can we have a reasonable expectation for privacy? A typical answer would be that we cannot have a reasonable expectation for privacy, but we also do not expect the government to be tracking our every move either. Since neither the Katz nor Jones cases answer this question, it is likely we will see future cases arising out of this advancement in technology.

Chapter 9 chronicles how Congress passed the ADA but also how it stifled progressive change. One recent example occurred December 4, 2012. Congress rejected passing a United Nations International Treaty, declaring its objection to discrimination for those with disabilities. One would think this was an easy call as 155 nations signed on to the treaty and it was ratified by 126 countries. It was seen as nothing more than a proclamation that countries around the world should strive for the American "gold standard" already set by the ADA. Republican opposition claimed such a treaty would 'infringe on American sovereign powers" (a claim debunked by its supporters), and it was rejected 61–38 in the Senate.

As the chapter in this section illustrates, politics is personal. It was personal in 1990 when the Americans with Disabilities Act was passed, and it was personal again that December 4th when former Republican Senator Bob Dole was wheeled by his wife onto the Senate floor in the hope that such a dramatic action would garner overwhelming support for the treaty as Dole had wanted. It did not. While old contemporaries praised his years of service and friendship, several of those longtime colleagues did not support the measure on grounds the international decree infringed on a family's effort to raise a disabled child as they wished—too much bureaucracy, they claimed. The rejection of the compact, which had no legal effect on the United States (as the ADA already addresses such issues), calls into question whether we truly have support for all citizens to have dignity, respect, and equality under the law. To recapture that culture of equality for all US citizens and those abroad, it is best to closely examine how the Americans with Disabilities Act was effectuated.[1]

---

1 For further information about this case and others similar to it, see *Floyd v. City of New York*, a class-action lawsuit against the NYPD.

Chapter Seven

Living Up to the Gideon Ideal

By Mark Walsh

In June 1962, when the U.S. Supreme Court granted review of the handwritten pauper's appeal from a Florida inmate named Clarence Earl Gideon, the court correspondent of the New York Times immediately knew he had a good news story on his hands. And, he thought, it was likely to be something more.

The correspondent was Anthony Lewis, then a 35-year-old Harvard graduate in his seventh year covering legal affairs in the Times' Washington bureau. Even before he got a good look at Gideon's appeal, in which the man convicted of breaking into and entering a pool hall had sought the aid of a lawyer at his trial, Lewis realized from the Supreme Court's order that it would consider overruling a key precedent on the provision of counsel to indigent defendants.

Lewis had recently been asked to write a children's book about the Supreme Court, and his initial thought was that Gideon's case might make for a good chapter or vignette in such a book. Luckily, for generations of readers, Lewis soon realized that the case was ripe for a full-fledged book of its own. That book was Gideon's Trumpet, which concisely tells the story of one of the most important criminal justice cases from the era of Chief Justice Earl Warren.

"The case had a lot of things going for it," says Lewis, who was interviewed in January, two months before the 50th anniversary of the Supreme Court's eventual decision in Gideon v. Wainwright. "First, how wonderful that it has a biblical name associated with it. And it's a case about one human being. It's not hard for anyone to relate to that."

In its Gideon decision, the justices unanimously overruled a 1942 case, Betts v. Brady, and held that the Sixth Amendment's guarantee of counsel was a fundamental right made applicable to the states through the 14th Amendment. Justice Hugo L. Black wrote for the court that it was an "obvious truth" that a fair trial for an indigent defendant could not be guaranteed without the assistance of counsel. The "noble ideal" that every defendant "stands equal before the law cannot be realized if the poor man charged with crime has to face his accusers without a lawyer to assist him," Black wrote.

Since that opinion—on March 18, 1963—and the publication of Gideon's Trumpet in 1964, many more words have been published about the legacy of the case for indigent defense in the United States. While the decision is being celebrated on its 50th anniversary, one report after another over the years has documented the nation's failure to truly live up to the ideal of Gideon.

A year ago, addressing the American Bar Association's National Summit on Indigent Defense, U.S. Attorney General Eric H. Holder Jr. said that across the country, "public defender offices and other indigent defense providers are underfunded and understaffed. Too often, when legal representation is available to the poor, it's rendered less effective by insufficient resources, overwhelming caseloads and inadequate oversight."

In short, Holder said, "the basic rights guaranteed under Gideon have yet to be fully realized."

Daniel T. Goyette, the chief public defender for Jefferson County in Kentucky, and a member of the ABA's Standing Committee on Legal Aid and Indigent Defendants, says that "despite some genuine efforts and notable advances, the criminal justice system and, more pointedly, the leadership of our executive, legislative and judicial branches of government—both state and federal—have largely failed to carry out the constitutional mandate of the Gideon decision."

He adds: "Sadly, it has not been a priority, and we are constantly taking one step forward and two steps back."

Humble Origin

The story began when Clarence Gideon believed he had a basic right to a lawyer for the felony charge he faced after breaking into and entering the Bay Harbor Pool Room in Panama City, Fla., in June 1961. (Coins were taken from the pool hall's jukebox and cigarette machine, and some beer and wine was reported missing.)

A state judge turned down Gideon's request, explaining that state-appointed counsel was a right only in capital cases. In fact, while counsel was guaranteed under the Supreme Court's 1932 decision in Powell v. Alabama (see "The Saga of the Scottsboro Boys Begins," page 72), the 1942 Betts ruling held that lawyers were provided in other felony cases only when there were "special circumstances," such as mental disability or illiteracy.

Gideon was 51 when he was convicted; he was sentenced to five years in state prison. As Lewis described him in the book, Gideon "bore the marks of a destitute life: a wrinkled, prematurely aged face, a voice and hands that trembled, a frail body, white hair. He had never been a professional criminal or a man of violence; he just could not seem to settle down to work, and so he had made his way by gambling and occasional thefts."

Gideon took to the prison library and filed his now-famous, five-page pauper's appeal claiming that his conviction violated his due process rights under the 14th Amendment. Gideon's punctuation and spelling were "full of surprises," as Lewis put it, and he failed to understand that the prevailing law under Betts did not guarantee him counsel without special circumstances. (Despite these faults, there is more recent evidence that Gideon was likely aided in writing his petition by a fellow inmate at the state prison in Raiford, Fla.—a former state judge who had been convicted in a murder plot.)

The Supreme Court, which had been signaling its move to overrule Betts, accepted Gideon's appeal and appointed distinguished Washington, D.C., lawyer (and future justice) Abe Fortas to represent him before the justices. Lewis, who had decided to go ahead with his book project, had frequent access to Fortas and others at his firm as they prepared Gideon's high court arguments.

As the book tells it, there was irony in that a defendant who faced all the machinery of the state at his trial without the aid of counsel now had top-notch representation in the highest court in the land, while Florida turned over the defense of its conviction to a young assistant state attorney general, Bruce R. Jacob, whose wife helped type up his legal briefs. (The other assistants in the criminal appeals division had all argued cases before the Supreme Court, and they recognized that the state was probably going to lose.)

"We knew immediately that this would probably be the case that would be used to overturn Betts v. Brady, because Gideon did not allege any special circumstances," says Jacob, who went on to become a defense attorney and a strong advocate for improving indigent defense.

An effort by Jacob to get other states to file an amicus brief extolling the dangers to federalism of requiring counsel for indigent defendants drew only two supporters (Alabama and North Carolina). Meanwhile, the letter from Jacob prompted a young, up-and-coming politician, Minnesota Attorney General Walter F. Mondale, to organize an amicus from states urging that Betts be overruled. Twenty-three states signed on.

After the Supreme Court ruled in his favor, Gideon was retried in Bay County, Fla. This time, with the aid of a savvy local criminal defense lawyer named W. Fred Turner (after Gideon had stubbornly rejected the help of two attorneys from the American Civil Liberties Union), he was acquitted.

Lewis had the storybook ending for Gideon's Trumpet. In fact, it would have almost ruined it if Gideon had again been convicted, Lewis says.

Supreme Expansion

The Supreme Court went on to expand Gideon's right to counsel to state juvenile delinquency proceedings, to state misdemeanor proceedings involving sentences of actual imprisonment, to proceedings involving suspended jail sentences, and the first appeal to a state appellate court. In addition, the court has recognized that the right to counsel is required at critical stages of the justice process, such as identification lineups, arraignments, preliminary hearings, plea negotiations and the entry of a guilty plea.

The bill of particulars about how the Gideon decision has failed to live up to its promise is familiar to many of those in the field, at least because each 10-year anniversary brings new lamentations.

A 2004 report by the ABA, Gideon's Broken Promise: America's Continuing Quest for Equal Justice, laid out the top concerns. The chief one is that indigent defense services are not adequately funded, leading to an inability to attract and compensate good lawyers, as well as to pay for experts and investigators. Meanwhile, defenders of the indigent are often inexperienced, fail to maintain proper contact with their clients, or are not competent to provide services that meet ethical standards. And judges sometimes fail to honor the independence of defense counsel and routinely accept representation of indigent defendants that is patently inadequate.

There were more specifics, of course, but the report's bottom line was that "40 years after Gideon v. Wainwright, indigent defense in the United States remains in a state of crisis, resulting in a system that lacks fundamental fairness and places poor persons at constant risk of wrongful conviction."

Fast-forward to 2009, and a report of the National Right to Counsel Committee and the Constitution Project found little progress. Despite an overall increase in funding, "inadequate financial support continues to be the single greatest obstacle to delivering 'competent' and 'diligent' defense representation," said the report, Justice Denied: America's Continuing Neglect of Our Constitutional Right to Counsel.

The most visible sign of such inadequate funding is public defenders with "astonishingly large caseloads," sometimes more than 100 clients per lawyer at a time. Such lawyers cannot interview their clients properly, file the appropriate motions, investigate their cases, responsibly negotiate with prosecutors, or perform other tasks.

Former Vice President Mondale, who was an honorary co-chair of the project, lamented in a 2009 op-ed essay in the Washington Post that if Clarence Gideon were hauled into court in Florida that year, he might well be denied a public defender because of the state's limits on assets to qualify as indigent.

"Sadly, Gideon's chances of getting counsel would be worse" in other states, Mondale wrote. Such barriers "effectively work to deny counsel to people who truly cannot afford to hire representation."

The Justice Denied report had a host of recommendations, including urging states to have a single statewide agency overseeing all aspects of indigent defense, the establishment of workload limits for defense attorneys (a position echoed in multiple reports and principles put forth by the ABA), and, where necessary, the filing of "systemic litigation" over excessive caseloads.

"There's a lack of political will" for properly providing indigent counsel, says Virginia Sloan, president of the Constitution Project in Washington, D.C. "There are lots of barriers to getting some of these indigent reforms into place."

This month, another book is coming out about the Gideon case and its legacy, though this one is more journalistic and anecdotal, and it puts more human faces on the issue than the dry policy reports on indigent defense.

In Chasing Gideon: The Elusive Quest for Poor People's Justice, journalist Karen Houppert focuses on four recent indigent defendants in Florida, Georgia, Louisiana and Washington state and their struggles with getting meaningful legal representation.

She details the story of one Spokane, Wash., public defender who risked a contempt-of-court citation to seek a continuance to have the proper time to prepare for a trial for one of her more than 100 clients. Another chapter examines a raft of challenges for indigent defense in New Orleans, made all the worse by disruption after Hurricane Katrina and a funding crisis that led one judge to appoint high-profile local lawyers, most of them inexperienced in criminal matters, to represent poor defendants in his courtroom.

In the book, Houppert attends a national conference of public defenders and legal aid attorneys, a "motley group" who wear "the resigned look and crumpled clothes of the system's legal workhorses. No power suits. No Brooks Brothers shirts. No Prada shoes." It was a group that understood good work was possible in public defense, but "that the greater context in which they labored made it a herculean effort that few could sustain," she writes.

"There have been many blue-ribbon commissions, and everyone is aware there is this huge crisis in indigent defense, yet not much has happened," Houppert says in an interview, and adds that her driving question in writing the book was: Why is this so hard to properly fund? Among the answers is that the problem is well-known in the legal community but not among the general public, whose image of the justice system was once shaped by crusading defense lawyers such as Perry Mason and Matlock but is now informed by pro-prosecution shows such as *Law & Order* and *C.S.I.*

Some in the academy have begun to question what they view as the traditional liberal outlook on Gideon—that extending it as far as possible should be the goal and more funding is a matter of right.

Donald A. Dripps, a law professor at the University of San Diego, argued in papers prepared for the 50th anniversary that the landmark decision has been both a failure and a paradox.

"It is generally agreed that Gideon was a great decision, yet it is also generally agreed that Gideon was not required by text and history and hasn't led to effective representation of typical indigent defendants," he argued in one paper.

"From my perspective, the cost of indigent defense ought to be thought of as part of the cost of criminal justice," Dripps adds in an interview. "We spend billions on police and prosecutions and prisons but then get pennywise for indigent defense."

Dripps and others argue that a new way to address the crisis would be to reduce the cost of effective representation for the indigent by increasing the supply and lowering the demand for such services. He proposes that the Supreme Court come up with a rule that would soften the requirement for counsel in felony cases, as long as incarceration was not a possible outcome of a prosecution.

He cites research by Erica J. Hashimoto of the University of Georgia law school showing that felony defendants who represented themselves experienced outcomes that were generally no worse, and were arguably better, than those experienced by indigent defendants with lawyers.

On the supply side, Dripps is joined by Stephanos Bibas, a law professor at the University of Pennsylvania and a former federal prosecutor, in arguing that the bar's monopoly on representation be loosened.

"Perhaps law schools and colleges could develop shorter paraprofessional training, akin to paralegal courses, to prepare people to handle unemployment compensation, disability claims, uncontested divorces, estate planning and similar specialized tracks," Bibas says. That would help free up the pool of appointed lawyers for cases of higher complexity, he says.

Bibas also suggests more legal triage to determine which cases really require lawyers. One possibility would be to limit the right to counsel only as far as the Sixth Amendment right to a jury, which covers all felonies and the most serious misdemeanors.
Bibas acknowledges that these reforms would require fundamental changes in law, and that they are still the views of a "very small minority" in the academy.

"The prevailing view is that Gideon was this great victory and the political branches are just not cooperating," Bibas says.

Goyette, the Louisville public defender and ABA committee member, expresses doubt about these more radical ideas. "Unless our justice system is fundamentally changed—and I think that is a dangerous proposition and unlikely to happen—limiting the right to counsel is not a wise approach or a viable solution."

One idea he favors is the reclassification of some offenses and the diversion of certain cases out of the criminal justice system, which would save money and relieve caseloads.

In June 2011 the Supreme Court issued its latest decision in the Gideon line, holding in Turner v. Rogers that the 14th Amendment's due process clause does not automatically require a state to provide counsel to an indigent person facing a civil contempt proceeding, even if the person faces incarceration.

The decision was largely a disappointment to the "civil Gideon" movement, the community of advocates who promote the appointment of counsel to indigent litigants in adversarial civil proceedings, particularly when such things as shelter, child custody, health or safety are at stake.

The movement took heart, though, that the high court required increased procedural safeguards in certain such cases. (The 5–4 decision held that a South Carolina man jailed for 12 months for nonpayment of child support should at least have been given alternative procedures that would have notified him that his ability to pay the overdue child support was the critical question in his contempt-of-court case.)

In January, just two months before the 50th anniversary of Gideon, the justices took up their latest criminal case involving indigent defense. The case was Boyer v. Louisiana, a factually messy dispute involving a capital defendant who faced a seven-year delay in being brought to trial, with five of those years awaiting the appointment of qualified state-appointed counsel.

The defendant, Jonathan Edward Boyer, contends in his court papers that the lengthy delay was caused by a "systemic breakdown in the funding of indigent defense" and violated his Sixth Amendment right to a speedy trial. Louisiana contends that the delay was not attributable to the state, and that Boyer always had effective representation. (Louisiana requires indigent capital defendants to receive two specially qualified lawyers.)

The justices wrestled during the Jan. 14 oral arguments with some of the thorny issues related to indigent defense. "Should the state be responsible when the funding problem is at a local level?" Justice Anthony M. Kennedy asked during the argument.

And Justice Sonia Sotomayor observed, "In the end, states are always strapped," but they make choices on how they allocate their criminal justice budgets, and even when they are broke they find ways to "pay the prosecutor."

Firsthand Remembrances

Observances of the 50th anniversary began last summer and run at least through late spring. Jacob, who is the dean emeritus at Stetson University College of Law in Tampa, Fla., will participate in at least 10 events, he says, including one in May sponsored by the Constitution Project that is celebrating him and three other original participants in the case who are still living: Lewis, Mondale and Abe Krash, who was a co-counsel to Fortas in representing Gideon.

"I feel like a historical relic," says Jacob.

After winning two Pulitzer Prizes while serving in the Washington bureau of the New York Times, Lewis moved to London in 1964 to become the paper's bureau chief there. He began writing an op-ed column from there in 1969 before moving back to the United States.

Gideon died in 1972 at age 61, having lived nine mostly uneventful years after his release from prison. Lewis recalls that he phoned the funeral parlor from London to learn the details, and he ended up talking with Gideon's elderly mother. She was upset with Lewis over a passage in Gideon's Trumpet, though it was really something Gideon had himself said about his mother's second husband in a letter about his life that he had written to his Supreme Court lawyers.

Lewis says that he hasn't followed all the complexities of the Gideon legacy in recent years.

"I said in the book that it would take a long time and a lot of difficulty to make representation for the poor a reality," Lewis says. "I'm not a lawyer and I never had to deal with all the realities of legislative support and so forth. I still look at the issue the way I did when I wrote the book—as an ideal.

"That's not enough, I know," he adds. "But you have to have an ideal. And it was the right ideal."

Chapter Eight

GPS Tracking, Smartphones, and the Inadequacy of *Jones* and *Katz*

By Monica Mark

Compared to a few decades ago, today's world is almost unrecognizable-at least technologically. Computers are not only portable but can store all the most intimate details of a person's life. People can stay connected to the Internet no matter where they are. Information can be transferred from person to person, countries apart, with the touch of a button or click of a mouse. As for phones? Well, phones keep getting smarter and smarter.

Technology is taking over. And not just any technology-this technology can pinpoint a person's location in seconds, reach hundreds of contacts with a single click, store a wealth of personal data, and compromise a person's finances, privacy, or identify if stolen. Inevitably, such a dramatic shift will result in new situations that may implicate a person's Fourth Amendment right to protection from unlawful search or seizure. It has happened before: with the advent of the "vital role that the public telephone [had] come to play in private communication" the United States Supreme Court recognized in the landmark case of *Katz v. United States* that it was time to acknowledge the Fourth Amendment as the protector of "people, not places." (389 U.S. 347, 351–52 (1967).) Technology has metamorphosed in the 45 years since then, when public phone booths dotted the landscape, and new Fourth Amendment questions are certain to again get their day in court.

In fact, certain questions are already making appearances in the courts. Forensic extraction devices that "allow law enforcement officials to crack suspects' mobile phones and mine them for incriminating information" are entering the arsenals of the federal government, the Pentagon, and police departments across the United States, including New York and Los Angeles. (Nick Taborek, *You're Under Arrest! Hand Over That iPhone*, Bloomberg Businessweek, Apr. 2–8, 2012, at 33.) Their advent raises questions as to whether a phone search requires a warrant—questions that are already dividing the states' highest courts. (*Compare* People v. Diaz, 244 P.3d 501 (Cal. 2011) (holding that a warrantless cell phone search incident to arrest was valid), *with* State v. Smith, 920 N.E.2d 949 (Ohio 2009) (holding that a warrantless cell phone search incident to arrest violated the defendant's Fourth Amendment rights).) However, one of the most alarming tools that smartphones have to offer has little to do with data or, at least, has little to do with data in the form of damning evidence. That tool? The global positioning system, or GPS. Unfortunately, the Supreme Court's decision in *United States v. Jones* did not address the crux of the problem; it also raises troubling possibilities as to what smartphones might soon be used to do.

Jones dealt with investigators' warrantless installation of a GPS device on the car of a suspect's wife. (132 S. Ct. 945, 946 (2012).) The government monitored the GPS for 28 days, gathering more than 2,000 pages of data, before arresting Jones for trafficking in narcotics. (*Id.* at 948.) The majority opinion, authored by Justice Scalia, reinvigorated the trespass doctrine, which dates back to the Constitution's adoption and constituted Fourth Amendment jurisprudence up until the mid-twentieth century. (*Id.* at 949.) Under this doctrine, property rights reigned supreme, and physical intrusion onto that property was thus a constitutional violation. (*Id*) The *Jones* Court used this principle to dispose of the problem before them. In essence, because the State "physically occupied private property for the purpose of obtaining information," the installation of the GPS was an unlawful search under the Fourth Amendment, as it was understood in the eighteenth century. (*Id*)

Justices Alito, Ginsburg, Breyer, and Kagan concurred in the result, but not without condemning the trespass doctrine, arguing that advances in technology since the eighteenth century have rendered the trespass-based theory of Fourth Amendment violation nearly meaningless. (*Id.* at 958 (Alito, J., concurring).) The Alito four advocated for the exclusive use of the formulation from *Katz v. United States,* which determined that the Fourth Amendment protects a person's "reasonable expectation of privacy." (389 U.S. 347 (1967).) The majority's response was, quite simply, that they did not need to address the question, that the trespass-based theory was *in addition to* the *Katz* test, and that "there is no reason for rushing forward" to address the thorny problems that *Katz* would create. (*Jones*, 132 S. Ct. at 954.)

Jones certainly disposes of cases in which the government attaches a GPS device to a person's vehicle: the majority's condemnation of physical trespass is unequivocal and, as the majority put it, provides "*at a minimum* the degree of protection [the Fourth Amendment] afforded when it was adopted." (*Id.* at 953.) However, thanks to innovations in mobile phones, that kind of physical intrusion is no longer necessary to track a person's location. By 2006, 100 million cell phone users already had phones that included GPS devices. (Melody Joy Kramer. *Somebody's Watching You—and It's Your Cell Phone*, NPR, http://tinyurl.com/9a8vns8 (last visited Oct. 27, 2012).) By 2015, according to the research firm In-Stat, 65 percent of the US population—or over 200 million people—will have a smartphone or tablet. (Don Reisinger, *In-Stat: Majority in U.S. to Have Smartphones, Tablets by 2015*, CNET News (Aug. 23, 2011), http://tinyurl.com/99lo8we.) Some numbers even suggest that there are already 322 million wireless devices in use in the United States. (*Jones*, 132 S. Ct. at 963 (Alito, J., concurring).)

And it is not only the number of phones that is increasing rapidly. New smartphones can reveal a person's location with far more accuracy even than older cell phone towers could. (Adam Cohen, *What Your Cell Phone Could Be Telling the Government*, Time (Sept. 15, 2010), http://tinyurl.com/93f8rym.) And, for reasons not necessarily relating to criminal law, the government is spurring on increased accuracy: the FCC mandates that 95 percent of 911 calls made from cell phones with GPS technology be capable of being tracked within 150 meters. (Kevin McLaughlin. *The Fourth Amendment and Cell Phone Location Tracking: Where Are We?*, 29 Hastings Comm. & Ent. L.J. 421, 427 (2007).) That level of accuracy, while remarkable, is only the tip of the iceberg: GPS tracking can potentially locate a phone to a level of accuracy within 50 feet. (*Id.*)

As noted, courts are already grappling with the question of whether data stored on a smartphone is open to warrantless search. But location can be a crucial bit of data in and of itself. Even before GPS units made their smartphone debut, cell phones could be used to determine a suspect's general location. An ordinary cell phone "pings" cell phone towers multiple times per minute, so it can make or receive calls. However, that data is stored by the company owning the towers, and can be accessed by the government if it wants to prove an individual was not where he or she claimed to be.

Courts have held that historical cell phone data such as this is not protected by the Fourth Amendment and does not require a warrant. (*E.g.*, United States v. Graham, 846 F. Supp. 2d 384 (D. Md. 2012).) In *Graham*, the district court noted that historical cell site data can only provide a suspect's previous locations and is less precise than GPS tracking. (*Id.* at 391–92.) However. *Graham*, like *Jones*, raises troubling possibilities that *Katz* cannot solve. Namely, what happens when instead of using cell site data—or a smartphone's GPS function—for evidence, the government uses it to track down a suspect in a crime?

Imagine: a crime scene, discovered by the police, immediately suggests a suspect. That suspect, however, is nowhere to be found. With a little digging, police determine the suspect's cell phone provider, and they learn that the suspect has a smartphone with a GPS unit inside. They call the provider, where an employee helpfully informs the officers of the exact location of the smartphone GPS unit. An arrest soon follows.

Efficient? Extremely. The larger and more critical question, however, is whether it violates the Fourth Amendment—and that question does not have quite so clear an answer.

This is where *Jones* falls short. The above scenario involves no physical trespass, particularly because Supreme Court precedent dictates that the suspect's acceptance of the phone with the GPS unit inside presents no problems at all, even if he or she is unaware the phone came equipped with such a unit. (*Cf.* United States v. Karo, 468 U.S. 705, 711–12 (1984) (holding that the placement of a beeper into a can not belonging to the defendant at the time of the placement "violated no one's Fourth Amendment rights").) But without physical trespass, a court must look to *Katz* for guidance—guidance that it realistically cannot provide.

The *Katz* question has developed into a twofold inquiry: first, whether a person had a subjective expectation of privacy, and second, whether society recognizes that expectation as reasonable. (*Katz* v. United States, 389 U.S. 347, 361 (1967) (Harlan, J., concurring).) However, as Justice Sotomayor noted in her separate concurrence in *Jones*, "the same technological advances that have made possible nontrespassory surveillance techniques will also affect the *Katz* test by shaping the evolution of societal privacy expectations." (United States v. Jones, 132 S. Ct. 945, 955 (2012) (Sotomayor, J., concurring).)

This evolution can cut both ways. As smartphones become ubiquitous, as people share more and more information voluntarily, and as more advanced monitoring techniques become possible, individuals may indeed lose any expectation of privacy they once had in their location. Even now, Facebook invites users to share their location (and sometimes their friends' locations, too); foursquare handles millions of check-ins per day; and few of the technology-savvy, if any, are surprised when someone seems to know, without asking, where they have been that day. But Justice Sotomayor tips the balance in the opposite direction: she asks whether individuals reasonably expect that their every movement will be freely accessible to the government—and heavily implies that the answer is "no." (*See id.* at 956.)

Either interpretation could turn out to be correct. This is assuming, of course, that Justice Sotomayor's other concern is addressed: that of third-party disclosure. It is long-established law that a person has no legitimate expectation of privacy in information voluntarily given to third parties. (Smith v. Maryland, 442 U.S. 735. 743-44 (1979).) In *Smith*, this applied to numbers dialed on a home telephone. Now, it could very well apply to a smartphone user's location, at least without modifying the broad language of *Smith. (See id.* at 745 ("[P]etitioner voluntarily conveyed to [the phone company] information that it had facilities for recording and that it was free to record. In these circumstances, petitioner assumed the risk that the information would be divulged to police.").) Such a case is not unimaginable. Indeed, it has already happened at least once, in Wisconsin, where police enlisted the help of a cell phone service provider, without a warrant, to determine a suspect's exact location. (Joe Forward, *GPS Tracking: U.S. Supreme Court Lays Foundation for Future Fourth Amendment Cases*, St. Bar Wis. (Feb. 15, 2012), http://tinyurl.com/8m5kt7q.) That case. *State v. Subdiaz-Osorio*, is currently on appeal before the Wisconsin Court of Appeals. (*Id.*) Meanwhile, the *Jones* majority left the third-party disclosure rule untouched, presumably to be revisited another day. (Carl Franzen, *What Does the Supreme Court Ruling against Warrantless GPS Tracking Mean?*, Tpmidealab (Jan. 23, 2012), http://tinyurl.com/9p7dp7v.)

Ultimately, even tried-and-true constitutional provisions provide little to no help in untangling the questions posed by the intersection of *Katz* and smartphones. For example, under *Kyllo v. United States*, the Fourth Amendment draws a bright line at the entrance to the home. (533 U.S. 27, 40 (2001).) However, individuals have no reasonable expectation of privacy in their movements when traveling on public roads. (United States v. Knotts, 460 U.S. 276, 281 (1983).) Under these two cases, location clearly affects *Katz* analysis, even though *Katz* held that "the Fourth Amendment protects people, not places." (Katz v. United States, 389 U.S. 347, 351 (1967).) Where a suspect is at any given moment, then, must logically have some effect on the GPS question.

Unfortunately, when law enforcement officials are unable to locate a suspect and need to turn to a cell phone provider for assistance, the suspect's location is the one thing they most certainly do not know. Suspects could be in their homes, or. more likely, if law enforcement cannot locate them, a temporary dwelling place such as a hotel or motel, which is likewise protected by the Fourth Amendment. (Stoner v. California. 376 U.S. 483–490 (1964).) However, a suspect could also be on a public road, albeit out of sight of those particular officers* eyes. The officers will not know which is true until they receive the data—and so they cannot be guided even by the decisions of the Supreme Court.

Katz analysis, then, could potentially result in a bizarre structure where the constitutionality of GPS tracking *cannot* be known until the tracking is complete. Before the cell phone provider reveals the suspect's location, police cannot know where the suspect will be, and so cannot know whether the person is in a public or private space. It is only afterward that the tracking can be deemed constitutional or otherwise, based wholly on where the suspect is at the moment of revelation—even though the police have obtained what they want in *both* cases. The only difference is that one search is retroactively unconstitutional—exactly the problem that some courts have identified [*39] with the "mosaic" theory of the Fourth Amendment, which, in GPS cases, looks to how long the monitoring took place to determine the likelihood that police could have observed all the suspect's movements during that time. (*See* United States v. Jones, 132 S. Ct. 945,954 (2012); United States v. Graham, 846 F. Supp. 2d 384, 402–03 (D. Md. 2012).) Though the police could not have known it at the time, the other search would be permissible simply because the suspect happened to be in a public place. This arbitrary distinction is no way to administer the Fourth Amendment.

Ultimately, as Justice Sotomayor points out, it may be time to modify the *Katz* test, at least to avoid results such as those explored above. She looks beyond the established rules of *Katz*, to the potential for abuse, asking "whether people reasonably expect that their movements will be recorded and aggregated in a manner that enables the Government to ascertain, more or less at will, their political and religious beliefs, sexual habits, and so on." (*Jones*, 132 S. Ct. at 956 (Sotomayor, J., concurring).) And she goes one step further, to the potential consequences of unlimited GPS access:

> Awareness that the Government may be watching chills associational and expressive freedoms. And the Government's unrestrained power to assemble data that reveal private aspects of identity is susceptible to abuse. The net result is that GPS monitoring—by making available at a relatively low cost such a substantial quantum of intimate information about any person whom the Government, in its unfettered discretion, chooses to track—may "alter the relationship between citizen and government in a way that is inimical to democratic society."
>
> (*Id.*)

Justice Sotomayor thus recognizes both the problems with GPS monitoring and the lack of guidance that *Jones* provides. And indeed, even those concerns barely scratch the surface of the struggles that could result from the intersection of technology and privacy. Though *Jones* was not the right time, according to the majority, to solve the question of *Katz* in the modern context, *Subdiaz-Osorio* in Wisconsin shows that time cannot be far away.

Given the confusing facets of *Katz* in this context, perhaps, as the court in *Graham* suggested about historical cell phone data, the solution to the smartphone conundrum is best determined by the legislature. (*Graham*, 846 F. Supp. 2d at 389-90.) One such effort has already been introduced the Geolocational Privacy and Surveillance Act, or the GPS Act. The Act would make it unlawful to "intentionally intercept, endeavor to intercept, or procure any other person to intercept or endeavor to intercept, geolocation information pertaining to another person." (S. 1212, 112th Cong. § 2602(a)(1)(A) (2011).) It provides exceptions for service providers in the normal course of business (allowing cell phone companies to continue their practice of recording locational data); foreign intelligence surveillance; information tracked consensually; public data (which would allow people to use services like Facebook and foursquare without breaking federal law); emergency information; theft or fraud; and, most importantly for the question at hand, officers having a warrant. (*Id.* § 2602(b)-(h).) Specifically, police "may intercept geolocation information or require the disclosure by a provider of a covered service of geolocation information only pursuant to a warrant" issued by proper procedures. (*Id.* § 2602(h)(2).)

The proposed law would set down a bright-line rule and remove the myriad problems of *Katz* from the picture. It would protect a person's privacy regardless of location at the time of search and in spite of phone companies" ability to locate the individual, down to the exact meter. But the remedy provided in section 2603 of the proposed law—suppression of evidence—leaves one more question open. (*See id.* § 2603.) Clearly, when police use GPS tracking to show a suspect was in a certain location at a certain time, suppression is an appropriate remedy. However, what of the situation in *Subdiaz-Osorio*, where a suspect is simply *heated* but not tried based upon GPS technology? Certainly, it makes no sense to release a crime suspect with the promise to try and legally track the suspect down again later. But the only other option is to proceed with investigation and, if the evidence supports it, prosecution, which provides the suspect no remedy for the infringement of Fourth Amendment rights. Neither option works, but a workable middle ground is hard to imagine.

The GPS Act is a positive step toward avoiding the inevitable complications that *Katz* will create if applied to smartphone tracking. However, even that Act is not enough—the remedy issue still remains. Perhaps fines or imprisonment upon violation (for which the Act provides, in section 2602(a)(2)) will be enough to encourage investigators to go the safest route and acquire a warrant for a suspect's location. And perhaps, if the Act is passed, service providers will quickly learn not to provide locational data to any caller who asks. But until then, criminal law practitioners need to be ever more aware of the potential problems that smartphone technology presents—the potential, in short, for a high level of monitoring and a high level of accuracy in that monitoring. *Jones* and *Katz* do not provide the guidance needed to resolve the multitude of questions that smartphones with GPS technology present. As the GPS Act moves through the legislature, practitioners should not only devote thought to these questions, they should make their voices and experience heard, particularly in developing an appropriate remedy should such monitoring be held unconstitutional.

Until then, they must recognize that *Jones* and *Katz* are not enough to pin down elusive GPS and smartphone technology into a neat Fourth Amendment category. As Justice Alito wrote, "The availability and use of [smartphones and tracking services] will continue to shape the average person's expectations about the privacy of his or her daily movements." (United States v. Jones, 132 S. Ct. 945, 963 (2012) (Alito, J., concurring).) Along the way, courts and practitioners alike must emphasize a workable analysis that avoids chilling the freedoms of citizens and infringing on privacy rights—even if that means leaving *Katz* behind.

Chapter Nine

Americans with Disabilities Act of 1990

Social Justice in American Policymaking

By Christopher M. Bellas, Ph.D.

The literature on social justice often chronicles legislative victories concerning racial and ethnic discrimination as well as the prevailing plight of women throughout the course of US history. These efforts are, of course, well justified and we are—and should be—proud of how changes in societal attitudes about these groups cleared the way for positive legal reform. This chapter focuses on a group that has received far less attention but is no less deserving of an examination of a social movement that also led to a legislative triumph for those with disabilities—the passage of the Americans with Disabilities Act.

Policy Overview

The Americans with Disabilities Act of 1990 is commonly referred to as the ADA or Public Law 101-336, and is codified as 42 U.S.C. §12101. The bill was passed by the Senate on September 7, 1989, and subsequently by the House of Representatives on May 22, 1990. The law was formally enacted when it was signed by President George H. Bush on July 26, 1990 (Mayerson, 1992). The ADA's basic definition of "disability" can be broadly defined as "an impairment that substantially limits one or more major life activities and that a person must possess a record of such impairment or be regarded as having such impairment" (42 U.S.C. §12102 (1)). A brief overview of the titles to the ADA is as follows. Title I states a covered entity under the ADA cannot discriminate against a qualified person who has a disability. This applies to promotion, job training, and other means of employment. It also restricts the use of pre-employment medical examinations and inquiries by employers and labor organizations when looking at a candidate for possible employment or employment benefits. Employers must also provide reasonable accommodations when applicants apply for such jobs. Title I also stipulates the powers and civil administrative remedies of the Equal Employment Opportunities Commission (EEOC) in handling employment discrimination based on disability, as well as race. Title II of the ADA prohibits state and local public entities from discriminating where physical access is reasonable in public transportation services. Title II also calls for fair housing for the disabled in the form of providing assistance and referrals to those seeking such housing (42 U.S.C. §12131-12165). Title III proclaims all areas of "public accommodation" (lodging, parks, restaurants, shops, etc.) must be made accessible. All public structures should be "barrier free" if possible and all structures under current or future construction were required to be accessible immediately after the 1992 passage. There are several exceptions regarding making historical structures barrier free if doing so would substantial alter the historical preservation of the structure. In 2010 there were even stricter standards put in place regarding public swimming pools becoming barrier free in order that people with physical disabilities have access to such pools (42 U.S.C. §12181-12189). Title IV of the ADA assures that the hearing- and speech-impaired will be able to use telecommunication services, by mandating that all telephone companies carry equipment necessary for disabled communication. Such mandating required modification to the Communications Act of 1934 and extended the Federal Communications Commission's regulatory authority (Americans with Disabilities Act of 1990, Public Law 101-336).

The Americans with Disabilities Act was amended on September 25, 2008, with an unusual move by Congress specifically challenging the United States Supreme Court in a number of cases for limiting the term "disability," and for providing an undue burden on disabled individuals for whom Congress intended to be covered by the 1990 law (Americans with Disabilities Act amended 2008, Public Law 110-325).

The ADA is comprehensive legislation and a modified version of the Rehabilitation Act of 1973, which is linked to the 1964 Civil Rights Act (Weber, 1995). The essential purpose of the Rehabilitation Act was to prohibit discrimination against the disabled by the federal government. There was greater interest group mobilization that occurred on behalf of the disabled community in the precursor to the ADA, which was not present in previous legislation such as the Rehabilitation Act. One reason for more interest could be attributed to a change in US demographics; an increasing elderly population, for example, which would create more disability awareness. There is evidence to support an increase in the disabled coalition from the alliance formed between victims suffering from the AIDS epidemic in the 1980s. Champions of AIDS awareness joined with disability advocates to form a partnership for legislative lobbying (Mayerson, 1992). Although many groups supported new legislation, the disabled movement had never had a political voice to rally support for their cause. Unlike previous civil rights movements that benefited from known faces such as Martin Luther King Jr., Jessie Jackson, Al Sharpton, and Gloria Steinem, there was no face associated to those with disabilities. This was, and still is, lacking in the disabled community even though more disabled people have become politically active over the past two decades (Pauley, 2012).

After extensive congressional subcommittee hearings and limited debate in both the House of Representatives and Senate, the ADA was signed into law. Although the law was passed in 1990, specific provisions in the bill were phased in during the following years. For example, the effective date for Title I employment discrimination was July

26, 1992, for businesses with twenty-five or more employees, and July 26, 1994, for employers with fifteen to twenty-four employees. Remedies for violating Title I include but are not limited to: hiring the particular individual, reinstatement, promotion, back pay, restored benefits, attorney's fees, and court costs (Americans with Disabilities Act of 1990, Public Law 101-336).

The vernacular of the ADA created changes to existing civil rights policies, which now included the disabled as a protected class (O'Day, 1996). In the language, Congress addressed a societal commitment to equality of opportunity, and that legislation was needed to combat discrimination that has plagued the disabled community for years. The introduction to the ADA made such a claim by stating, "historically society has tended to isolate and segregate individuals with disabilities, and despite some improvements, such forms of discrimination continue to be a serious and pervasive problem" (42 U.S.C. §12101 (a)(2), Chapter 126). Congress further stated that the disabled have existed in a social class that has been deemed inferior and has been continuously subjected to outright exclusion. Specifically, it said "the Nation's proper goals regarding individuals with disabilities are to ensure equality of opportunity, and to ensure their full participation in daily living through economic independence and independent living" (42 U.S.C. §12101 (a)(7-8), Chapter 126). Congress made clear that as an institution it would insist on rules and regulations to change the prior pattern of unacceptable behavior experienced by those with disabilities. Congress's purpose in eradicating discrimination via the ADA was to provide clear, strong, consistent, and enforceable standards to address the needs of individuals with disabilities and to ensure that the federal government would play a central role in enforcing those standards.

Although the ADA was strongly supported, it was not without critics. Many opponents of the policy argued that vague language in the law, such as "undue hardship" or "reasonable accommodation," would allow for excessive litigation against businesses (Clegg, 1999; Deleire, 2000). Those in opposition to the bill worried about the potential burden placed on businesses having to deplete themselves of resources to comply with the law.

New Ideas Surrounding the Passage of the ADA

Hillary Appel (2000) states, "ideologies are first and foremost belief systems ... and provide an interpretation of the world both as it is perceived and as it should be" (p. 527). To fully understand the importance of the ADA, one must examine the historical attitudes of society regarding the disabled and trace the evolution in thought.

Throughout history people with disabilities were seen as inferior and much of society's attitude toward the disabled stemmed from a Darwinian ideology advocating that the weak (especially the physically weak) were inferior, unproductive, and hence unwanted members of society (Darwin, 1859). In the thirteenth and fourteenth centuries as American society became more industrialized, physical laborers were in greater demand while those who could not contribute to the community's economic survival were deemed expendable. Although many did not intentionally discriminate against those with disabilities, many classified disabled individuals as "sick," "deformed," and "pitiful" people who needed to be segregated from mainstream society. There is even historical legal evidence barring the disabled from participating in social and civil events. Anita Silvers (1996) cites a Wisconsin Supreme Court case that upheld the exclusion of a boy with cerebral palsy from attending school because the boy produced what the court called "a depressing and nauseating effect on the teachers and school children" (p. 211). Society's general belief system about people with disabilities seemed to be one of persistent inferiority, not only because of their physical appearance but also because of their inability to engage in the labor force.

Productivity is a valuable commodity in any society and one's importance is often based on that individual's economic contribution. Entrepreneurs assign value to workers based on whether the worker can contribute to the overall success of the business. Success is often defined economically (profits) under a cost-benefit analysis, a utilitarian idea. Susan Hoffmann (2001) discusses among numerous public philosophies the concept of utilitarianism—the notion of deciding on moral action from a cost-benefit approach. Jeremy Bentham (1789), the noted father of utilitarianism, created a mathematical formula for calculating individual happiness, which he measured in units referred to as utils. A person's action, according to Bentham, will depend on the pleasure one gets from engaging in a particular behavior. If, after weighing all the factors, a person's perceived pain or unhappiness outweighs their pleasure, then he or she will choose not to engage in such action. As happiness and personal satisfaction weigh on the mind of a disabled person, Amartya Sen (1973), a proponent of utilitarian moral theory, asserts those with disabilities will in the final analysis be disconsolate. He states that a nondisabled person (A) will always derive exactly twice as much utility from a given income than a disabled person (B), merely because B has a disability. Thus, because of possible income disparity, a disabled person's overall general happiness (personal utility) will be diminished (1973). Sen's notion, however, presupposes that happiness derives from economic self-worth alone and omits any qualitative examination of a happy, satisfying life.

Still, the requirements of industrial capitalism systematically have segregated the fit from the unfit (Russell, 2000, p. 14). Specifically with respect to employment, the emerging market economy required a maximization of workers' mechanical ability. The competitive market did not allow employers to offer the slightest accommodation for the disabled. As with most rational choice decisions, businesses had to account for the fact that the disabled may be less productive, while at the same time cost-prohibitive. Businesses could also expect elevated insurance premiums, as well as the threat of worker compensation lawsuits. These were legitimate business concerns feared by many (Russell, 2000).

Interest Groups and the ADA

There were few advocacy groups for the disabled prior to the 1980s. The exceptions were the Coalition for Citizens with Disabilities (CCD), the National Organization on Disability, and the Consortium for Citizens with Disabilities (West, 2000). It appeared that no matter how much these organizations advocated, the only way they could become a catalyst for significant change in disability policy would be to team up with other civil rights activists. Civil rights groups such as the black, Hispanic, and women's caucuses, the Civil Rights Leadership Coalition (CRLC), as well as numerous religious organizations and gay/lesbian coalitions were invaluable as they already had connections in Washington from prior lobbying efforts (West, 2000). There was no greater cause of the 1980s than the growing population of AIDS victims. While people with disabilities were trying to overcome their own negative image and did not necessarily want to be associated with the AIDS cause, they knew that building an alliance with such a large group could only strengthen their efforts in Congress. Thus, a kinship was formed with AIDS advocacy groups only after negotiating the language of the ADA to cover AIDS under the definition of disability; in return, the advocacy groups would guarantee passage of the law using their already powerful and persuasive message through high-profile mediums of communication (Mayerson, 1992).

The criticism and struggles of the ADA seemed to only mirror the fact that the disability movement was carried out in unconventional ways. To note one example, the key stimulus in agenda setting was a detailed logging of the activities of disabled Americans, called "diaries of discrimination." These diary authors collected their writings and came to Washington and testified before congressional committees about their experiences and the effects such discrimination had on their lives. Major Owens, a member of the House of Representatives, appointed Justin Dart, a prominent albeit still unknown national leader in the disability community, to lead a task force and present the findings to Congress (Mayerson, 1992). Dart traveled across the country holding town hall meetings and "diary parties," which offered the disabled community an opportunity to voice their grievances and frustrations. Although Dart was able to rally support for the disabled movement through national discussions, the cause still needed someone who understood the politics of American policy making in order to reach members of Congress, and thus get the future ADA on the legislative agenda.

Pat Wright, director of the Disability Rights Education and Defense Fund (DREDF), became the intermediary between interest groups and Congress. Soon advocacy groups were meeting weekly, becoming more organized and disciplined and devising strategies on how to target members of Congress. They agreed on a tactic to gain empathy from congressional leaders who could most identify with people with disabilities (West, 2000). In doing so, members of Congress who eventually introduced the first draft of the bill on May 9, 1989, included Democratic Representative Tony Coelho of California, who suffered from epilepsy, and Republican Senator Lowell Weicker of Connecticut, whose son suffered from a developmental disability (Mayerson, 1992). One reason these individuals were sought out by the National Council on Disability (NCD) was that little time was needed educating these congressional members on existing barriers for the disabled population; they had their own personal experiences to draw upon. Due to defeat in the next election, Senator Weicker was replaced by Democrat Tom Harkin of Iowa, who also had a family member with a disability. Harkin became the new chair of the Subcommittee on Disability Policy, while Democratic Senator Ted Kennedy of Massachusetts, having a sister with a developmental disability, chaired the full Committee on House and Labor (overseeing the Subcommittee on Disability Policy). The chair of any Senate committee has a great deal of influence in setting the legislative calendar, so spotlighting disability issues was nearly certain (Mayerson, 1992; West, 2000).

Lawyers who were experts on a variety of legal topics also came together to draft the legislation, including Arlene Mayerson, lead attorney for the DREDF, who had fifteen years' experience with disability rights laws; Chai Feldblum, counsel for the American Civil Liberties Union and an expert on AIDS discrimination; Bonnie Milstein of the Bazelon Center on Mental Illness; and Jim Weisman of the Paralyzed Veterans of America (West, 2000).

Opposition to the ADA came primarily from the business community. Groups that testified before the House Committee on Small Business in February 1990 included National Small Business United, the U.S. Chamber of Commerce, and the National Federation of Independent Businesses (Mandel, 1990). These organizations testified that the excessive costs for small businesses to comply with the ADA, not only in architectural modification but also in newly mandated employment practices, would do nothing but drive up human resource expenditures (DeLeire, 2000).

The perspectives of those opposed to the ADA relied on the notion that the law's effect would interfere with businesses' ability to compete in the marketplace by creating excessive financial burdens to provide accommodation (Seligman & Llosa, 1992; Clegg, 1999). Opponents of the ADA contended that the government should not legislate employment practices; rather it was more appropriate to let the market forces decide who is the "best" employee to hire, regardless of whether or not the person had a disability (Clegg, 1999). The government's response to such concerns would be to offset the expenditure with a tax credit. Businesses, however, still argued that the tax credit would not compensate for the litigation and administrative expenses incurred. Therefore, if the goal of the ADA was to eradicate discrimination, its unintended consequences might, ironically, have had the opposite effect. If a business envisioned hiring a person with a disability, it might recoil for fear of ongoing federal anti-discrimination lawsuits once the person is hired. It became clear that both groups would not budge and the battle between these competing interest groups would be indefinite. As such, ADA advocates now had the task of not only pushing back against industrial opposition, but also navigating the waters of political institutions.

Congress, the Presidency, and the Courts

Institutions are the values, rules, and patterns of behavior in which actors engage in political discourse. Such a prototype is useful to gain a better understanding of these institutions and the people who function within them (Peters, 2001; Lowndes, 2002). Studying the behavioral process of the actors both inside and outside Congress, the presidency, and the courts reveals how the Americans with Disabilities Act came to fruition.

Congressional committees are institutions that have a tremendous influence on policy outcomes (Krehbiel, 1992; Schickler, 2001). Disability advocates knew the rules of Congress and committee assignments well enough to know which members in both Houses were not only powerful within the boundaries of their committee roles, but also those who would be most sympathetic in assigning the cultural meaning of respect, dignity, and equality to those with disabilities. These powerful leaders are rational actors who carefully consider which policies receive committee attention. Members of Congress who want to get reelected are keenly aware of which issues are salient enough to bring to the table at any given period of time (Polsby, 1968; Mayhew, 1974). Therefore, the American adherence to equality, represented by the ADA, left little opposition when it came to public opinion. The American public's overwhelming support of helping those with disabilities along with the congressional goal of gaining reelection were rational considerations nudging Congress to support the law.

Similarly, the institution of the presidency played a significant role in the passage of the ADA. Presidents from George H. Bush, to Bill Clinton, to George W. Bush have supported the disabled community through multiple workforce policies. Each of these presidents used the power of the presidency to support passage or reaffirmation of the ADA and similar statutes. In particular, President Clinton signed Executive Order 13078, which created a presidential task force on the employment of adults with disabilities. President George W. Bush signed the 2008 amended Americans with Disabilities Act of 1990, and President Barack Obama redoubled efforts of his administration to advocate the spirit and letter of the ADA on the anniversary of the Supreme Court's ruling in *Olmstead v. L.C.*, a 1999 case giving those with mental disabilities the right to be deinstitutionalized and become part of their local community. The Obama administration also took steps to require public recreational facilities that have swimming pools and/or spas to have lifts for those with disabilities. Whether Republican or Democrat, presidents have been supportive of disability policies and used the institution of the presidency to make a statement about contemporary cultural values, norms, and beliefs regarding equality for the disabled population.

Courts have also been influential in changing social policy based on contemporary social values (O'Brien, 2000). From racial discrimination cases such as *Brown v. Board of Education* (1954) to *Roe v. Wade* (1973), the Supreme Court has created social change based on contemporary cultural norms through modifications to existing law, as well as striking down laws as unconstitutional (O'Brien, 2000). There have been times, however, when the judiciary has stifled the application of social legislation on constitutional grounds. For example, the ADA was challenged by Alabama in the US Supreme Court, with the state university arguing that citizens suing the state of Alabama under the law violated the Eleventh Amendment's sovereign immunity clause to the Constitution, which prohibits a lawsuit by one of its citizens (Amendment XI, US Constitution; *Board of Trustees of the University of Alabama v. Garrett*, 2001). The court had to consider whether an individual could sue a state for monetary damages in federal court under the ADA, or whether such an action violated the Eleventh Amendment to the Constitution. The court held that such suits are in fact barred by the Constitution. While one could agree with the court on a strict constitutional basis, it was the majority's opinion that was most revealing. The court stated that unlike the Voting Rights Act of 1965, Congress had fallen far short of showing a pattern of discrimination by states and failed to show that the incidences of discrimination that were demonstrated could not have been corrected by less invasive remedies (*Board of Trustees of the University of Alabama v. Garrett*, 2001, p. 10–17). Prior to this court ruling, another case (one that would eventually catch the attention of Congress), regarded the language of the ADA as opposed to whether one could sue a state under the ADA. The Supreme Court in *Sutton v. United Airlines* (1999) declared that to make a determination that one meets the definition of a disabled person under the ADA, one must also take into account any mitigating steps utilized by the person to correct their ailment. More interesting, and for which Congress later corrected, the court stated that Congress did not mean to include those with "correctable impairments" in the meaning of persons with disabilities under the ADA. Congress in the 2008 amended ADA and denounced the court's interpretation of its supposed intent.

Another challenge in the Supreme Court that Congress later addressed came in *Toyota Motor Manufacturing v. Williams* (2002). In that case the court narrowed the definition of the term "substantially limits" when referring to one's ability to perform job-related tasks. Again, Congress in its amended version of the ADA in 2008 specifically argued the Supreme Court had placed an overly restrictive interpretation to the meaning of "substantially limits" in the law. Congress also took that opportunity to broaden the terms "major life activities" and "major bodily functions." The reasons Congress gave for amending the original ADA cannot be understated for it was a direct aim at the court for misinterpreting Congress's legislative intent and to officially correct the record while, in turn, expanding the scope of the ADA.

While we often think of judicial intervention as advancing social change, it can also be used to depress the extension of American social policy on legal grounds. Yet in 2008 the 110th Congress took the unusual step of reinvigorating the original purpose of the ADA. And in doing so it broadened the number of citizens covered by the law.

Conclusion

This chapter has given an overview of the Americans with Disabilities Act of 1990, as well as analyzed the role ideas, interests, and institutions played in contributing to the passage of the law. Although prior legislation such as the Civil Rights Act of 1964, as well as the Rehabilitation Act of 1973, showed modest recognition that society had begun to change its perception of those who suffered from disabilities, the disabled were still viewed as inferior in the workforce (Hahn, 1993). The passage of the ADA, much like the passage of the Civil Rights Act of 1964, exhibited a continuing evolution in our ideology about minority populations. The ideas of integration, empowerment, and equality were asserted through the enactment of the ADA, which served to codify these principles.

The ADA became a legalized response to changing beliefs about the importance of people with disabilities. While still recognizing the significance of capitalism, the ADA brought a human qualitative perspective to public policy making by incorporating a "values-based" policy approach (Hahn, 1993). The ADA was a realization that the disabled are not to be feared or ostracized for their physical appearance, but rather the idea that they can make valuable contributions to the labor force by being a part of its productivity (Hahn, 1993). Thus, the ADA as a social policy is a legal example of the change in ideology about a population that had for so long been obscured.

Similarly, a coalition of rational actors mobilized a powerful social movement. Political advocates seized on the changing ideas about the disabled, and strategic actors outside as well as inside the political arena lobbied those in positions of power to recognize the importance of the ADA (O'Day, 1996). The policy's development reflects movements both in thought and in action concerning the disabled population, and these ideas and actions were supported by members within American political institutions. Thus, the Americans with Disabilities Act of 1990 reveals how American ideas, interests, and institutions are needed for social as well as legal change.

References

Amendment XI, U.S. Constitution.

Americans with Disabilities Act of 1990, P. L. 101-336, 104 Stat. 327 (1990).

Americans with Disabilities Act of 1990, 42 U.S.C. § 12101, Chapter 126 (1990).

American with Disabilities Act, amended 2008, P. L. 110-325 (2008)

Appel, H. (2000). The ideological determinants of liberal economic reform: The case of privatization. *World Politics, 52(4)*, 520–549.

Bentham, J. (1789). *An introduction to the principles of morals and legislations.* New York: Hafner Publishing Co.

Board of Trustees of the University of Alabama v. Garrett, 531 U.S. 356 (2001).

Civil Rights Act of 1964, P. L. 88-353, 78 Stat. 241 (1964).

Clegg, R. (1999). The costly compassion of the ADA. *Public Interest, 136*, 100–112.

Communication Act of 1934, P. L. 416, 48 Stat. 1064 (1934).
Executive Order No. 13,078, 63 F.R. 13111 (1998). Retrieved June 20, 2007, from http://janweb.icdi.wvu.edu/cap/13078.htm
Darwin, C. (1859). *On the origin of the species by means of natural selection.* New York: Appleton.
DeLeire, T. (2000). The unintended consequences of the Americans with Disabilities Act. *Regulation, 23(1),* 21–24.
Hahn, H. (1993). The political implications of disability definitions & data. *Journal of Disability Policy Studies, 4(2),* 41–52.
Hoffman, S. (2001). *The politics of banking: Ideas, public policy, and the creation of financial institutions.* Baltimore: John Hopkins University Press.
Jane Roe, et al. v. Henry Wade, District Attorney of Dallas County, 410 U.S. 113 (1973).
Krehbiel, K. (1992). *Information and legislative organization.* Ann Arbor: University of Michigan Press.
Lowndes, V. (2002). Institutionalism. In D. Marsh & G. Stoker (Eds.), *Theory and methods in political science* (pp. 90–107). New York: Palgrave Macmillan.
Mandel, S. (1990). Disabling the GOP. *The National Review, 42(11),* 23–24.
Mayerson, A. (1992). *The history of the ADA: A movement perspective.* Retrieved February 20, 2013, from http://dredf.org/publications/ada_history.shtml
Mayhew, D. R. (1974). *Congress: The electoral connection.* New Haven: Yale University Press.
O'Brien, D. (2000). *Storm center: The Supreme Court in American politics.* New York: W.W. Norton.
O'Day, B. (1996). Reauthorization of the Rehabilitation Act: Comprehensive solutions or political satisficing? *Disability & Society, 11(3).* 411–27.
Oliver Brown et al. v. Board of Education of Topeka et al, 347 U.S. 483 (1954).
Olmstead v. L.C. 527 U.S. 581 (1999).
Pauley, J. (2012). *Fifteen years of the Americans with Disabilities Act.* Retrieved December 30, 2012, from http://abilitymagazine.com/american_disabilities.html
Peters, B. G. (2001). *Institutional theory in political science.* London: Continuum.
Polsby, N. (1968). The institutionalization of the U.S. House of Representatives. *The American Political Science Review, 62,* 144–168.
Rehabilitation Act of 1973, P. L. 93–112, 87 Stat. 394 (1973).
Russell, M. (2000). The political economy of disablement. *Dollars & Sense,* 13–15, 48–49.
Schickler, E. (2001). *Disjointed pluralism: Institutional innovation and the development of the U.S. Congress.* Princeton: Princeton University Press.
Seligman, D., & Llosa, P. (1992). Disability legislation. *Fortune, 125(12),* 160–162.
Sen, A. (1973). *On economic inequality.* Oxford: Oxford University Press.
Silvers, A. (1996). (In)equality, (Ab)normality, and the Americans with Disabilities Act. *Journal of Medicine and Philosophy, 21(2),* 209–224.
Sutton v. United Airlines 527 U.S. 471 (1999).
Toyota Motor Manufacturing v. Williams 534 U.S. 184 (2002).
Voting Rights Act of 1965, 42 U.S.C. § 1973–1973aa-6 (1965).

Weber, M. C. (1995). Disability discrimination by state & local government: The relationship between section 504 of the Rehabilitation Act and the ADA. *William and Mary Law Review, 36(3),* 1089–1134.

West, J. (2000). *When to hold 'em and when to fold 'em: Lessons learned from enacting the Americans with Disabilities Act.* Retrieved February 25, 2013, from http://dredf.org/international/paper_w-w.html

Section IV

Social Ills and Social Justice

Introduction to Section IV

Social Ills and Social Justice

By Michelle Foster

The final section in this book entails other problems and concerns in society that raise social justice issues. Drug crimes had been on the political agenda for decades but have interestingly almost disappeared from political discourse in recent years. Chapter 10 provides insight about directions that should be taken to achieve an end to the war on drugs and reach a position of peace. The war on drugs on the whole has been a failure to society. The portrayal of the crack addict in the 1980s as a violent, unstable person who kills people without remorse was a "sham" perpetuated in political rhetoric and the media. Addicted individuals were demonized in the name of justice and so began the call for harsh, retaliatory punishments. The results of this "war" have been longer prison sentences, institution of mandatory minimums, and prisons overcrowded with non-violent offenders. Today, society is left with the "fallout" from this "war." Michael Keane suggests a new approach needs to be taken. It should be recognized that individuals are both criminals and victims of addiction. They are criminals because they are knowingly violating the law; they are victims because they are addicts and cannot typically just stop using drugs. Hence, just throwing addicts in prison does not benefit anyone. Keane advises a compromise needs to be achieved between both sides (liberals and conservatives alike). Bargaining and compromise is the normal process of politics and even applies to the war on drugs. If society can find some middle ground on the drugs issue, then it is possible to realize the goal sought by both sides—a reduction in addiction and drug offending.

Chapter 11 includes a global perspective about violence and poverty, common problems today both in US society and throughout the world. How poverty is judged, however, is relative. It is dependent upon the person's perception of what it means to be "poor." In the United States, the focus on material wealth is common, and how rich or how poor a person appears to be is based on material goods. People sometimes judge themselves poor or unworthy or unequal if they do not have the newest, nicest phone, clothes, car, etc. This focus on material wealth can be considered relative poverty.[1] Conversely, absolute poverty is what individuals in Third World countries feel. It is the state of not being able to provide even the most basic necessities of life (i.e., starvation, life-threatening illnesses that are easily curable). Taking this information into account, *some* countries that are suffering from absolute poverty experience less violence than those that experience relative poverty. This focus on material goods and experiencing relative poverty creates a strain in society,[2] with individuals feeling pressure to obtain those goods.

Chapter 12, the final chapter, looks at public attitudes toward defensive gun use. Moving beyond the debate about individuals having the right to bear arms to whether the public favors gun use for self-defense is worthy of consideration. A common argument by those who favor using guns for protection is that "guns don't kill people, people kill people." While this argument is valid, the question that still remains is what lengths should people go for protection? Do we all start carrying guns? Should only some of us, and if so who is considered "safe" to carry a gun? Or if no one is allowed to have a gun do we rely solely on the strapped resources of law enforcement for our protection?

1 See Elliott Currie's book *The Roots of Danger: Violent Crime in Global Perspective* (2009) for his discussion about relative and absolute poverty and their effects on violence.

2 See Robert Merton's book *Social Theory and Social Structure* (1957) for his discussion about strain theory.

Chapter Ten

A Roadmap to Peace in the War on Drugs

By Michael Keane

The war on drugs has been raging for decades. Tens of millions of lives have been lost or ruined. Because both the effect of the drugs and the effect of criminalisation have contributed to the toll, both prohibitionists and those for liberalisation are genuine in their conviction that they are on the right side of morality and history. To end this war we need a roadmap to peace.

However, like an intransigent territorial dispute, it is impossible to say what the peace should entail. Should peace entail a situation where minimum lives are lost? Or should an outcome optimise personal freedom? What about finding an optimal balance between personal freedom and lack of harm? Harm to innocent third parties is generally given considerably more weight than harm to wilful participants.

Some believe that peace in the war on drugs simply by achieved by minimising harm to third parties. The counter argument is that healthcare and welfare expenditure (even loss of a person's maximum productivity) are representative of harm to third parties (taxpayers), and thus it is impossible to segregate an individual's harm from the rest of society. Clearly then, both conservatives and progressives need to cede ground if there is any hope of finding a way to break the stalemate.

Unease about the awkward ideological bedfellows that have formed in response to the war on drugs is, in part, driving some willingness to make concessions amongst progressives. For example, the American Society of Addiction Medicine's (ASAM) opposition to legalisation of marijuana is leading many younger leftist, public-health types to question the use of Nanny State solutions to alcohol, fast food and gambling, in light of what has happened in the war on drugs.

Conservatives should also recognise that the reverse equally applies. They should see that the fundamental rationale for prohibiting drugs is very similar to the Nanny Statists': neurobiologically naïve, quasi-cult-like insistence that many 'lifestyle choices' (like gambling or drinking) can now be labelled as 'addictions'.

Summarising its opposition to legalisation, ASAM says that 'addiction should be primarily treated as a health issue rather than a criminal justice issue.' The same people that describe violence, lack of work ethic, drink driving and a variety of criminal activities as merely 'alcohol related harm' are now telling us the same thing about marijuana.

The dominance of this 'disease model' within academe has solidified conservative opposition to drug liberalisation. If the sometimes devastating consequence of drug use is a disease, no different from malaria, HIV or diabetes, then any moral and rational person would advocate prohibition of the drug and tough sanctions against those spreading the 'disease'. Ironically, therefore, it is the ideology of the left that is most responsible for the stalemate in the war on drugs.

Before ever rationally compromising towards liberalisation, conservatives need measures to be implemented that provide confidence that any outbreak of the 'disease' won't affect them. Crucially this must involve measures that target individuals and remove them from situations in society which affect others. For instance, lengthy prison sentences for drug-related violent behaviour; shared responsibility co-payments for drug-related healthcare; at least some degree of reasonable drug screening for government welfare recipients and an assortment of other measures. Some libertarians might balk at such measures. However, not conceding ground on these issues is not an option if libertarians ever want conservatives to make concessions.

To establish the roadmap we must be informed about the basic pharmacology of illicit drugs. But as we have seen in many debates, the often disingenuous misapplication of science can be used to usurp what are fundamentally value judgments and philosophical constructs. Hence we need to incorporate into our roadmap not only pharmacology, but also place the neuroscience of addiction in the context of our most sophisticated understanding of our political and cultural heritage.

Consistent with the science and biology, it is crucial to justify the intellectual argument that individuals should be held responsible for the consequences of drug use. Without this philosophical construct, the measures outlined above could not be justified and we would necessarily have to resort back to the extreme 'disease' model and endless stalemate. Conservative values recognise the necessity of personal freedom to generate a fair and vibrant society and also the impossibility that an individual's behavioural choices can be anticipated and controlled by a central authority made up of society's elite.

But do the effects of drugs prevent people from assuming responsibility? From the scientific evidence, the answer is a resounding 'no' for practically every modern recreational drug. Sadly, there has been an intellectual retreat by conservatives in this area, and the void this retreat leaves inevitably leads to a free pass for the most egregious of reckless behaviour.

Drugs do alter how you feel and how you perceive life. There are acute intoxicating, withdrawal and chronic effects of drugs. But the crucial point for the war on drugs is that whatever the effects of the drugs, there is an enormous range of reserve in which people retain the ability to know right from wrong. Importantly, we should expect adults to utilise that reserve of character. Relevant to the conservative construct of individual responsibility and to the roadmap, the headline messages are that across a range of different drugs the vast majority of people exposed to drugs (i) do not act recklessly;

(ii) take measures that prevent the drugs from impinging on their functioning; and (iii) the reckless drug users are not innocent victims of a disease but are most definitely culpable.

It is particularly within the realm of drug-driving, psychosis and violent rage that there is understandable opposition to drug liberalisation. Consistent with the roadmap, society already expects adults take reasonable measures to avoid situations where they can harm third-parties. Although it goes to their very core, progressives must make concessions concerning their all-consuming disease-and-no-responsibility model.

Drug driving is often perceived as the most concerning aspect of drug liberalisation. Although most drugs cause less driving impairment than alcohol, nonetheless it would be reasonable for penalties for drug driving to be an order of magnitude harsher than for drink driving; as a genuine good-faith concession on the part of progressives to allow 'peace talks' to continue.

Another major obstacle to liberalisation concerns the rare propensity for drugs to cause true psychosis where people are not reasonably in control of their actions (the term psychosis is often misused when a person is merely aggressive but still in control). It must be stressed that even in those absolutely rare occasions where people have got themselves into a situation where the acute intoxicating effects of drugs make it impossible for them to reasonably control their actions, they remain morally and legally culpable. Consider the severe epileptic who stops taking their meds, parties without sleep for days, drinks buckets of caffeine, drives a large semi-trailer, has a seizure and crashes into a car killing a family. During the seizure the person has zero control over their behaviour and therefore much less than a drug user has. Do we blame the epilepsy? No, this is a straight-down-the-line criminal justice issue, not a health issue. Just like the driver with epilepsy, the drug user with the rare propensity for psychosis who repeatedly uses drugs should be removed from society. It is not a health issue.

Similarly, you've all seen the clichéd, stethoscope-clad, innercity Emergency Department doctor despairing at the scourge of methamphetamine ('meth' or 'ice'); probably the same pained, noble, healer that was assuring us that the alcopops tax was vital in stopping the scourge of alcohol. Except for rare instances, ice does not cause violence. Frustration? Yes, as can peak-hour traffic. Adults are expected to control their frustration. The liberal ideology would have us revise the children's song to 'if you're angry and you know it ... punch someone's lights out (and then blame society)'. Violent 'meth-heads' should not be utilising the scarce resources of paramedics, police and Emergency Departments; they should be in jail.

Until and unless we re-invigorate the concept of character and until progressives can allow society to identify some of the worst of the worst in our society as criminals and not victims of a health phenomenon, then there will never be an end to the stalemate in the war on drugs.

Because the concept of addiction and disease is so thoroughly entwined with the war on drugs, we cannot allow it to be hijacked by those whose ultra-simplistic ideology recklessly ignores the neurobiological, historical and sociopolitical concept of character.

It's Been Tried Before: The Portugese Experience

By Chris Berg

Portugal decriminalised drug use and possession in July 2001. It was not the first country to do so. Various nations have experimented with decriminalisation since the drug prohibition began more than 100 years ago. But the Portuguese experiment is important as it was explicitly intended to tackle what was seen as a rising drug problem—for policymakers, the purpose of decriminalisation was to limit drug abuse.

It has been a resounding success. Overall drug use has not increased—as critics feared—but has actually declined slightly. The riskiest forms of drug taking are in sharp decline: the number of injecting drug users has decreased 40 per cent. New HIV cases in drug users declined from 907 in 2000 to 267 in 2008. Obviously, incarceration for drug related crime has decreased dramatically as well.

However, we should strike a caution here. The Portuguese decriminalisation model is both complex, paternalistic and expensive.

It is still technically illegal to possess drugs, even for personal use. The 2001 reform made the penalty no longer criminal but administrative. Individuals found in possession of an amount judged for personal use (ten days worth of an average daily dose of drugs) are referred to a three person board of medical, social and legal assessors to gauge their needs. They can dismiss without sanction, require medical treatment, or impose a fine. The Portuguese model is centred around treatment: drug use is a public health problem, and the goal of decriminalisation is to get users into the health system.

In many ways, this is the opposite to a 'liberal' drug regime. Portugal treats all drug use as a medical problem. According to this model, the decision to use drugs is not a question of individual choice and responsibility, but framed through public health and addiction.

Portugal is not alone, however. A large number of South American countries—who have been ravaged and corrupted as collateral in the war on drugs—have called for, and experimented with, different legalisation and decriminalisation approaches. Belgium, the Czech Republic, Estonia, Germany, Italy, the Netherlands, Poland, and Spain have all varying degrees of decriminalisation. Here in Australia, marijuana is partially decriminalised in a number of states.

The broad consensus in the academic literature is that these experiments have been positive. Drug use does not appreciably increase after decriminalisation, and the negative consequences of prohibition (criminality, disease transmission, high-risk use and abuse) substantially decline.

It is the recognition of the importance of character where we have seen the progressive elitist agenda unchallenged by conservatives. This is especially so as it relates to projections of what might happen to the total harm caused by drugs if criminal sanctions were lifted.

Extrapolating the drug-related behavioural patterns of mostly functional people based on those of established addicts is absurd. Homogenising human behaviour is politically correct but completely without any academic merit. Furthermore, the 'politically -correctisation' of dysfunctional behaviour in relation to drugs by using non-judgmental, neutral, non-prejudicial descriptors is not in any way morally sophisticated and is costing millions of lives by propagating the war on drugs. Compassion is noble and justified; deliberately ignoring what we know about the human condition is not.

To conservatives who may say that this is all very well but I just don't want the availability of drugs to increase because it might affect me; that is an entirely rational and valid concern. I too have been that stethoscope clad doctor working in the inner city hospital on a Saturday night seeing what drugs do. However, I have also been the DJ at big dance parties and the white-coated, drug-use researcher.

It is the overwhelming number of ordinary people: doctors, lawyers, trades-people, accountants, policemen, students, musicians, military personnel, and small business owners who do not behave like selfish, reckless, zombie-monsters that provide the imperative for large sections of the community to fight for the decriminalisation of drugs. There is a war because people are fighting on the other side. If we don't develop a reasonable and rational roadmap to peace, conservatives will end up with a completely ineffectual solution being imposed on them; where their safety and property will be contemptuously disregarded in an effort to placate outdated moral relativism.

Chapter Eleven

Violence, Identity and Poverty

By Amartya Sen

Violence is omnipresent in the world around us. On the root causes of contemporary global violence, theories abound—as theories are prone to. However, two particular lines of theorizing have come to receive much more attention than most others: one approach concentrates on the culture of societies, and the other on the political economy of poverty and inequality. Each approach has some plausibility, at least in some forms, and yet both are, I would argue, ultimately inadequate and in need of supplementation. Indeed, neither works on its own, and we need to see the two sets of influences together, in an integrated way.

I begin with the cultural approach—or more accurately, cultural approach. Different cultural theories have something in common—they tend to look at conflicts and violence as they relate to modes of living as well as religious beliefs and social customs. That line of reasoning can lead to many different theories, some less sophisticated than others. It is perhaps remarkable that the particular cultural theory that has become the most popular in the world today is perhaps also the crudest. This is the approach of seeing global violence as the result of something that is called 'the clash of civilizations'. The approach defines some postulated entities that are called 'civilizations' in primarily religious terms, and it goes on to contrast what are respectively called 'the Islamic world', 'the Judeo-Christian' or 'the Western world', 'the Buddhist world', 'the Hindu world' and so on. Divisions among civilizations make them prone, we are informed, to clash with each other.[1]

Underlying the approach of civilizational clash is an oddly artificial view of history, according to which these distinct civilizations have grown separately, like trees on different plots of land, with very little overlap and interaction. And today, as these disparate civilizations, with their divergent histories, face one another in the global world, they are firmly inclined, we are told, to clash with each other—a tale, indeed a gripping tale, of what can be, I suppose, called 'hate at first sight'. This make-believe account has little

1 The fullest exposition of this theory can be found in Huntington (1996). For very different readings of world history, see for example Russett, Oneal & Cox (2000) and Sen (1997, 2002, 2006).

use for the actual history of extensive—and persistent—interactions through history, and constructive movements of ideas and influences across the borders of countries, in so many different fields—literature, arts, music, mathematics, science, engineering, trade, commerce and other human engagements.

Theorists of civilizational clash also seem convinced that coming closer to each other as human beings must somehow *aggravate* the anxiety about foreigners, rather than helping to allay it. This is at odds with the rather ancient arguments of those who have tried, over millennia, to write about foreign countries, hoping to generate interest and understanding, rather than exacerbating distrust across the borders. This was part of the motivation of that remarkable Iranian traveller and mathematician, Al Beruni, who came to India in the late tenth century and wrote his classic Arabic book on India in the early years of the eleventh century, called *Tarikh al Hind* ('The History of India'), noting that he wanted to contribute to overcoming the terrible influences of the fact that a 'depreciation of foreigners not only prevails among us and [the Indians], but is common to all nations towards each other' (Embree, 1971: 20). Other historical writers on world culture, from Megasthenes and Faxian to Ibn Batuta and Marco Polo, had looked to more contact and understanding as ways of reducing prejudice and tension.

What is perhaps the most limiting feature of the civilizational approach—even more limiting than missing out a great deal of world history—is the mind-boggling shortcut it takes in trying to understand our sense of identity. Ignoring the immense richness of the multiple identities that human beings have, given their diversity of affiliations, attachments and affinities, the civilizational approach attempts to put each of us into a little box of a single sense of belonging, to wit, our alleged perception of oneness with our respective 'civilization'. It is through this huge oversimplification that the job of understanding diverse human beings of the world is metamorphosed, in this impoverished approach to humanity, into looking only at the different civilizations: personal differences are then seen as being, in effect, parasitic on civilizational contrasts. Violence between persons is interpreted, in this high theory, as animosity between distinct civilizations. Thus, in addition to its dependence on an imaginary history of the world, the civilizational explanation of global violence is firmly moored on a particular 'solitarist' approach to human identity, which sees human beings as members of exactly one group defined by their native civilization, defined mainly in terms of religion (Sen, 2006).

A solitarist approach is, in general, a very efficient way of *mis*understanding nearly everyone in the world. In our normal lives, we see ourselves as members of a variety of groups—we belong to all of them. The same person can be, without any contradiction, a Norwegian citizen, of Asian origin, with Bangladeshi ancestry, a Muslim, a socialist, a woman, a vegetarian, a jazz musician, a doctor, a poet, a feminist, a heterosexual, a believer in gay and lesbian rights, and one who believes that many of the most important problems that Norway faces today could be resolved if Norwegians could be made to take an interest in the game of cricket. Each of these identities can be of significance to the person, depending on the problem at hand and the context of choice, and the priorities between them could be influenced by her own values as well as by social pressures. There is no reason to think that whatever civilizational identity a person has—religious, communal, regional, national or global—must invariably dominate over every other relation or affiliation he or she may have.

Trying to understand global violence through the lens of clashing civilizations does not bear much scrutiny, because the reasoning on which it is based is so extraordinarily crude. And yet, it must also be recognized that reductionist cultivation of singular identities has indeed been responsible for a good deal of what we can be call 'engineered bloodshed' across the world. However, this results from the fomenting and cultivation of targeted differences, rather than being just a spontaneous outcome from an inescapable 'clash'. We may be suddenly informed by instigators that we are not just Yugoslavs but actually Serbs ('we absolutely don't like Albanians'), or that we are not just Randans or Kigalians or Africans, but specifically Hutus who must see Tutsis as enemies. I recollect from my own childhood, in immediately pre-independent India, how the Hindu-Muslim riots suddenly erupted in the 1940s, linked with the politics of partition, and also the speed with which the broad human beings of summer were suddenly transformed, through ruthless cultivation of segregation, into brutal Hindus and fierce Muslims of the winter. Hundreds of thousands perished at the hands of people who, led by the designers of carnage, killed others on behalf of—for the cause of—those who they abruptly identified as their 'own people'.

This too is a cultural theory—based on the vulnerability of human beings to propaganda and instigation that make use of racial, ethnic, religious, or some other cultural themes that carry the potential of exploitability. However, we must note that the thesis of engineering bloodshed by playing up one divisive identity, excluding all others, is a very different theory from that of an inescapable clash of civilizations, based on the idea that civilizational identities must have an intrinsic priority.

Let me, for the moment, leave the cultural approaches there. What about the other approach, the one of political economy? This line of reasoning sees poverty and inequality as the root cause of violence, and it certainly is—or at least seems like—a momentous approach that rivals cultural explanations of violence. It is not hard to see that the injustice of inequality can generate intolerance and that the suffering of poverty can provoke anger and fury. That connection has been pointed out extensively in the social approach to understanding the prevalence of violence and disorder. There have been some statistical attempts to bring out the factual basis of this 'economic reductionism', but the connection has appeared to be so obviously credible that the paucity of definitive empirical evidence has not discouraged the frequent invoking of this way of understanding the recurrence of violent crime in countries with much poverty and inequality.

And there is indeed considerable plausibility in seeing a connection between violence and poverty.[2] For example, many countries have experienced—and continue to experience—the simultaneous presence of economic destitution and political strife. From Afghanistan and Sudan to Somalia and Haiti, there are plenty of examples of the

2 Some of these connections have indeed been empirically investigated; see for example Collier (2007) and the references cited there.

dual adversities of deprivation and violence faced by people in different parts of the world. To look at a different set of events, it would be hard to think that the outbursts of political violence in France in the fall of 2005 had nothing to do with the economic and social deprivation of some people living in parts of the country, often living in the outskirts of Paris and other cities, who felt badly treated and neglected. Given the co-existence of violence and poverty, it is not at all unnatural to ask whether poverty kills twice—first through *economic privation,* and second through *political carnage.*

Poverty can certainly make a person outraged and desperate, and a sense of injustice, related particularly to gross inequality, can be a good ground for rebellion—even bloody rebellion. Furthermore, it is not uncommon to presume that an enlightened attitude to war and peace must go beyond the immediate and to seek instead 'deeper' causes. In looking for such underlying causes, the economics of deprivation and inequity has a very plausible claim to attention. The belief that the roots of discontent and disorder have to be sought in economic destitution has, thus, been fairly widely favoured by social analysts who try to look beyond the apparent and the obvious.

The straightforward thesis linking poverty with violence has another significant appeal: it is available for use in the humane political and moral advocacy of concerted public action to end poverty. Those trying to eradicate poverty in the world are, naturally enough, tempted to seek support from the apparent causal connection that tics violence to poverty, to seek the support of even those who are not moved by poverty itself. There has, in fact, been an increasing tendency in recent years to argue in favour of policies of poverty removal on the ground that this is the surest way to prevent political strife and turmoil. Basing public policy—international as well as domestic—on such an understanding has some evident attractions. It provides a politically powerful argument for allocating more public resources and efforts to poverty removal because of its presumed political rewards, taking us much beyond the direct moral case for doing this.

Since generic physical violence seems to be more widely loathed and feared, especially by well-placed people, than social inequity and the deprivation—even extreme deprivation—of others, it is indeed tempting to be able to tell all, including the rich and those well placed in society, that terrible poverty will generate terrifying violence, threatening the lives of all. Given the visibility and public anxiety about wars and disorders, the indirect justification of poverty removal—not for its own sake but for pursuing peace and quiet—has become, in recent years, a dominant part of the rhetoric of fighting poverty.

While the temptation to go in this direction is easy to appreciate, one of the difficulties here lies in the possibility that if the causal connection proves to be not quite robust, then economic reductionism would not only have impaired real knowledge and understanding of the world (a serious loss in itself, for science and objectivity have importance of their own), but it would also tend to undermine the social ethics of public commitment to remove poverty. This is a particularly serious concern, since poverty and massive inequality are terrible enough in themselves to provide more than ample reason for working for their removal—even if they did not have any further ill effects through indirect links. Just as virtue is its own reward, poverty is at least its own punishment. To look for some ulterior reason for fighting poverty through its effects on violence and conflict may make the argument broader with a larger reach, but it can also make the reasoning much more fragile.

To see this danger is not the same as denying that poverty and inequality can—and do—have far-reaching connections with conflict and strife (more on this presently), but these connections have to be investigated and assessed with empirical strongmindedness. The temptation to summon economic reductionism may sometimes be effective in helping what we may see as a right cause, particularly in getting support even from the ethically obtuse who are unmoved by the poverty of others but are scared of bloody violence affecting their own lives as well. It can, however, be an unsound way to proceed and can indeed be seriously counterproductive for political ethics, if the empirical picture is, in fact, rather murky.

And murky the picture certainly is, at least at the level of immediacy that is sometimes presumed in these causal reasonings. The claim that poverty is responsible for group violence draws on an oversimplification of empirical connections that are far from universal. The relationship is also contingent on many other factors, including political, social and cultural circumstances, which make the world in which we live far more complex.

Let me give an example. When recently I gave the Lewis Mumford Lecture at the City College of New York, entitled 'The Urbanity of Calcutta', I had the opportunity to comment on the rather remarkable fact that Kolkata—as the name of that city is now spelled in English in order to sound closer to the Bengali word for it—is not only one of poorest cities in India, and indeed in the world, but it also has an exceptionally low rate of violent crime—absolutely the lowest violent crime rate of all Indian cities. This applies by a long margin to the incidence of homicide or murder. The average incidence of murder in Indian cities (including all the 35 cities that are counted in that category) is 2.7 per 100,000 people—2.9 for Delhi. The rate is 0.3 in Kolkata.[3] The same low level of violent crime can be seen in looking at the total number of all violations of the Indian Penal Code put together. It also applies to crimes against women, the incidence of which is very substantially lower in Kolkata than in all other major cities in India.

It also emerges that, while Kolkata is by a wide margin the city with the lowest homicide rate in India, Indian cities in general are strikingly low in the incidence of violent crime by world standards, and are beaten only by much richer and more well-placed cities like Hong Kong and Singapore. Here are some numbers, relating to 2005 or the closest year for which we could get data: Paris has a homicide rate of 2.3, London 2.4, Dhaka 3.6, New York 5.0, Buenos Aires 6.4, Los Angeles 8.8, Mexico City 17.0, Johannesburg 21.5, Sao Paulo 24.0, and Rio de Janeiro an astonishing 34.9.[4] In India, only Patna, in the troubled state of Bihar, is in the big league with a figure of 14.0 as the homicide rate—no other Indian city reaches even half that number, and the average of Indian cities is, as mentioned earlier, only 2.7. Even the famously low-crime Japanese

3 The data are taken from National Crime Record Bureau (2006) of India.

4 The data for the different cities have been collected from the respective municipal and national publications and official sources. I am very grateful to my research assistant, Pedro Ramos Pinto, for undertaking the rather exacting task of getting and placing in a comparable framework, the information from the different cities. I also take this opportunity of thanking him for his general advice and help in this work.

cities have more than three times the murder rate of Kolkata, with 1.0 per 100,000 for Tokyo and 1.8 for Osaka, and only Hong Kong and Singapore come close to Kolkata (though still more than 60% higher), at 0.5 per 100,000 compared with Kolkata's 0.3.

If all this appears to us to be an unfathomable conundrum, given Kolkata's poverty, that may be a reflection of the limitation of our thought, rather than a paradox of nature. Kolkata does, of course, have a long distance to go to eradicate poverty and to put its material house in order. It is important to remember that the low crime rate does not make those nasty problems go away. And yet there is something also to celebrate in the fact that poverty does not inescapably produce violence, independently of political movements as well as social and cultural interactions.

Explanation of crime is not an easy subject for empirical generalizations, but there are some possible connections that seem suggestive. While there have been some attempts recently to understanding the nature and incidence of crime in terms of the characteristics of the respective neighbourhoods, it is quite clear that there is still a long way to go for a fuller understanding of the picture (see, e.g., Wilkstrom & Sampson, 2006).

In my Mumford Lecture, I have tried to argue that Kolkata has, among other causal factors, benefited from the fact that it has had a long history of being a thoroughly mixed city, where neighbourhoods have not had the feature of ethnic separation that exists in some cities—in India as well as elsewhere. There are also many other social and cultural features that are undoubtedly relevant in understanding the relation between poverty and crime. For example, in trying to understand the high rate of violent crime in South Africa, where I spoke, *inter alia,* about some of these issues in my Nadine Gordimer Lecture in April 2007, it would be hard to overlook the connection between the high incidence of urban violent crime and the legacy of the apartheid. The linkage involves not only the inheritance of racial confrontation, but also the terrible effects of separated neighbourhoods and families that were split up for the economic arrangements that went with apartheid policies. But it would not be easy to explain why the belated attempts to generate mixed communities have also had the immediate effect of fostering crime committed *within* the newly mixed neighbourhoods; perhaps the legacy of history is harder to wipe out than we hope it might be.

I do not think we know enough about the empirical relations to be confident of what the exact causal connections are, and I am acutely aware that there is need for humility here that social sciences invariably invite and frequently do not get. It does, however, seem fairly clear that the tendency to see a universal and immediate link between poverty and violence would be very hard to sustain. There is certainly a more complex picture that lies beyond the alleged straightforwardness of the poverty—violence relationship.

More specifically, if we look, in particular, at violence related to religion, ethnicity and community (the direction to which we are dispatched by many cultural theorists), the role of conscious politics as a barrier also demands a fuller recognition. For example, the prevailing politics of Kolkata and of West Bengal, which is very substantially left of centre (West Bengal has the longest history in the world of elected communist governments, based on free multiparty elections—for 28 years now), has tended to concentrate on deprivation related to class and, more recently, gender. That altered focus, which is very distinct from religion and religion-based community, has made it much harder to exploit religious differences for instigating riots against minorities, as has happened, with much brutality, in some Indian cities, for example Mumbai (or Bombay) and Ahmedabad. Kolkata did have its share of Hindu-Muslim riots related to the partition of India, which were rampant across the subcontinent. But since then, over more than four decades, there have been no such riots in this large city, unlike in many other urban conglomerates in India. Indeed, the whole sectarian agenda of cultivating communal divisiveness seems to have been substantially overturned by the new political and social priorities that dominate the city.

And in this political development, the focus on economic poverty and inequality seems to have played a constructive role in bringing out the ultimate triviality of religious differences in preventing social harmony. In the recognition of plural human identities, the increased concentration on class and other sources of economic disparity has made it very hard to excite communal passions and violence in Kolkata along the lines of a religious divide—a previously cultivated device that has increasingly looked strangely primitive and raw. The minorities, mainly Muslims and Sikhs, have had a sense of security in Kolkata that has not been possible in Mumbai, Ahmedabad or Delhi.

If identities related to left-wing politics and class have had the effect of vastly weakening violence based on religious divisions and community contrasts in the Indian part of Bengal, a similar constructive influence can be seen on the other side of the border in Bangladesh, coming from the power of identities of language, literature and music, which do not divide Muslims and Hindus into different—and exploitably hostile—camps. The more general point here is that an understanding of multiplicity of our identities can be a huge force in combating the instigation of violence based on a singular identity, particularly religious identity, which is the dominant form of cultivated singularity in our disturbed world today.

To return to economic reductionism, it may be not be quite as crude and gross as an approach as the thesis of the clash of civilizations, and yet it too is far too simple, isolated and deceptive. We do need a fuller and more integrated picture. For example, the violent history of Afghanistan cannot be unrelated to poverty and indigence that the population have experienced, and yet to reduce the causation of violence there entirely to this singular economic observation would be to miss out the role of the Taliban and the politics of religious fundamentalism. It would also leave out the part played by the history of Western military support—and incitement—to strengthen religious militants in Afghanistan against the Russians at a time when the Western leaders saw the Soviet Union as a single-handed 'axis of evil'. And, at the same time, to dissociate the rise of fundamentalism and sectarian violence from all economic connections would also be a mistake. We must try to understand the different interconnections that work together, and often kill together. We need some investigative sophistication to understand what part is played by the economic components in the larger structure of interactions here.

In the context of discussing the low crime rate in Kolkata, I commented on the constructive role of radical politics that concentrates on class, gender and poverty. Poverty can be connected with low violence for a very different reason as well, namely, the effect of extreme impoverishment in making people too debilitated even to protest and rebel. Indeed, destitution can be accompanied not only by economic debility, but also by political impotence.

Severe famines have, in fact, occurred without there being much rebellion or strife or warfare. For example, the famine years in the 1840s in Ireland were among the most peaceful, and there was little attempt by the hungry masses to intervene even as ship after ship sailed down the river Shannon laden with food, carrying it away from starving Ireland to well-fed England, by the pull of market forces (the English had more money to buy meat, poultry, butter and other food items than the blighted Irish had). As it happens, the Irish do not have a great reputation for excessive docility, and yet the famine years were, by and large, years of law and order and peace. London not only got away with extreme misgovernance of Ireland, they did not even have to face, then, the violence of Irish mobs, who were busy looking for ways and means of escaping hunger. As Calgacus, the rebellious Scottish chief, said about Roman rule of first-century Britain (as reported by Tacitus): 'They make a wilderness and they call it peace.'

This does not, however, indicate that the poverty, starvation and inequity of the Irish famines had no long-run effects on violence in Ireland. Indeed, the memory of injustice and neglect had the effect of severely alienating the Irish from Britain, and contributed greatly to the violence that characterized Anglo-Irish relations over more than one and a half centuries. Economic destitution may not lead to an immediate rebellion, but it would be wrong to presume from this that there is no connection between poverty, on the one hand, and violence, on the other. There is an important need here to look at connections over time, often a very long time. It is also important to understand how the grievances of deprivation and maltreatment get merged with other factors, including, in the Irish case, a championing of national identity that seeks distancing from the English. The offensive nature of English caricatures of the Irish, going back all the way to Edmund Spenser's *Faerie Queene* in the 16th century, would be strongly reinforced by the experience of the famines of the 1840s under British rule, generating deep resentment against Ireland's more powerful neighbours who did so little to stop the starvation, and in many ways, even helped to aggravate it.

Let me consider another example, this time from the Middle East today. There are, of course, many influences that make the situation as terrible as it is there right now, including the apparent inability of the US administration to think clearly—not to mention wisely and humanely—on the subject. But among the many connections, it is hard to ignore the memory of ill treatment of the Middle East by Western powers during colonial times, when the new masters could subdue one nation after another and draw and redraw the boundaries between countries in ancient lands just as the colonial superpowers wanted. That abuse of power did not cause many riots then and there in the 19th century, but the silence of the vanquished—the peace of the trampled—did not indicate that the subject matter was gone forever, and would not leave behind a terrible memory of ill-treatment. Even the new episodes of trampling and pulverization today—in Iraq and Palestine and elsewhere—will not, I fear, be easily forgotten for a long time in the future.

The general message here is to accept that poverty and inequality arc importantly linked with violence and lack of peace, but they have to be seen together with divisions in which other factors, such as nationality, culture, religion, community, language and literature, play their parts. Deprivation is not a 'lone ranger'—to use that well-known character from Western movies—in generating violence. The influence of poverty and inequality has to be understood not through an exclusive concentration on deprivation and destitution in isolation from society and culture, but through looking for a larger and much more extensive framework with interactive roles of poverty and other features of society. The linking of poverty and injustice to violence does indeed have some plausibility, but there is neither any immediacy nor any inevitability there.

We also have to appreciate how ideas of identity and culture add to the reach of political economy, rather than competing with its influence in an '*either* this, *or* that' form. The categories around which the provoked violence may proceed would have cultural and social relevance of their own (linked with ethnicity, nationality or social background), but the possibility of instigating anger can be dramatically increased and magnified by historical association with economic and political inequity and poverty. Indeed, even the brutality of the Hutu activists against the Tutsis made effective use of the fact that Tutsis had a more privileged position in Rwanda than the Hutus typically had. This would not, of course, have done anything whatsoever to justify what happened, but the existence of that historical connection is relevant for empirical studies of violence.

Similarly, while the fierce nastiness of Al-Qaeda against Western targets cannot be justified by any invoking of history, the fact that those in whose name the terrorists act have had unequal treatment in the past from Western colonialists makes the invitation to barbarity that much easier to sell. The absence of an ethical justification of such a linkage does not eliminate the fact that it can, nevertheless, have much power in moving people to blind rage. The tolerance of terrorism by an otherwise peaceful population is another peculiar phenomenon in some parts of the contemporary world, where many people feel that they were very badly treated in the past: the violence that is tolerated is often seen as some kind of a retaliation for past injustices.

There is no inevitability here, but the conquest of potential violence does demand a powerful vision. Indeed, but for the leadership of Mahatma Gandhi and others in working for the acceptance of what Nadine Gordimer (1995) calls the 'common pursuit that doesn't have to be acknowledged in any treaty',[5] it would be hard to imagine a multi-religious India that is so radically different today from the rioting days of the 1940s, despite the ceaseless efforts of some sectarians to stir up passions against minorities, which the Indian voters firmly rejected in the general elections of 2004. In the context of the familiar British colonial thesis of an irreparable division between Indian

---

5 Gordimer (1995) is talking here, in her essay called 'Zaabalawi: The Concealed Side', about three great writers. Naguib Mahfouz, Chinua Achebe and Amos Oz, respectively from Egypt, Nigeria and Israel: they 'do not expound the obvious, divided by race, country and religion, they enter by their separate ways territory unknown, in a common pursuit that doesn't have to be acknowledged in any treaty'.

communities, which played such a big role in the colonial policy of divide and rule, it would have been hard to expect that with its more than 80% Hindu population, the country could still choose, as it has, non-Hindus for all three principal positions in the country in charge of Indian political affairs: a Muslim President (Abdul Kalam), a Sikh Prime Minister (Manmohan Singh), and a Christian leader of the ruling party (Sonia Gandhi).[6]

Similarly, but for the political vision that inspired South Africa's anti-apartheid movement led by Nelson Mandela. South Africa today would be full of violent revenge against what had been one of the crudest and most brutal segregationist regimes in the world. Those prospects have been successfully avoided, in a way that was barely imaginable when the whole world was worried not only about injustice in South Africa, but also about what seemed the likelihood of an inescapable blood-bath when the chains binding the blacks would ultimately break.

That understanding has implications for other issues as well that worry us, If there is still far too much violence of a more 'ordinary' kind in any country in the world (including South Africa), a discernment of its causal connections must call for a serious integration of political, social and cultural analysis with investigations of the hard realities of economic deprivation. Disparity and deprivation do, of course, demand urgent and concentrated attention, for they are terrible curses on their own, but the need for that urgency does not have to be justified by the further claim that they are inescapable and straightforward generators of crime and violence. It would be, I think, a huge mistake to see economic inequality and poverty as being automatically responsible for violence—indeed, it would be just as serious a mistake as the assumption that inequality and poverty have nothing to do with the possibility of violence.

So what are my general conclusions? First, economic, social and cultural issues related to violence demand serious efforts at integration, an exercise that is spurned both by the fatalistic theorists of civilizational clash and by the hurried advocates of economic reductionism. Cultural and social factors, as well as features of political economy, are all quite important in understanding violence in the world today. But they do not work in isolation from each other, and we have to resist the tempting shortcuts that claim to deliver insight through their single-minded concentration on some one factor or another, ignoring other central features of an integrated picture.

Second, while identity politics can certainly be mobilized very powerfully in the cause of violence, that violence can also be effectively resisted through a broader understanding of the richness of human identities. Our disparate associations may divide us in particular ways, and yet there are other identities, other affiliations, that encourage us to defy the isolationist demands of any singular division, no matter how lionized that division might be in some particular versions of identity politics. A Hutu who is recruited in the cause of chastising a Tutsis is, in fact, also a Rwandan, and an African, possibly a Kigalian, and indubitably a human being—identities that the Tutsis

6 Since this lecture was given in May 2007, the term of President Kalam expired, and a new President has now been chosen, a Hindu woman (Pratibha Devisingh Patil).

also share. The process of such cultivated violence cannot be readily translated into the unfolding of something like human destiny.

Third, even as far as identity divisions are concerned, no matter how momentous the religious differences may appear to be in the context of warfare today, there are other divisions that also have the potential for creating strife and carnage. The violence of solitarist identity can have a tremendously varying reach. Indeed, the obsession with religions and so-called civilizations has been so strong in contemporary global politics that there is a tendency to forger how other lines of identity divisions have been exploited in the past—indeed, not so long ago—to generate very different types of violence and war, causing millions of deaths.

For example, appeals to country and nationality played an intoxicating role in the immensely bloody war in Europe between 1914 and 1918, and a shared Western or European background of Christianity did nothing to stop the Germans, the British and the French from tearing each other apart. The identities that were championed then were those of nationalities, with the patriotic fervour that they generated. Before the horrors of the First World War took the life or Wilfred Owen, he wrote his own protest about values that glorify violent combat in the cause of one's identity with ones nation and fatherland:

> My friend, you will not tell with such high zest
> To children ardent for some desperate glory,
> The old lie: Dulce et Decorum est
> Pro Patria Mori.

Horace's ringing endorsement of the honour of death for (or *allegedly* for) one's country could be seen as catering to the violence *of* nationalism, and it was this invocation against which Wilfred Owen was emphatically protesting.

Europeans today may not easily appreciate Owen's profound sense of frustration, pessimism and protest. The Germans, the French and the British work with each other today in peace and tranquillity and sit together to decide what to do in their continent without reaching for their guns. This would have seemed highly implausible when Owen was writing his poem of protest. A similar vulnerability is present in many other divisions of identities that may, at one level, be made to look like an unstoppable march of violence based on its unique claim of importance, but which, at another broader level, may be nothing other than an artificially fostered avowal that can be disputed and displaced by a great many other solidarities and loyalties associated with different identities, including, of course, the broad commonality of our shared humanity.

Fourth, some of the divisions between people linked with distinct racial or ethnic or other non-economic identities are made more tangible and serious through their association with poverty and inequality. It is mainly through those associations that economic deprivation and social humiliation can become a lethal cause of violence. It is important for us to probe closely how the connection of poverty and inequality with violence works, and why non-economic features of social description have to be brought in to explain the working of the process.

Purely economic measures of inequality such as the Gini coefficient or the ratio of incomes of top and bottom groups, do not bring out the social dimensions of the disparity involved. For example, when the people in the bottom income groups also have different non-economic characteristics, in terms of race (such as being black rather than white), or in immigration status (such as being recent arrivals rather than older residents), then the significance of the economic inequality is substantially magnified by its 'coupling' with other divisions, linked to non-economic identity groups. It would be hard, for instance, to have an adequate understanding of the turmoil in the suburbs of Paris and other French cities in the autumn of 2005 only in terms of poverty and deprivation, without bringing in race and immigration. It would be similarly unsatisfactory to try to base a causal explanation only on race and immigration, without bringing in inequality and economic disparity.

I conclude by emphasizing the need for avoiding isolationist programmes of explaining violence only through concerns of economic and social inequality and deprivation, or exclusively in terms of identity and cultural factors. None of these individual influences, important as they very often are in a fuller picture, can provide an adequate understanding of the causation of widespread violence and the absence of societal peace. The interconnections are as important as the elements that have to be connected.

References

Collier, Paul, 2007. *The Bottom Billion.* Oxford: Oxford University Press.

Embree, Ainslee Thomas, ed., 1971. *Alberuni's India,* translated by Edward C. Sachau. New York: Norton.

Gordimer, Nadine, 1995. *Writing and Being.* Cambridge, MA: Harvard University Press.

Huntington, Samuel, 1996. *The Clash of Civilizations and the Remaking of World Order.* New York: Simon and Schuster.

National Crime Record Bureau, 2006. *Crime in India 2005.* New Delhi: Government of India.

Russett, Bruce M.; John R. Oneal & Michaelene Cox, 2000. 'Clash of Civilizations, or Realism and Liberalism Déjà Vu? Some Evidence', *Journal of Peace Research* 37(5): 583–608.

Sen, Amartya, 1997. 'Human Rights and Asian Values,' *New Republic* 217(2–3), 14 July: 33–40

Sen, Amartya, 2002. 'Civilizational Imprisonments: How To Misunderstand Everybody in the World', *New Republic,* 226(22) 10 June: 28–33.

Sen, Amartya, 2006. *Identity and Violence: The Illusion of Destiny.* New York: Norton; London & Delhi: Penguin.

Wilkstrom, Per-Olof H. & Robert J. Sampson, eds, 2006. *The Explanation of Crime: Context, Mechanisms and Development.* Cambridge: Cambridge University Press.

Chapter Twelve

Willingness to Shoot

Public Attitudes Toward Defensive Gun Use

By Liqun Cao, Francis T. Cullen, Shannon M. Barton, Kristie R. Blevins

Introduction

Writers (Lacayo, 1998; Wright, Rossi, & Daly, 1983) often portray the United States as a nation "under the gun." This characterization reflects not only America's high rates of gun-related violence, but also the widespread ownership of and relatively easy access to firearms (Cook & Ludwig, 2000; Zimring & Hawkins, 1997). It is estimated that Americans possess in the vicinity of 200 million guns (Cook & Ludwig, 1997, 2000; Kleck, 1991; Zimring & Hawkins, 1987). Depending on the survey, 35% to almost half of those polled report that a firearm is present in their household (Cook & Ludwig, 1997; Gibbs, 1993; Kleck, 1991; Maguire & Pastore, 1995, p. 186). It is estimated that 14 to 17 million adults carry a gun outside their homes for self-protection over the course of a year (Cook & Ludwig, 1997; Kleck & Gertz, 1998). There also is a move afoot to relax prohibitions against having a firearm in public. With recent legislative changes, 31 states now issue permits that allow citizens, with few restrictions, to carry a concealed firearm (Ludwig, 2000). Ten states have passed these laws in the last five years (Ludwig, 2000). Most controversially, Lott (1998) presents data purporting to show that crime decreases in jurisdictions following the implementation of concealed handgun laws. His claim is that "more guns" lead to "less crime" (for alternative views, see Black & Nagin, 1998; Ludwig, 2000; McDowall, Loftin, & Wiersema, 1995).

The prevalence of firearms, however, is not *prima facie* evidence that a "gun culture" fully determines how Americans think about firearms (Zimring & Hawkins, 1987). One can detect cleavages between people who do and who do not favor limiting access to guns (Brennan, Lizotte, & McDowall, 1993; Kleck, 1991). On a broader level, reviews of public opinion suggest that most Americans take a balanced, rather than a *laissez faire,* approach to firearms control. Although some people balk at proposals to make gun ownership illegal, believe they have a constitutional right to bear arms, and are ambivalent about whether gun laws will reduce crime, a clear majority favors tightening gun control laws, especially if restrictions do not greatly inconvenience law-abiding citizens who wish to secure a firearm (Adams, 1996; Bordua, 1984; Gibbs, 1993; Kleck, 1991; Roberts & Stalans, 1997; Wright et al., 1983).

Most of the research on firearm-related attitudes focuses on gun-control issues such as requiring a permit to purchase a firearm, handgun registration, and a waiting period to check whether a potential gun purchaser has a criminal record (Brennan et al., 1993; Kleck, 1991; Roberts & Stalans, 1997; Wright & Marston, 1975). This research thrust is understandable given the ongoing policy debate over gun control in the United States (Cottrol, 1994; Gibbs, 1993; Jacobs & Potter, 1995; Kleck, 1991; Van Biema, 1995; Zimring & Hawkins, 1987). Even so, the near-exclusive attention given to public views on gun control may limit research unnecessarily on the full panorama of attitudes that citizens possess about firearms and their use.

Given this background, the current project builds upon Whitehead and Langworthy (1989) by investigating public attitudes in a closely related, but nonetheless distinct, domain: the willingness of citizens to shoot offenders during the commission of a crime (hereinafter referred to as "willingness to shoot"). Phrased differently, this research explores public views on the defensive use of guns. As Ludwig (2000, p. 379) recently observed, "no systematic data are available on public attitudes toward defensive gun use." An attempt is made in this study to help fill this void in the current literature.

This area holds interest for several reasons. First and most speculative, survey data on "willingness to shoot" may be a broad indication of the propensity of citizens to use firearms in self-defense generally and in specific situations. The extent to which guns are employed in self-defense is hotly disputed (Cook & Ludwig, 1997; Kleck, 1988, 1991; Kleck & Gertz, 1995; Ludwig, 2000; McDowall, 1995). Estimates regarding the defensive use of guns are widely disparate, ranging from less than 65,000 incidents a year to 2.5 million annually (Cook & Ludwig, 2000; Kleck & Gertz, 1995; McDowall, 1995). There is the possibility that methodological difficulties in securing accurate reports about when weapons are used and for what purpose may inflate these figures (Cook & Ludwig, 1997; Ludwig, 2000). Even so, the existing research is clear in showing that, at minimum. Americans annually use guns to thwart tens, if not hundreds, of thousands of victimizations. Further, willingness to shoot varies in these incidents. Kleck and Gertz's (1995) study of defensive gun use suggests that potential victims are not "trigger happy" but exercise restraint in discharging their firearms. In their survey, only about one-fourth of "gun defenders" fired their weapons, with 8.3% wounding or killing their assailants.

The current authors recognize, as Kleck and Gertz (1995, p. 167) point out, that "having access to a gun and being willing to use it against criminals is not the same as actually doing so." Still, social psychological research reveals a moderate connection between expressions of behavioral intentions and future conduct when opportunities to act are present (Albrecht & Carpenter, 1976; Davis, 1985; Fishbein, 1995; Fishbein & Ajzen, 1975; Murray & Erickson, 1987). This connection is higher when the intention or attitude being assessed is behaviorally specific and is measured through surveys constructed to capture such intentions (e.g., through vignettes that describe a scenario in some detail). Following this logic, researchers now are measuring propensities to offend through items and vignettes that focus on specific behaviors (see, e.g., Grasmick &

Bursik, 1990; Mazerolle & Piquero, 1998; Murray & Erickson, 1987; Nagin & Paternoster, 1993). In a similar vein, the current project uses scenarios describing varying situations to probe propensities to defend oneself with a gun. Although one should view the results with appropriate caution, they furnish beginning insights into the circumstances under which people are willing to use guns in self-defense.

Second, researchers in other attitudinal domains, such as public punitiveness toward crime, have explored the normative principles that guide people's evaluations (Jacoby & Cullen, 1998; Rossi & Berk, 1985). In a similar way, attitudinal data on willingness to shoot may provide insight into the conditions under which the use of firearms is seen as socially normative and legally justified. For example, if most respondents state they would shoot an assailant in a given situation, this finding would indicate a degree of consensus on when the use of deadly force is approved and unlikely to be sanctioned with criminal penalties. As a side note, this research also would provide an opportunity to discern whether the standards for citizen use of deadly force differ or coincide with the regulations applied to the police (Cullen et al., 1996). Thus, it is possible that certain normative standards organize public sentiment about when it is appropriate to use a firearm against an offender, regardless of whether it is a citizen or a police officer wielding the potentially lethal weapon.

Third, examining willingness-to-shoot views has relevance to theoretical debates about gun ownership and gun-related attitudes. Previous research reveals that owning a firearm is a major predictor of attitudes toward gun control (Brennan et al., 1993; Kleck, 1991; Wright & Marston, 1975). Kleck (1991, pp. 374–375) attributes this relationship to self-interest. Owners oppose gun control out of a fear that their access to firearms may be restricted or eliminated in the future. "Rational choice," in essence, is held to shape policy views. It is not clear, however, whether the divide between gun owners and non-owners will materialize in an attitudinal domain in which self-interest is not manifestly linked to owning a firearm. Indeed, gun attitudes may be due to a host of conditions, including cultural factors, crime-related experiences, assessments of collective security, and political orientations. As will be explained in more detail, the current study examines these competing perspectives on public support for the use of guns in self-defense. Again, the results will be particularly informative to the debate over whether gun ownership is a salient social status, perhaps even demarcating a proclivity to be "trigger happy."

Research Strategy

The present study is an attempt to extend the research by Whitehead and Langworthy (1989), who explored the sources of willingness to shoot among gun owners by reanalyzing the nationwide 1982 ABC News Poll of Public Opinion on Crime. They found that about 70% of gun owners answered "yes" to the question, "Do you think you would try to use your firearm if a burglar broke into your house at night?" Using this item to assess "willingness to shoot," they discovered that several factors increased the propensity to use a firearm against a night-time burglar. For example, willingness to shoot was significantly higher among men, those fearful of crime, those perceiving crime to be on the rise in their neighborhoods, the less educated, and residents of the South.

The analysis here is informed by, but also differs from, the Whitehead and Langworthy (1989) study. First, the measure of willingness to shoot is more detailed and asks specifically whether a respondent would shoot the offender. The question in the ABC Poll data asks only if the respondent "would use your firearm." The term "use," however, might include not only firing a weapon, but also brandishing a gun to scare the offender away (Kleck & Gertz, 1995).

Second, the ABC Poll asked only gun owners if they would be willing to shoot a burglar. In contrast, this question is presented to all respondents in the current survey. In this way, it is possible to discern whether views on using deadly force to thwart a criminal victimization are unique to gun owners or common to all citizens. Furthermore, the ABC Poll measured only whether a gun was in the household and not whether the individual being surveyed owned a firearm. The current project used a measure of personal gun ownership so that the unit of analysis, the individual, is consistent across all variables.

Third, because the sample is drawn from a midwestern city, it not feasible to explore regional differences in willingness to shoot. Previous research suggests that Southerners have distinct views on gun control (Brennan et al., 1993; Kleck, 1991) and willingness to shoot (Whitehead & Langworthy, 1989). This attitudinal cleavage is usually attributed to cultural differences in the South regarding firearms and the use of deadly force to resolve problems (Brennan et al., 1993). The weakness in previous research, however, is that it often uses the variable of "living in the South" as a proxy for these cultural variables. In contrast, the current survey is designed to measure a range of potential cultural influences directly (e.g., childhood socialization into a gun culture, adult participation in a gun culture, and endorsing violent values). In this way, it is possible to assess whether gun-related attitudes, as Brennan et al. (1993, p. 304) suggested, have a "cultural component." As far as the present researchers can determine, no other study of gun-related attitudes has explored this issue with this degree of specificity.

Fourth, beyond cultural factors, there may be other determinants which affect support for the use of firearms to prevent a crime. Similar to Whitehead and Langworthy (1989), the present study explores whether willingness to shoot is a reaction to concerns about crime and about collective security. There is a large body of research that links ownership and protective use of weapons to fear of crime and to a belief that the state is unable to ensure order (see, e.g., Cao, Cullen, & Link. 1997; McDowall, 1995). A range of variables are included to test this proposition. It is also possible that willingness to shoot is a byproduct of political ideology. Accordingly, the potential influence of conservatism on attitudes in this domain are explored. Finally, whether racial attitudes might affect willingness to shoot is assessed.

Fifth, although the main concern is with the use of guns for defense against crime, the project also incorporated a measure of "defensive violence" that assesses the willingness to use non-gun violence ("hit someone") in defense against crime (Dixon & Lizotte, 1987). This measure attempts to make possible a comparative analysis of whether the predictors of using guns for defense, a potentially lethal form of protection, differ from the predictors of using non-gun violence for defensive purposes, a form of protection that would be non-lethal in most cases.

Taken together, these considerations hopefully allow for one of the more comprehensive analyses of gun-related attitudes. It is important to recognize, of course, that the findings are limited by the use of a sample drawn from one social context. This methodological choice involves a trade-off. Secondary analysis of national data allows for broader generalization and for the ability to test for regional effects. In contrast, primary data collection in a specific site provides the opportunity to design fairly detailed measures of central theoretical variables. Both kinds of analyses have merit and, when merged, have the potential to provide a clearer understanding of the nature of American attitudes toward guns.

Methods

Sample

A random sample of 1,000 households in the City of Cincinnati were sent a questionnaire titled the "1992 Cincinnati Crime Survey" during the fall of 1992. In an attempt to minimize nonresponse due to population transiency, the sample was drawn through a service provided by the Cincinnati Bell Telephone Company, which updates its listings every two weeks. Because males are more likely to be listed in telephone books (e.g., women are more likely than men to be listed under their spouses' name), an attempt was made to balance the gender of respondents. Thus, half the surveys carried the instruction that the survey should be completed by an adult female over the age of 21, while the other half were to be completed by an adult male 21 or older. In the event that an adult of the sex requested was not present at the address, then any adult residing at the address was asked to complete the survey. Age 21 was used because it is the minimum legal age in Ohio to purchase a handgun.

Following Dillman (1978), the sample was sent an initial mailing of the survey, a reminder letter, and two additional mailings of the survey. The time intervals between the follow-up mailing were guided by Dillman's "Total Design Method." Due a shortage of funds, however, the researchers were unable, as Dillman (1978, pp. 180–191) recommends, to send the third follow-up by certified mail. This inability may have reduced the response rate among those persons reluctant to participate in the study. As a potential counterbalance, after the contacts specified by the Dillman method were completed, nonrespondents were telephoned to urge them to complete and return the survey. In all, 544 questionnaires were received, 539 of which were usable; thus, the response rate was 53.9%. If the response rate is calculated on the population minus the number of potential respondents who had moved, were deceased, and the like ($n = 66$), the response rate would climb slightly to 57.7% (539 of 934).

Table 12.1 compares the sample characteristics with census data on Cincinnati. The sample is representative on gender, but under-represents nonwhites, the undereducated and the poor. If the sample composition introduces biases, the findings reported by

Whitehead and Langworthy (1989) would suggest that race would decrease, but education would increase, the level of willingness to shoot expressed by the sample. Income had no effect in their study.

Finally, it is important to reiterate that one should exercise appropriate caution when interpreting these results. Not only is the sample drawn from one community, but also the data are now a decade old. Although crime-related attitudes tend to be stable (Cullen, Fisher, & Applegate, 2000; Cullen, Pealer, Fisher, Applegate, & Santana, in press), one cannot rule out the possibility that the causal relationships might be specified by events during the intervening years. Mail surveys also are less likely than other data collection strategies to secure the views of potential respondents who are transient and/or uncomfortable with paper-and-pencil tasks. Further, the use of the term "Cincinnati Crime Prevention Survey" to describe the current research, while enhancing the legitimacy of the survey to some respondents, inadvertently might have caused others to refrain from completing their questionnaires.

Dependent Variables

Willingness-to-Shoot Measure

The dependent variable, willingness to shoot, is an index of four items ($\alpha = .705$). The respondents were given the following instructions: "Let's assume that you have a loaded gun in your hand and within reach. For each of the following situations, *would you use the gun to shoot the criminal?*" (italics used in the survey instrument). Note that the instructions on the survey instrument were intended to read "have a loaded gun in your hand *or* within reach" not "*and* within reach." Although the effect of this error cannot be known for certain, it is likely that the meaning of the instructions, including the directions that followed, were clear. Thus, the use of "and" rather than "or" should have little substantive influence on the results. There was no evidence (e.g., excessive missing cases) that the respondents were troubled by the minor incorrect wording of the instructions.

In any event, after reading the instructions, the respondents were asked to answer "yes" or "no" to the question, "Would you shoot?," for each of these scenarios:

1. You come home and find a criminal running out of your home with your television set. (Scenario label: Shoot unarmed, non-threatening burglar.)
2. You come home and find a criminal who not is armed with a weapon, in your home. The criminal sees you and turns toward you. (Scenario label: Shoot unarmed, but threatening burglar.)
3. You come home and find a criminal, who is armed with a knife, in your home. The criminal sees you and turns toward you. (Scenario label: Shoot armed and threatening burglar.)
4. Two men, one having a knife, stop you on the street and demand you give them your money. (Scenario label: Shoot armed robbers.)

Table 12.1. Selected Sample (n = 539) and Adult Population Characteristics

Characteristic	Sample	Cincinnati
Gender:		
Female	56.7%	55.3%
Male	43.3	44.7
Race:		
White	79.2%	64.9%
Non-while	20.9	35.0
Education:		
Did Not Graduate from High School	9.7%	30.4%
Graduated from High School	20.8	25.0
Some College	26.4	22.5
Graduate from College	21.9	13.4
One or More Years of Graduate School	21.2	8.7
Median Family Income	$36,259	$26,006
Mean Age	47.0	35.0

These items are referred to as "Scenarios 1 to 4" in the results section. A respondent's score on this index was computed as a 1 for each scenario given a "yes" answer. Thus, scores on this index ranged from 0 to 4. OLS regression was employed in the multivariate analysis. However, as a check on this analysis, the dependent variable also was coded dichotomously, with those scoring 0 on the index in one category and those showing any willingness to shoot (an index score of 1 to 4) in the other category. Logistic regression was used to examine this outcome measure.

These scenarios obviously do not exhaust the many types of victimization that the survey might have asked. Even so, these items do reflect situations (burglary, the potential of assault, and robbery) in which a person might reasonably employ a gun for self-protection. In their study of defensive gun use, for example, Kleck and Gertz (1995, p. 185) found that "crime defenders" used their guns most often in or near their homes (73.2%) and to stop a burglary (33.8%), robbery (20.5%), and assault (30.4%).

Defensive Violence

Building on previous research by Dixon and Lizotte (1987; see also, Cao et al., 1997), the researchers developed three items to measure the willingness to use non-gun violence in response to a crime. This measured is termed "defensive violence." These items were answered on a six-point scale ranging from "1" (very strongly disagree) to "6" (very strongly agree). The scale was additive and had an alpha of .678. The three scale items the respondents rated are:

1. I think it is okay to hit someone if they are breaking into my house.
2. I think it is okay to hit people in self-defense.
3. I think it is okay to hit someone if they are committing a crime against someone else.

Independent Variables

Existing research (Lizotte & Bordua, 1980) notes the potential importance of distinguishing gun ownership that is personal from the presence of a firearm in the household, especially when individuals are the unit of analysis. Accordingly, the present study measured personal gun ownership by asking "Do you *personally* own any kind of gun?"(italics used in the survey instrument). It is noteworthy that compared to cities of similar size (see Kleck, 1991, p. 57), the sample's level of personal gun ownership is only slightly lower (17.5% versus 19.3%).

A summary of the remaining measures used in the analysis, including the items and response categories for each variable, appears in the Appendix. This appendix presents the measures according to five general categories: socialization/cultural variables, crime-related variables, collective security variables, political ideology variables, and demographic variables. The scales were pretested on college students. The independent variables are not highly intercorrelated, thus mitigating concerns about multicollinearity.

First, six variables were included in an attempt to assess cultural values that might influence attitudes about guns. Growing up in the South and community size where one resided at age 16 were utilized because cultural values favorable to guns are hypothesized to be more prevalent in the South and in rural areas (Kleck, 1991). Building on Lizotte and Bordua (1980; see also Lizotte, Bordua, & White, 1981), seven items were used to measure childhood socialization into a gun culture ($\alpha = .795$). A three-item "gun subculture" scale ($\alpha = .615$) assessed recent involvement in gun-related activities. Since training in the use of firearms occurs in the armed forces, respondents were asked if they had served in the military. Relying on Dixon and Lizotte (1987), the study also incorporated a measure of "violent attitudes" ($\alpha = .741$).

Second, five variables were included that relate to crime fear and victimization. Previous research often has operationalized "fear" with items that do not tap actual feelings of anxiety about being victimized. In contrast, the measure asked respondents to report how many times in the past month they had been afraid or worried that they might become a crime victim. An eight-item index was used to assess whether the respondent had been a victim of a crime. An attempt also was made to capture vicarious victimization by asking whether the respondent knew a crime victim personally (see Luxenburg, Cullen, Langworthy, & Kopache, 1994; Skogan & Maxfield, 1981). The study incorporated "perceived risk of victimization," which measured the respondents' judgment of their chances of being a crime victim in the future (Whitehead & Langworthy, 1989). "Crime trends" assessed whether the respondents perceived crime in their neighborhood to be increasing (Whitehead & Langworthy, 1989).

Third, the collective security model argues that citizens take private protective action when they doubt the ability of institutionalized, collective means of security—in particular, the criminal justice system—to protect them. Consistent with previous research (Cao et al., 1997; Luxenburg et al., 1994; Smith & Uchida, 1988; Whitehead & Langworthy, 1989; Young, McDowall, & Loftin 1987), collective security is operationalized with a five-item measure of "confidence in the police" (α = .775). The advantage of this scale is that it asks specifically about the ability of the police to enhance citizen security and not about general confidence or satisfaction with law enforcement. A measure of neighborhood disorder or incivilities was also used (Lewis & Salem, 1986) on the assumption that perceptions of disorder may indicate a breakdown in formal and informal collective security and prompt protective attitudes. This measure is based largely on items developed by Skogan (1987, 1990), which measured physical and social disorder. These types of disorder were combined into a single measure because, similar to Skogan's (1987, p. 109) research, they are highly intercorrelated (α = .882).

Fourth, general "conservative political ideology" was measured with an item adopted from the General Social Survey which asks respondents to self-report their degree of conservatism or liberalism. The measure of "conservative crime ideology," which largely assesses support for harsher punishments, drew items from previous research (α = .806) (Cullen, Bynum, Montgomery, & Greene, 1985; McGarrell & Flanagan, 1987).

Fifth. previous research on gun ownership has explored, with mixed results, whether securing firearms is affected by race-related attitudes (Cao et al., 1997; Lizotte et al., 1981; Kleck, 1991; Whitehead & Langworthy, 1989; Young, 1985). In this vein, the study assessed whether willingness to shoot is increased by the perception that one's neighborhood is changing its racial make-up due to the influx of more black residents.

Sixth, the study included as control variables the demographic variables of race, gender, age, education, and household income. For the household income variable, 107 subjects did not respond. Rather than delete this variable or the cases from the analysis, the researchers substituted income values for the missing answers based on a regression analysis of factors significantly related to income in the sample. Given these nonresponses, one should interpret any results regarding household income cautiously. Note also that a measure of household income is used rather than individual income because an individual's class status is typically measured by the economic resources present in the household (e.g., a homemaker who is not remunerated for family-related tasks is given the class status of his or her spouse).

Results

Table 12.2 presents the extent to which the respondents stated that they were willing to shoot by each scenario and then across the scenarios. The data reveal that nearly 7 in 10 members of the sample answer affirmatively to at least one of the scenarios. There is not, however, a uniform willingness to shoot under all conditions. The data suggest that willingness to shoot is tied to whether a perceived physical threat is present. A fleeing or unarmed burglar does not elicit a pervasive willingness to shoot. In contrast, when offenders are armed and

Table 12.2 . Willingness to Shoot (n = 539)

	Percent		
Scenario	Yes	No	Total
Willingness to Shoot:			
Shoot unarmed, nonthreatening burglar	12.6%	87.4%	100.0%
Shoot unarmed, but threatening burglar	28.9	71.1	100.0
Shoot armed and threatening burglar	65.1	34.9	100.0
Shoot armed robbers	44.2	55.8	100.0
Total	68.4	31.6	100.0
Willingness to Shoot:			
One Scenario	17.8%		
Two Scenarios	27.0		
Three Scenarios	15.6		
Four Scenarios	8.0		

appear menacing, support for the use of deadly force rises markedly in Scenarios 3 and 4. Similarly, only a relatively few respondents say they would shoot under all four conditions.

As explained earlier, the current study includes a defensive violence scale largely as a way of comparing whether the predictors of using guns for defensive purposes is similar to the predictors for non-gun violence for protection. When the distribution of responses for the three items in this measure is examined, it can be seen that respondents mostly support the use of violence across the items. Support is highest for the notion of hitting someone in self-defense (88%), second highest for striking a person breaking into one's house (74%), and lowest for those committing a crime (66%). The respective mean scores for these three items were 4.86, 4.33, and 3.91 on a six-point scale. Making direct comparisons to the willingness-to-shoot measure is difficult because one set of items uses scenarios and the other does not. Still, on a broad level it appears that respondents are more likely to believe it is permissible to use non-gun violence against burglars than to shoot them. If this interpretation has merit, it would mean that the participants differentiate gun from non-gun means of defense and have more stringent criteria for when lethal force is warranted.

Table 3 presents the multivariate analyses. With respect to willingness to shoot, gun ownership approaches, but does not achieve, statistical significance. Furthermore, the relationship is a negative one. Gun owners are less likely than non-gun owners to say they would shoot. When this relationship is examined for males and females separately, it is non-significant for females but significant and negative for males. This finding suggests that the image of gun-toting males being "trigger happy" is likely misplaced. In addition, gun ownership is not related to defensive violence.

Two socialization variables have statistically significant effects. Willingness to shoot is increased by childhood socialization into a gun culture (but not current involvement

Table 12.3. Determinants of Willingness to Shoot and Defensive Violence, OLS Summary (n = 539)

	Willingness to Shoot		Defensive Violence	
Independent Variables	*b*	β	*b*	β
Gun Ownership	–.288	–.084	–.052	–.006
Socialization Variables:				
Grew Up in South	.050	.014	.133	.014
Community Size	.029	.025	–.220	–.072
Childhood Gun Socialization	.109	.165*	–110	.062
Gun Subculture	–.014	–.008	.126	.025
Violent Attitudes	.121	.200*	.325	.198*
Military Experience	.231	.067	–.151	–.016
Crime-Related Variables:				
Fear of Crime	.054	.050	.082	.028
Crime Victim	.037	.026	.297	.079
Crime Trend	.165	.099*	.326	.072
Perceived Victimization Risk	.173	.107*	–.115	–.026
Vicarious Victimization	.127	.049	.152	.022
Collective Security Variables:				
Confidence in Police	–.013	–.045	–.048	–.060
Neighborhood Disorder	–.029	–.082	–.091	–.097
Conservative Ideology Variables:				
Politics	.044	.070	–.112	–.066
Crime	.021	.083	.099	.142*
Changes in Racial Make-Up	.248	.097*	.692	.101*
Demographic Variables:				
Race	–.279	–.088*	.626	.073
Age	–.006	–.085	–.033	–.172*
Gender	.285	.109*	1.436	.204*
Education	–.039	–.065	.058	.036
Household Income	.000	.086	.000	.109*
Constant	–.721		7.240*	
R^2	.191		.228	
Adjusted R^2	.157		.195	
F	5.541		6.929	
Significance	.000		.000	

*$p < .05$

in a gun subculture) and by violent attitudes. Willingness to shoot also is increased by perceptions that crime in one's neighborhood is rising and that one is more at risk for victimization. Holding a conservative political ideology (p = .066), being male, and being nonwhite foster support for using deadly force against offenders. The analysis also reveals that perceptions that the racial make-up of a neighborhood is becoming more black is positively related to willingness to shoot.

To test for the robustness of the results, a reduced analysis of the model is conducted for the willingness-to-shoot scale that includes only the significant predictors in Table 3. With one exception, all variables that are significant in the full model are also significant in this reduced analysis. The one exception is race, which is now statistically significant only at the .067 level. As a further check, the analysis was reanalyzed using a dichotomous measure of willingness to shoot (those never willing to shoot versus those willing to shoot in at least one of the scenarios). Based on logistic regression analysis, the results are substantially the same. Thus, gun ownership continues to be unrelated to willingness to shoot, while the variables of childhood socialization, violent attitudes, perceived risk of victimization, and change in racial make-up retain a significant relationship with the dependent variable. The only changed results are that crime trend, race, and gender lose their statistical significance, whereas age achieves statistical significance (negatively, but weakly, related to willingness to shoot).

Defensive violence is predicted by several different factors that are unrelated to willingness to shoot. Thus, it is positively associated with conservative crime ideology, being younger, and having a higher house-hold income. In contrast to the previous analysis, childhood socialization in a gun culture is unrelated to defensive violence. Similar to the willingness-to-shoot analysis, however, the defensive use of violence is supported more by males and by those with violent attitudes. All the significant variables in Table 3 retain their prominence in a separate reduced analysis. Finally, gun ownership has no relationship with defensive violence.

Discussion

Almost 70% of the respondents express a willingness to shoot an offender in at least one of the scenarios presented for their assessment. It is possible that this level of protective action could be heightened considerably if the respondents rated scenarios in which the danger was more imminent, such as such as an offender making life-threatening comments, charging toward them, or attempting to harm one's child or family member. Willingness to shoot also might be shaped by contextual factors, such as whether the crime is being committed under the cover of darkness. There is some evidence that items pertaining to shooting a criminal who has intruded into a house during the night elicit high levels of willingness to use a gun (Cullen et al., 1996; Whitehead & Langworthy, 1989). In short, respondents generally endorse employing violence to protect themselves against crime.

The results, however, do not suggest that the United States is so "under the gun" that citizens embrace shooting offenders under virtually any circumstance. The central normative structure (Jacoby & Cullen, 1998; Rossi & Berk, 1985) guiding the willingness to shoot is the physical threat posed by the offender. Consensus favoring the use of deadly force is high when the risk of bodily harm is present, but declines substantially when victims arc not in imminent physical danger (see Cullen et al., 1996 for similar results on police use of deadly force).

The data buttress the conclusion that views toward gun use may have a cultural component (Brennan et al., 1993). The present study suggests there might be utility to moving beyond proxy measures of culture, such as being in the South, and to measuring socialization experiences and cultural attitudes more directly (see also, e.g., Cao et al., 1997; Dixon & Lizotte, 1987; Lizotte & Bordua, 1980; Lizotte, Tesoriero, Thornberry, & Krohn, 1994). Three observations are pertinent here. First, childhood socialization into a gun culture, but not adult participation in a gun subculture, is significantly and positively related to willingness to shoot. It appears that people who have grown up around firearms are more likely to see themselves as able to use a gun as a decisive way to end a victimization episode. This predisposition to shoot may reflect a general belief in the utility of firearms to protect life and property and, perhaps, self-confidence that they could use deadly force effectively.

Second, building on Dixon and Lizotte (1987), this study includes a measure of violent cultural attitudes that assesses whether people see physical violence as an appropriate response to disputes, attempts to tarnish one's honor, displays of opposing viewpoints, and the like. The analysis reveals that people who endorse violent attitudes are more supportive of using guns for defense. They also are more supportive of the general use of violence for defensive purposes. The results suggest, then, that expressions of willingness to shoot and to hit someone to prevent crime may be part of a broader cultural domain that defines violence as appropriately serving defensive and offensive functions across a variety of situations, of which shooting and hitting an offender are but two instances.

Third, males are more likely to favor both willingness to shoot and defensive violence. Criminologists often focus on the illegitimate invocation of violence by males. However, it appears that men also are more oriented to using violence legitimately. One can link this male proclivity towards violence to such theoretical considerations as gender-role socialization and patriarchy. As Messerschmit (1993) explains, "maleness" is not an undifferentiated construct. There are different "masculinities." Accordingly, researchers may wish to explore how willingness to shoot and defensive violence are influenced by cultural and structural factors, not only between men and women, but also within each gender group.

Willingness to shoot is also rooted in concerns about crime and a breakdown in collective security. Respondents who believe that crime is rising in their neighborhood and who perceive themselves to be more at risk of becoming a crime victim express a higher level of willingness to shoot. The analysis also reveals that living in a neighborhood that is absorbing more black residents is related to both dependent variables and, quite possibly, reflects racial prejudice. Young (1985), for example, reports that aggressive reactions to criminals—from support for tougher sanctions to gun ownership—are related to racially tainted views. Although these observations are only beginning insights, they provide a basis for encouraging future researchers to explore whether support for defensive violence is a function of racial prejudice.

Nonwhites, predominantly African Americans, are more willing to shoot and exhibit a border-line significant relationship with defensive violence. It may be that urban minorities are more likely to favor "self-help" measures against crime. Such self-help advocacy might stem from the historical tendency of minorities to mistrust the police to provide adequate protection against crime (Cao, Frank, & Cullen, 1996). Related research suggests that African Americans are less supportive of police use of deadly force, a finding that again may reflect a lack of confidence in law enforcement officials (Cullen et at., 1996). The current study, however, does not find that confidence in the police predicts willingness to shoot or defensive violence, even when separate analyses are conducted for whites and minorities and when the effects of an interaction term of involving race and confidence in the police are explored. Further investigations, perhaps using a wider array of confidence measures, are needed to confirm whether mistrust of the police is, in fact, implicated in minority support for defensive gun use.

An exclusive focus on gun control policies, where self-interest is paramount, risks fostering the mistaken contention that owners and non-owners are so distinct that common ground between them is nonexistent. The current study provides no evidence that these groups differ in their assessments of when deadly force should be used against offenders. Indeed, a potentially important finding is that support for willingness to shoot is unrelated to being a gun owner. In fact, if anything, the data indicate that gun owners are *less likely* to say that they would shoot an offender. It is possible, of course, that this finding is specific to an urban environment where the present study was conducted. That is, gun owners in rural areas may be quicker to "pull the trigger." Still, it also is possible that owning a gun is not a central determinant of all firearm-related attitudes.

The cleavage between gun owners and non-owners may emerge only when clear self-interests are at stake (see Kleck, 1991). For owners, such a situation may arise when they see gun control laws as limiting their access to firearms. For non-owners, it may occur when they view proposed laws as putting people at risk by permitting unrestrained access to weapons that seem to have no other purpose than to kill human beings. In this case, attitudes reflect rational choice. Outside this realm of discourse, however, owners and non-owners may be more alike than different. They may agree on when offenders committing a crime should be shot or on whether law-breakers who use a firearm should serve extra time in prison. The broader theoretical point is that gun owners may not, as some believe, have distinct personalities or diverge from non-owners in social attitudes (Kleck, 1991). This conclusion receives additional credence from the finding that gun ownership in this study also is unrelated to support for defensive violence.

Future research might benefit from exploring more systematically the factors that structure normative judgments about when shooting an offender is warranted, whether by citizens or by law enforcement officials. One promising strategy for assessing normative judgments is the factorial design survey in which one can combine vignette components at random (see, e.g., Jacoby & Cullen, 1998). Again, the current study suggests that willingness to use guns for defense is influenced substantially by perceptions of imminent danger or risk. Although the concept of risk has objective qualities, it is also a social construction. For example, perceptions of risk may vary depending on offender characteristics (age, gender, size, number of assailants), type of weapon involved (gun, knife, or bat), victim characteristics (age, gender, size, number present), and context (day versus night, possibility or no possibility of escape, at home or on the street). A factorial vignette survey could help assess how certain factors and their combination (e.g., interaction of victim-offender characteristics) shape perceptions of risk and the willingness to shoot.

Conclusion

Due to the prevalence of firearms and the controversy over gun ownership in the United States, research on public attitudes about weapons is important both in its own right and for what it potentially reveals about American society. Discourse in this area, however, is often highly charged and polarized. One side depicts gun owners as "trigger happy" and the other side paints non-owners as liberal elites who wish to deprive others of fundamental constitutional rights. The current study, however, suggests that these portrayals mask what Americans have in common when dealing with the use of lethal force for self-protection. Both gun owners and non-owners embrace the view that guns should be used judiciously for defensive purposes. There is a consensus that lethal and non-lethal violence are appropriate means of self-defense. There is also a shared belief that lethal force should not be used indiscriminately but only when imminent physical danger is present. Like other attitudinal domains, views about guns are a social product. This study shows that willingness to shoot is shaped by cultural factors, concern about crime and security, and structural location. Whereas the common expectation might be that gun ownership would be the factor that accounts for extant attitudinal variation, the current analysis reveals such is not the case.

References

Adams, K. (1996). Guns and gun control. In T. J. Flanagan & D. R. Longmire (Eds.), *Americans view crime and justice: A national public opinion survey* (pp. 109–124). Thousand Oaks, CA: Sage.

Albrecht, S. L., & Carpenter, K. E. (1976). Attitudes as predictors of behavior versus behavior intentions: A convergence of research traditions. *Sociometry, 39*, 1–10.

Black, D. A., & Nagin, D. S. (1998). Do right-to-carry laws deter violent crime? *Journal of Legal Studies, 27*, 209–219.

Bordua, D. J. (1984). Gun control and opinion measurement: Adversary polling and the construction of social meaning. In D. B. Kates, Jr. (Ed.), *Firearms and violence: Issues of public policy* (pp. 51–70). San Francisco: Pacific Institute for Public Policy Research.

Brennan. P. G., Lizolte, A. J., & McDowall, D. (1993). Guns, southernness, and gun control. *Journal of Quantitative Criminology, 9*, 289–307.

Cao, L., Cullen, F. T., & Link, B. G. (1997). The social determinants of gun ownership: Self-protection in an urban environment. *Criminology, 35,* 629–657.
Cao, L., Frank, J. & Cullen, F. T. (1996). Race, community context, and confidence in the police. *American Journal of Police, 15,* 3–22.
Cook, P. J., & Ludwig, J. (1997). *Guns in America: National survey on private ownership and use of firearms.* Washington, DC: U.S. Department of Justice, National Institute of Justice.
Cook, P. J., & Ludwig, J. (2000). *Gun violence: The real costs.* New York: Oxford University Press.
Cottrol, R. J. (1994). *Gun control and the constitution: Sources and explorations on the Second Amendment.* New York: Garland,
Cullen, F. T., Bynum. T. S., Montgomery, K. G., & Greene, J. R. (1985). Legislator ideology and criminal justice policy: Implications from Illinois. In E. S. Fairchild & V. J. Webb (Eds.), *The politics of crime and criminal justice* (pp. 57–76). Beverly Hills, CA: Sage.
Cullen, F. T., Cao. L., Frank, J., Langworthy, R. H. Browning, S, L., Kopache, R., & Stevenson, T. J. (1996). "Stop or I'll shoot:" Racial differences in support for police use of deadly force. *American Behavioral Scientist. 39,* 449–60,
Cullen, F T., Fisher, B. J., & Applegate, B. K. (2000). Public opinion about punishment and corrections. In M. Tonry (Ed.), *Crime and justice: A review of research, volume 27* (pp. 1–79). Chicago: University of Chicago Press.
Cullen, F. T., Pealer, J. A., Fisher, B. K., Applegate, B. K., & Santana, S. A. (in press). Public support for correctional rehabilitation in America: Change or consistency? In J. Roberts & M. Hough (Eds.), *Changing public attitudes to punishment: Findings from around the globe.* Devon, UK: Willan Publishing.
Davis, R. A. (1985), Social structure, belief, altitude, intention, and behavior: A partial test of Liska's revisions. *Social Psychology Quarterly, 48,* 89–93.
Dillman, D. A. (1978), *Mail and telephone surveys: The total design method.* New York: John Wiley.
Dixon, J., & Lizotte, A. J. (1987). Gun ownership and the southern subculture of violence. *American Journal of Sociology, 93,* 383–405.
Fishbein, M. (1995). Developing effective behavior change interventions: Some lessons learned from behavioral research. In T. E. Backer, S. L. David, & G. Soucy (Eds.). *Reviewing the behavioral science knowledge base on technology transfer* (pp. 246–261). Rockville, MD: National Institute of Health, National Institute on Drug Abuse.
Fishbein, M., & Ajzen, I. (1975). *Belief, attitude, intention, and behavior.* Reading, MA: Addison-Wesley.
Gibbs, N. (1993, December 20). Up in arms. *Time,* pp. 18–26.
Grasmick, H. G., & Bursik, R. J. (1990). Conscience, significant others, and rational choice: Extending the deterrence model. *Law & Society Review, 24,* 837–861.
Jacobs, J. B., & Potter, K. A. (1995). Keeping guns out of the "wrong" hands: The Brady Law and the limits of regulation. *Journal of Criminal Law & Criminology, 86,* 93–120.
Jacoby, J. E., & Cullen, F. T. (1998). The structure of punishment norms: Applying the Rossi-Berk model. *Journal of Criminal Law & Criminology, 89,* 245–312.
Kleck, G. (1988). Crime control through the private use of armed force. *Social Problems, 35,* 1–21.
Kleck, G. (1991). *Point blank: Guns and violence in America.* New York: Aldine de Gruyter.

Kleck, G., & Gerlz, M. (1995). Armed resistance to crime: The prevalence and nature of self-defense with a gun. *Journal of Criminal Law & Criminology, 86,* 150–187.

Kleck, G., & Gertz, M. (1998). Carrying guns for protection: Results from the national self-defense survey. *Journal of Research in Crime & Delinquency, 35,* 193–224.

Lacayo, R. (1998, July 6). Still under the gun. *Time,* pp. 34–35.

Lewis, D. A., & Salem, G. (1986). *Fear of crime: Incivility and the production of a social problem.* New Brunswick, NJ: Transaction.

Lizotte, A. J., & Bordua, D. J. (1980). Firearms ownership for sport and protection: Two divergent models. *American Sociological Review, 45,* 229–244.

Lizotte, A. J., Bordua, D., & White, C. S. (1981). Firearms ownership for sport and protection: Two not so divergent models. *American Sociological Review, 46,* 499–503.

Lizotte, A. J., Tesoriero, J. M., Thornberry, T. P., & Krohn, M. D. (1994). Patterns of adolescent firearms ownership and use. *Justice Quarterly, 11,* 51–74.

Lott, J. R. (1998). *More guns, less crime: Understanding crime and gun control laws.* Chicago: University of Chicago Press.

Ludwig, J. (2000). Gun self-defense and deterrence. In M. Tonry (Ed.). *Crime and justice: A review of research, volume 27* (pp. 363–417). Chicago: University of Chicago Press.

Luxenburg, J., Cullen, F. T., Langworthy, R. H., & Kopache, R. (1994). Firearms and Fido: Ownership of injurious means of protection. *Journal of Criminal Justice, 22,* 159–170.

Maguire, K., & Pastore, A. L. (1995). *Sourcebook of criminal justice statistics, 1994.* Washington, DC: U.S. Department of Justice, Bureau of Justice Statistics.

Mazerolle, P., & Piquero, A. (1998). Linking exposure to strain with anger: An investigation of deviant adaptations. *Journal of Criminal Justice, 26,* 195–211.

McDowall, D. (1995). Firearms and self-defense. *Annals of the American Academy of Political and Social Science, 539,* 130–140.

McDowall, D. Loftin, C., & Wiersema, B. (1995). Easing concealed firearms laws: Effects on homicide in three states. *Journal of Criminal Law & Criminology, 86,* 193–206.

McGarrell, E. F., & Flanagan, T. J. (1987). Measuring and explaining legislative crime control ideology. *Journal of Research in Crime & Delinquency, 24,* 102–118.

Messerschmidt, J. W. (1993). *Masculinities and crime: Critique and reconceptualization of theory.* Totowa, NJ: Rowman and Littlefield.

Murray, G. F., & Erickson, P. G. (1987). Cross-sectional versus longitudinal research: An empirical comparison of projected and subsequent criminality. *Social Science Research, 16,* 107–118.

Nagin, D. S. & Paternoster, R. (1993). Enduring individual differences and rational choice theories of crime. *Law & Society Review, 27,* 467–496.

Roberts, J. V., & Stalans, L. J. (1997). *Public opinion, crime, and criminal justice.* Boulder, CO: Westview.

Rossi, P. H., & Berk, R. A. (1985). Varieties of normative consensus. *American Sociological Review, 50,* 333–347.

Skogan, W. G. (1987). *Disorder and community decline.* Evanston, IL: Center for Urban Affairs and Policy Research. Northwestern University.

Skogan, W. G. (1990). *Disorder and decline: Crime and the spiral of decay in American Neighborhoods.* Berkeley: University of California Press.

Skogan, W. G., & Maxfield, M. G. (1981). *Coping with crime: Individual and neighborhood resources.* Beverly Hills, CA: Sage.

Smith, D. A., & Uchida, C. D. (1983). The social organization of self-help: A study defensive weapon ownership. *American Sociological Review, 53,* 94–102.

Van Biema, D. (1995, March 27). License to conceal. *Time,* pp. 26–29.

Whitehead, J. T., & Langworthy, R. H. (1989). Gun ownership and willingness to shoot: A clarification of current controversies. *Justice Quarterly, 6,* 263–282.

Wright, J. D., & Marston, L. L. (1975). The ownership of the means of destruction: Weapons in the United States. *Social Problems, 23,* 93–107.

Wright, J. D., Rossi, P. H., & Daly, K. (1983). *Under the gun: Weapons, crime, and violence in America.* New York: Aldine.

Young, R. L. (1985). Perceptions of crime, racial attitudes, and firearms ownership. *Social Forces, 64,* 473–486.

Young, R. L., McDowall, D. & Loftin, C. (1987). Collective security and the ownership of firearms for protection. *Criminology, 25,* 47–62.

Zimring, F. E., & Hawkins, G. (1987). *The citizen's guide to gun control.* New York: Macmillan.

Zimring, F. E., & Hawkins, G. (1997). *Crime is not the problem: Lethal violence in America.* New York: Oxford University Press.

Appendix

Summary of Measures

Measure	Question
Gun Ownership:	
Gun Ownership	Do you personally own any kind of gun? 0 = No, 1 = Yes *M* = .17, *SD* = .28
Socialization:	
Grew up in South	What state were you living in at age 16? 0 = Non-South, 1 = South *M* = .15, *SD* = .36
Community Size	What kind of a community were you living in at age 16? 1 = rural and not near a city 2 = rural but not far from a city 3 = suburb 4 = small city 5 = big city *M* = 3.43, *SD* = 1.14
Childhood Gun Socialization Scale	Before the age of 18, parent or other family member member: a. kept a gun in the home for hunting or something like that. b. kept a gun in the home and said they would use it to shoot any criminal. e. showed me how to shoot a gun. d. took me hunting. e. gave me a gun. f. I went shooting or hunting with friends. g. most of the people you knew had a gun in their home. 0 = No, 1 = Yes (sum of 6 items) *M* = 1.69, *SD* = 1.96, α = .79
Gun Subculture Scale	Over the last 12 months, a. a friend or family member took you to a gun show or to a store that sold mainly firearms. b. someone gave you a magazine on guns or hunting to read. c. you had friends or family members talk to you about why they like guns. 0 = No, 1 = Yes (sum of 3 items) *M* = .33, *SD* = .69, α = .61
Violent Attitudes Scale	a. If some stranger was making a lot of noise in some protest march I disagreed with, I might hit him. b. If some stranger insulted me and swore at me, I might hit or slap him. c. If some stranger was drunk and bumped into me, I might hit or slap him. 1 = Very Strongly Disagree, 2 = Strongly Disagree, 3 = Disagree, 4 = Agree, 5 = Strongly Agree, 6 = Very Strongly Agree (sum of 3 items) *M* = 3.48, *SD* = 2.13, α = .68
Military Experience	Have you ever served in the military? 0 = No, 1 = Yes M = .17, SD = .38

Crime-Related:	
Fear of Crime	Think back to those times when you might have felt afraid that you might be a crime victims. How many times have you felt afraid of crime in the last month? 1 = Once, 2 = Two to Three, 3 = Three to Five, 4 = Over Five *M* = 2.01, *SD* = 1.19
Crime Victim	In the last two years, have any of the following crimes been committed against you; a. someone broke into your house; b. had property stolen from your house or yard; c. someone stole, broke into, or vandalized your car; d. someone held you up on the street and robbed you; e. someone threatened to beat you up or threatened you with a knife, gun, or other weapon; f. someone actually beat you up; g. some other crime not listed here happened to you. 0 = No, 1 = Yes *M* = .44, *SD* = .5
Crime Trend	In the last 12 months, do you think that crime in your neighborhood has 1 = Decreased a Lot, 2 = Decreased a Little, 3 = Stayed about the Same, 4 = Increased a Little, 5 = Increased a Lot *M* = 3.33, *SD* = .77
Perceived Victimization Risk	In the next 12 months, what do you think the chances are that you will be a victim of a crime? 1 = None, 2 = A Little, 3 = About 50–50, 4 = High, 5 = Very High *M* = 2.14, *SD* = .8
Vicarious Victimization	In the past two years, do you personally know anyone who has been a victim of a crime that injured or scared them? 0 = No, 1 = Yes *M* = .36, *SD* = .48
Collective Security:	
Confidence in Police	a. There are not enough police in my neighborhood to deal with crime. b. When people in my neighborhood call the police, they come right away. c. The police do a good job in my neighborhood in making sure that no one disturbs the peace. d. The police care a lot about the safety of the people in my neighborhood. e. The police do a good job in protecting me against crime. 1 = Very Strongly Disagree, 2 = Strongly Disagree, 3 = Disagree, 4 = Agree, 5 = Strongly Agree, 6 = Very Strongly Agree (sum of 5 items) *M* = 16.8, *SD* = 4.36, α = .77

Neighborhood Disorder	How much of a problem is each of the following: a. noisy neighbors—people who play loud music, have late parties, or have noisy fights? b. garbage or litter on the streets or sidewalks? c. people not keeping up their houses or apartments—like not painting or fixing windows that break? d. groups of teenagers hanging out on the corners or in the streets? e. people selling or using illegal drugs in the neighborhood? f. vandalism—like kids breaking windows or writing on walls or things like that? g. teenage gangs who commit crime? h. people who say insulting things or bother people as they walk down the street? 1 = Not a Problem, 2 = Some Problem, 3 = Big Problem (sum of 8 items) $M = 4.68$, $SD = 3.75$, $\alpha = .88$
Conservative Ideology:	
Political	How would you rate yourself on a scale of 1 to 9? 1 = Extremely Liberal, 9 = Extremely Conservative $M = 5.7$, $SD = 2.16$
Crime	a. Stiffer jail sentences are needed to show criminals that crime does not pay. b. Juvenile criminals are treated too leniently by the courts. c. Crime has increased in recent times because society has become too permissive. d. These days, criminals have too many legal rights. e. If we really cared about crime victims, we would make sure that criminals were caught and given harsh punishment. 1 = Very Strongly Disagree, 2 = Strongly Disagree, 3 = Disagree, 4 = Agree, 5 = Strongly Agree, 6 = Very Strongly Agree (sum of 5 items) $M = 18.7$, $SD = 5.04$, $\alpha = .81$
Racial Attitude:	
Changes in Racial Make-Up	Has the racial make-up of your neighborhood changed much lately? 1 = My neighborhood has more white residents than before, 2 = the neighborhood has stayed about the same, 3 = My neighborhood has more black residents than before $M = 2.24$, $SD = .51$
Demographics:	
Race	0 = Non-white, 1 = White M = .79, SD = .41
Age	In years $M = 47.12$, $SD = 18.0$
Gender	0 = Female, 1 = Male $M = .43$, $SD = .5$
Education	1 = Did Not Graduate From High School, 2 = Graduated From High School, 3 = Some Years of College, 4 = Graduated From College, 5 = Finished One or More Years of Graduate School $M = 3.25$, $SD = 1.26$
Household Income	1 = \$2,000 and Below; 2 = \$2,0001–\$6,000; 3 = \$6,0001–\$10,000; 4 = \$10,0001– \$15,000; continues in \$4,999 increments; 14 = \$60,001–\$70,000; continues in \$9,999 increments; 17 = \$90,001–\$120,000; 18 = \$120,000+ *M* = 8.78, *SD* = 4.25

Credits

Marcus Felson and Rachel Boba, "Chemistry for Crime," *Crime and Everyday Life*, pp. 25–48. Copyright © 2010 by Sage Publications. Reprinted with permission.

Travis C. Pratt, "Misinformation about the Crime Problem," *Addicted to Incarceration*, pp. 29–44. Copyright © 2009 by Sage Publications. Reprinted with permission.

Matthew B. Robinson, "Assessing Criminal Justice Practice Using Social Justice Theory," *Social Justice Research*, vol. 23, no. 1, pp. 77–97. Copyright © 2010 by Springer Science+Business Media. Reprinted with permission.

Frank Butler, "Rush to Judgment: Prisoners' Views on Juvenile Justice," *Western Criminology Review*, vol. 12, no. 3, pp. 106–119. Copyright © 2011 by Western Society of Criminology. Reprinted with permission. Provided by ProQuest LLC. All rights reserved.

Heather Schoenfeld, "Mass Incarceration and the Paradox of Prison Conditions Litigation," *Law & Society Review*, vol. 44, no. 3/4, pp. 731–767. Copyright © 2010 by John Wiley & Sons, Inc. Reprinted with permission.

Cynthia Jones, "Confronting Race in the Criminal Justice System," *Criminal Justice*, vol. 27, no. 2, pp. 10–15. Copyright © 2012 by American Bar Association Publishing. Reprinted with permission.

Mark Walsh, "Living Up to the Gideon Ideal," *American Bar Association Journal*, vol. 99, no. 3, pp. 45–49. Copyright © 2013 by American Bar Association Publishing. Reprinted with permission.

Monica Mark, "GPS Tracking, Smartphones, and the Inadequacy of Jones and Katz," *Criminal Justice*, vol. 27, no. 4, pp. 36–39. Copyright © 2013 by American Bar Association Publishing. Reprinted with permission.

Michael Keane, "A Roadmap to Peace in the War on Drugs," *IPA Review*, pp. 41–45. Copyright © 2012 by Institute of Public Affairs. Reprinted with permission.

Amartya Sen, "Violence, Identity and Poverty," *Journal of Peace Research*, vol. 45, no. 1, pp. 5–15. Copyright © 2008 by Sage Publications. Reprinted with permission.

Liqun Cao, Francis T. Cullen, Shannon M. Barton, and Kristie R. Blevins, "Willingness to Shoot: Public Attitudes Toward Defensive Gun Use," *American Journal of Criminal Justice*, vol. 27, no. 1, pp. 85–109. Copyright © 2002 by Springer Science+Business Media. Reprinted with permission.

Cover images: Copyright © 2010 by Depositphotos Inc./Fedor Selivanov. Copyright © 2010 by Depositphotos Inc./Andrey Burmakin.

www.ingramcontent.com/pod-product-compliance
Ingram Content Group UK Ltd.
Pitfield, Milton Keynes, MK11 3LW, UK
UKHW051330130926
15127UKWH00013B/94